DEMOCRATIC DEFENCE

Dedicated to the memory of Tom Wintringham – a forgotten socialist who deserves to be remembered for reminding us that 'Freedom is a gain for which to fight . . . Freedom is also, or can be, a weapon with which to fight'.

PETER TATCHELL

DEMOCRATIC DEFENCE

a non-nuclear alternative

First published March 1985 by GMP Publishers Ltd,
P O Box 247, London N15 6RW.

a Heretic book

Distributed in North America by Alyson Publications Inc.,
40 Plympton Street, Boston, MA 02118, USA.

by the same author:

The Battle for Bermondsey

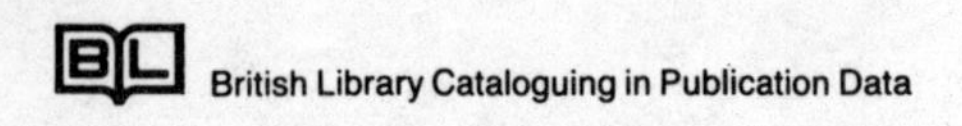

Tatchell, Peter
Democratic defence.
1. Warfare, Conventional 2. Great Britain
——Military policy
I. Title
355'.0335'41 UA647

ISBN 0-946097-16-X

Cover by Louis Mackay
Photoset by M. C. Typeset, 34 New Road, Chatham, Kent
Printed and bound by Book Plan (Billing & Sons Ltd), Worcester

Preface

This book has been conceived as a socialist contribution to the debate within the Labour and peace movements concerning the development of an alternative non-nuclear defence strategy.

Whilst it is not intended as an exhaustive survey of all the arguments and alternative options, I trust it will demonstrate the desirability and feasibility of a democratic non-nuclear defence policy, act as a catalyst for further and wider debate and, by so doing, add some small contribution to the efforts of millions of others who are striving to rid the world of the threat of nuclear extermination.

Peter Tatchell
London, January 1985

At various points in this book I have drawn on the recollections, research and published works of the following people to whom I am grateful: Alternative Defence Commission, *Defence Without the Bomb*, Taylor & Francis, 1983; British Medical Association, *The Medical Effects of Nuclear War*, John Wiley & Sons, 1983; Bill Brooks for his recollections of radical agitation in the armed forces during the Second World War; David Fernbach, 'Tom Wintringham and Socialist Defence Strategy', *History Workshop*, no. 14, Autumn 1982; Jim Garrison and Pyare Shivpuri, *The Russian Threat – Its Myths and Realities*, Gateway Books, 1983; Owen Greene, Barry Rubin, Neil Turok, Philip Webber and Graeme Wilkinson, *London After the Bomb*, Oxford University Press, 1982; David Lamb, *Mutinies: 1917–1920*, Solidarity, undated; Lawyers Versus The Bomb, *The Illegality of Nuclear Warfare*, undated; Adam Roberts (ed.), *The Strategy of Civilian Defence – Non-Violent Resistance to Aggression*, Faber & Faber, 1967; Adam Roberts, *Nations In Arms – The Theory and Practice of Territorial Defence*, Chatto & Windus, 1976.

I am particularly indebted to those members of the armed forces who contributed their experiences, ideas and criticisms. Owing to military regulations which forbid their involvement in the public discussion of these issues, they must remain anonymous.

Many thanks also to Pat Francis and Andrew Bryan at the Labour Party library, and to the staff of the Marx Memorial Library.

Chapter One:

Why a Non-Nuclear Alternative?

The Consequences of Nuclear War

> There were voices, and thunderings, and lightnings, and an earthquake . . . there followed hail and fire mingled with blood . . . and the third part of trees was burnt up and all green grass was burnt up . . . a great mountain burning with fire was cast into the sea: the third part of the sea became blood. And the third part of the creatures which were in the sea and had life, died; and the third part of the ships were destroyed . . . and the third part of the sun was smitten, and the third part of the moon, and the third part of the stars; so as the third part of them was darkened, and the day shone not for a third part of it, and the night likewise.
>
> *Revelations 8:5–12.*

On 6 August 1945, the United States dropped an atomic bomb, code-named 'Little Boy', on the Japanese city of Hiroshima. An area of 13 square kilometres was instantly flattened and 20 square kilometres was turned into a blazing inferno. Sixty thousand buildings were crushed to dust and burnt to ashes, including 95 per cent of all hospitals. More than 90 per cent of the city's doctors and nurses were blasted to death or incinerated in the ensuing firestorm. By the end of 1945, 130,000 people – representing 40 per cent of Hiroshima's population – were dead.

The tragic fate of Hiroshima provoked Arthur Koestler to conclude: 'If I were asked to name the most important date in the history of the human race, I would answer without hesitation, 6 August 1945. From the dawn of consciousness until the 6 August 1945, man had to live with the prospect of his death as an individual; since the day when the first atomic bomb outshone the sun over Hiroshima, he has had to live with the prospect of his extinction as a species.'[1]

Perhaps the most chilling thing about Hiroshima is that such vast devastation was achieved by one very small and unsophisticated atomic bomb with an explosive power equivalent to only 12,500 tons of TNT. By comparison, today the superpowers' nuclear arsenals include 'grim reaper' bombs as much as one thousand times more powerful than Hiroshima. Even their average-sized nuclear warheads have an explosive strength 80 times greater than 'Little Boy', amounting to one megaton (the equivalent of one million tons of TNT).

The awesome scale of the arms race is best illustrated by the following startling facts and figures: the world's stockpile of nuclear weapons today totals 50,000 warheads with an explosive power of 20,000 megatons (20 thousand million tons of TNT), i.e. the equivalent of five tons of TNT for every man, woman and child on earth! This is 4,000 times the total explosives used by all countries during the whole of the Second World War. It represents an explosive capacity equal to 1.6 million Hiroshima-size bombs. If all the world's nuclear stockpile was compressed into bombs the size of the Hiroshima blast and one was exploded every day, it would take nearly 4,400 years to get rid of them all.

The United States alone turns out eight new nuclear bombs every day. According to Garrison and Shivpuri, by 1978, well before the latest expansion of the arms race, the US had enough explosive power in its nuclear arsenal to obliterate 41 times over all 229 Soviet cities with populations over 100,000 – causing a death toll of between 100 and 170 million. Likewise, the Soviets had the capacity to obliterate all American cities of similar size 23 times over.[2]

Just two of Britain's existing Polaris submarines, each armed with 160 Poseidon nuclear warheads, could destroy 75 per cent of the Soviet population and economy. Even more deadly, our proposed new Trident submarines will each carry 408 nuclear warheads and each of these warheads will be 40 times more powerful than the bomb which destroyed Hiroshima. Between them, Britain's proposed four Trident submarines will carry a total of 1,632 warheads with the capacity to reduce every major city in the world to ruins.

In 1982, world military expenditure totalled $600 billion, or more than a million dollars a minute. Over $100 billion of this was spent on new nuclear weapons, i.e. $274 million a day on 'nukes' alone. At the same time, 870 million adults cannot read or write, 500 million are unemployed or only partly employed, 450 million people suffer from starvation and malnutrition, 250 million live in urban slums and 2,000 million people do not have a safe, clean water supply. A mere two weeks of global military expenditure would be sufficient to eradicate all this poverty and to feed, clothe and house every human being on earth. Alas warfare is more profitable than welfare.

What we are witnessing in the world today is a monstrous military overinsurance and overkill capacity which far exceeds what any nation requires for self-defence or deterrence. It even goes beyond what any megalomaniac would require to destroy the whole world a hundred times over. Whereas military strategists argue that weapons parity between East and West guarantees peace and stability, this quest for parity has in fact been the driving motor which is pushing the arms race to such absurd lengths that in order to 'keep up with the Russians', the Americans are now proposing to spend by 1989 a staggering $1,800 billion a year on 'defence' to ensure the development of projects such as the MX missile, B–1 bomber and 'star wars' killer satellites.

The so-called balance of forces is increasingly a *balance of terror* which threatens to exterminate human civilisation on planet Earth.

To begin to understand the Armageddon-like implications of nuclear war, it is worth looking at the effects of just a *single* nuclear missile. In *London After the Bomb,* five university researchers estimate that a one megaton warhead air-burst above Trafalgar Square would decimate an area of London ten miles in diameter. The same bomb burst on the ground would create a gigantic crater 1,300 feet across, 250 feet deep and big enough to contain ten Wembley Stadiums.[3]

In the former case, a one megaton bomb air-burst at an altitude of 6,000 feet would look something like this. Instantly after detonation, a brief flash of dazzling white light would be emitted. It would be sufficiently intense to blind anyone within a couple of miles who happened to be looking towards it. Within three seconds a scorching fireball 6,000 feet across would be formed. At the centre, this would reach temperatures of 3,000 degrees centigrade; hot enough to vapourise everything within it and melt steel and glass within a two-and-a-half mile radius. The heat would be so intense that the exposed skin of people four miles away would be charred with third degree burns and their clothes would burst into flames. Firestorms would begin as far away as five miles from ground-zero as curtains, carpets, upholstery and painted and wooden surfaces spontaneously caught fire. Within twelve seconds, a blast wave travelling faster than the speed of sound would spread outwards from the epicentre with a pressure so great that buildings within a two mile radius would be instantly razed to the ground, burying people alive and blocking the streets with rubble. The blast would be accompanied by double hurricane-force winds of 200 mph laden with lethal flying projectiles such as uprooted trees and street lamps, cars, glass and house roofs. Even nine miles out from the blast centre, people's eyesight would be damaged by the flash and their skin severely burned and blistered by the heat. At this distance, the arrival of the blast wave would blow in doors and windows, dislocate roofs and fracture housing foundations and internal walls.[4]

The effects of a much larger bomb are detailed in the Campaign for Nuclear Disarmament booklet *Civil Defence and Nuclear War.* Based on the government *Civil Defence Manual Pamphlet No. 1* and the US Department of Defence book *The Effects of Nuclear Weapons,* it gives the following impression of the aftermath of a ten megaton bomb exploded on the ground at King's Cross station, London:

> We are travelling towards London from the outside. We might see the first damage to houses as far away as Peterborough and Southampton, 80 miles away, where the windows would be smashed. At Luton, Chelmsford, Guildford and Maidstone, 30 miles away, doors and windows would be blown in and interior partitions cracked. At St Albans, Slough, Sevenoaks and Brentwood, 20 miles away, we would begin to see debris in the roads. At Epping, Watford, Uxbridge, Epsom and Dartford, 15 miles away, a few houses would be burning, and people who had been out in the open at the time of the explosion would be seriously or fatally burned by the heat-flash of the explosion.
>
> At Romford, Waltham Abbey, Stanmore, Harrow, Surbiton and Chislehurst, 12 miles away, the main fire zone would begin. Inside this zone, 24 miles across, almost every building exposed to the heat-flash would have been set on fire at the moment of the explosion. There would be so much blast damage that it would be difficult to make our way along the streets even if there were no fires. People who had been in the open in this area when the bomb exploded would have been charred by the flash.
>
> Mass fires would stop us going any further into this area. Inside, there would be increasing blast damage, and in the ring bounded by Tottenham, Highgate, Fulham and Greenwich, five miles away from the explosion, all houses would have collapsed and the streets would be impassable until cleared by bulldozer. The area from Hampstead to Stepney and from Stoke Newington to Battersea, seven miles across, would be completely flattened, a mass of dust and rubble.
>
> King's Cross itself would be in the middle of a crater nearly a mile wide and deep enough to hold Nelson's Column and to penetrate the deepest part of the London Underground.

As far as Nottingham, Birmingham, Bristol and Bournemouth (100–150 miles away) anyone who had been looking in the direction of the explosion when it happened would have had their eyesight permanently damaged because the lens of the eye focuses the heat-flash on the sensitive lining of the eye, burning a hole in it.

The enormous number of separate fires that would be started simultaneously over hundreds of square miles would not stay isolated.

In the big fire raids of World War II when thousands of incendiaries were dropped on Hamburg, Tokyo, Dresden and other cities, the fires all joined together to make a single holocaust or 'fire storm'. These huge pillars of fire caused winds of up to 150 mph, strong enough to uproot trees, to rush in towards the burning area. Only the contents of basements escaped burning. People caught in the street in the fire storm were soon burned to death. The fate of people in fireproof shelters was not much better. The air that they breathed had to come in from the street, and the temperature of that air was 1,400 degrees fahrenheit, or nearly as hot as molten glass. This forced some people to rush out of the shelters into the flames outside. Others were killed by carbon monoxide, a poisonous gas produced by the enormous fire. The fires burned for days and some areas were so hot that they could not be entered for weeks. Even then, the insides of some shelters burst into flames when they were forced open, and some were even red-hot.[5]

Even in the smallest nuclear exchange, the casualties would totally overwhelm and outstrip the capacity of the health service. The British Medical Association's 1983 report on *The Medical Effects of Nuclear War* suggested that a *single* one megaton bomb air-burst over St Paul's Cathedral in London at night would result in 1.6 million blast injuries alone. On the assumption that only 1 per cent of the local population were outdoors at the time, there would be 26,000 major burn cases. If, however, the same bomb was dropped in daytime when a quarter of the population were in the open, there would be 650,000 serious burn injuries.[6]

The BMA report pointed out that there are only 106 beds for acute burns in the entire National Health Service and the total number of beds for all kinds of casualties amounts to just 160,000.

There have been several recent studies on the probable effects of *limited* and *localised* nuclear attacks. In *Ground Zero,* A. Qasrawi and the West Midlands branch of Scientists Against Nuclear Arms estimate that if Birmingham, Wolverhampton and Coventry were each hit by a one megaton nuclear missile (two ground-burst and one air-burst), this would result in 603,000 blast deaths and 665,000 blast injuries; plus anywhere between 18,600 and 466,000 major burn cases depending on the numbers of people outdoors at the time.[7]

So far as London is concerned, the researchers who authored *London After the Bomb* looked at the consequences of a nuclear attack on six targets on the periphery of the Greater London Council area. They calculate that three ground-burst and three air-burst bombs would cause 4.5 million to 5.3 million deaths and 464,000 to 765,000 injuries from blast and radiation fallout within two months. In addition, there would be 50,000 serious burn casualties.[8]

Other studies have concentrated on the nationwide effects of a full nuclear war. Both the Home Office in 1977 and 1981 and the government's 1980 civil defence exercise Square Leg assumed that in a nuclear war Britain would be hit by 200 megatons – the equivalent of 16,000 Hiroshima-size bombs.

Since then, with the arrival in Britain of Cruise missiles, many strategic experts have suggested that the destruction of these missiles would be a priority in an enemy attack, and that to ensure this, a very much larger megatonnage would be dropped. Indeed, Geoffrey Pattie, Secretary of State for Defence (Air Force), stated in 1981 that to destroy dispersed Cruise missile-launchers would require a blanket-bombing of the deployment area totalling 1,000 megatons.

Nevertheless, Openshaw and Steadman based their calculations of the nationwide effects of nuclear war on the more conservative estimates used by the government in its Square Leg exercise. In this scenario, a combination of military and civilian targets are hit by a 200 megaton attack. Openshaw and Steadman suggest that 58 air-burst and 67 ground-burst missiles totalling 196.5 megatons would result in 2.5 million burn deaths, 13 million blast deaths, 11.2 million fallout deaths and 6.8 million serious injuries – an overall casualty figure of 33.5 million amounting to well over half of the British population.[9]

Openshaw and Steadman also made projections for a variant scenario of a smaller attack concentrated on 50 cities and involving 50 air-burst bombs adding up to 50 megatons. They predict that such an attack would result in between 17 million and 26.7 million fatalities from the initial blast alone.[10] In a 'worst case' attack, if the blitz was targeted on 200 towns and cities and consisted of 200 air-burst missiles averaging one megaton each, they estimate that between 33.1 million and 43.3 million people would be killed by the immediate blast.[11]

Openshaw and Steadman's final case study was based on the nuclear bombing of primarily military targets, plus some industrial centres, with a large number of relatively small warheads with an average yield of 0.65 megatons. They predict that 119 air-burst and 221 ground-burst weapons, with a combined megatonnage of 222, would cause a total of 38.6 million fatalities broken down as follows: 3.1 million burn deaths, 20.2 million blast deaths, 15.3 million radiation deaths; plus a further 4.3 million people seriously injured.[12]

Butler's studies were slightly more optimistic, though the vast scale of death and devastation is broadly confirmed. His report on the casualties following a nationwide nuclear attack was based on estimates by the Home Office Scientific Advisory Branch. Assuming a mixture of military and civilian targets involving 179 nuclear weapons totalling 193 megatons, Butler suggested that there would be 17 million fatalities from blast, fallout and burns; plus 3.5 million major injuries.[13]

Butler also drew up predictions for other possible scenarios as well: an attack on a 'stay put' population with 84 nuclear warheads amounting to 180 megatons would kill 5.6 million if primarily military targets were involved, 15.7 million if a combination of military installations and population centres were hit, and 19 million if the missiles fell mainly on towns and cities.[14]

As to the global consequences of a large-scale nuclear war: in a nuclear exchange involving 5,000 to 10,000 megatons (i.e. the equivalent of between 450,000 and 900,000 Hiroshima-size bombs) 750 million people would die instantly from the blasts, according to studies by Carl Sagan and other scientists. They calculate that a 5,000 megaton nuclear war would result in at least 30 per cent of all people living in the mid latitudes of the northern hemisphere receiving a fatal or near-fatal dose of radiation. Overall, the total global fatalities from blast, fire and fallout would amount to 1,100 million with a further 1,100 million people seriously injured. This would mean that nearly 50 per cent of the world's population would be casualties in a major nuclear war, many of whom would be people in neutral countries uninvolved in the conflict.[15]

What would it be like in Britain immediately after a nuclear war? The survivors would face a Hobbesian nightmare where life was poor, nasty, brutish and short.The mass of unburied corpses, uncollected garbage and broken drains and sewers would result in a plague of rats, flies, cockroaches and maggots. Widespread epidemics of cholera, typhoid and hepatitis would follow. Up to 100 miles downwind from the blasts, unprotected people, crops and livestock would receive a lethal dose of radiation from fallout. Millions of 'luckier' people would be afflicted by radiation sickness causing nausea, vomiting, diarrhoea, blood blisters, loss of hair, skin scaling and ulceration, exhaustion, fever and convulsions. With the body's immunity system damaged by the effects of radiation, secondary infections would soon set in and illnesses such as diphtheria, poliomyelitis, rheumatic fever and tuberculosis would become commonplace. In the longer term, leukaemia and other cancers would strike down much of the surviving population, and hideous birth deformities and genetic mutations would occur on a massive scale.

Few of these 'survivors' would get any medical attention because most of the hospitals would be destroyed and the majority of doctors and nurses killed. According to fairly conservative estimates by A.P. Haynes, a nuclear attack on London following the pattern anticipated in the Home Office's 1980 Square Leg exercise would leave each surviving doctor with between 400 and 900 serious casualties and 175 major burn cases (on the calculation that 25 per cent of the population were outdoors at the time of the explosion).[16]

The BMA point out that even the best organised surgical team could perform only nine operations a day under ideal conditions. Assuming the lower estimate of 575 casualties per doctor and one doctor per surgical team working seven days a week, it would take each doctor at least nine weeks to treat all the injured patients. Long before then, most of them would be dead, including the doctor if he or she had been exposed to large amounts of radiation.

In reality, of course, after a nuclear attack most surviving doctors would themselves be injured and therefore unable to operate at full efficiency. Few surgical teams would be intact and operating theatres would quickly run out of drugs, dressings and sterilised instruments. In London, there are only 5,000 pints of blood ready for emergency use – just enough to give transfusions to 2,500 people. Clearly, as official government policy tacitly admits, the majority of the injured would simply be left to die.

With many fire stations in ruins and their firefighters dead, the fire storms ignited by the nuclear blasts would rage unchecked through our cities and forests for weeks on end. Communications and power supplies would be virtually nonexistent, creating a total blackout in many areas. The electromagnetic pulse emitted from the nuclear explosions would knock out the electricity grid, computers, radios, televisions and telephones hundreds of miles from the blast centre. A high proportion of gas, electricity and telephone lines would be broken. Oil, gas and coal fields would be ablaze and individual power stations and telephone exchanges would be razed by blast and fire.

Many water pipes would be burst. Even where piping remained intact, water would be unavailable to most survivors because nearly all Britain's supplies are dependent on pumping and this would be impossible owing to the destruction of the power grid. Emergency water deliveries would be negligible because our existing tanker fleet only has a capacity to supply 2 per cent of the population. In the absence of essential purification processing, any remaining fresh water would quickly become polluted with bacteria, resulting in outbreaks of dysentery and gastroenteritis. Even far from where the bombs dropped water supplies would be contaminated by radioactive fallout – as would crops and livestock.

The distribution of disaster relief in the form of food, water, blankets and fuel for cooking and heating would be severely hampered by impassable rubble-strewn roads and a shortage of petrol and undamaged vehicles. Many survivors would die of starvation or, in winter, freeze to death. The agony and trauma would drive others to mental illness and suicide. Life would not be worth living.

But there would be some who would battle to survive against all these odds. Across the country, huge wailing columns of blind and bleeding refugees would trek out from the blast zones. In desperation for food and shelter, many of these hungry and homeless would turn to looting. Fearful of disease, radiation and pillaging, communities which had escaped the full ravages of the holocaust would resort to repelling the destitute hordes with armed force. Law and order would collapse and civilisation would revert to the survival of the strongest.

Britain would become a virtual military dictatorship with the army and police ruling the ruins of the nation. Martial law would be imposed and civil liberties suppressed. Regional military commanders would assume the power to direct people where to live, compel them to undertake forced labour and, in cases of protest and rebellion, invoke the power of summary execution. It is a fate so ghastly as to be almost beyond human comprehension.

But if all this was not bad enough, the recent revelations by Carl Sagan and other eminent international scientists add a new apocalyptic dimension to the consequences of nuclear war.[17] Their studies on the long-term environmental and climatic changes following a nuclear conflict are based on the data acquired during volcanic eruptions and the global dust storms on Mars which were observed by the American Mariner 9 spacecraft in late 1971. This data showed that the injection of large volumes of dust into the atmosphere reduces the penetration of sunlight and causes a drop in surface temperatures.

Sagan's team applied this information to a computer model of a 5,000 megaton war in the northern hemisphere involving 25 per cent of the world's nuclear stockpile. They came up with the following catastrophic predictions. An attack of this 'standard' proportion would throw up into the earth's atmosphere several hundred million tons of dust, soil particles, smoke and lethal pyrotoxins. These would be produced by a combination of the initial explosions, firestorms in forests and cities, and blazing chemical plants, oil wells, gas fields and coal mines. They would shroud virtually the whole northern hemisphere, and much of the southern hemisphere as well, in a thick envelope of pollution.

For at least several weeks, most normal sunlight would be blocked out, resulting in a constant 'nuclear night'. At first, the midday sun would be little brighter than the moon, and even a year later, the sunlight would still be below normal ambience.[18] By blocking out the sun's warming rays, the blanket of dust and smoke would also precipitate a 'nuclear winter' of Siberian intensity in which temperatures fell below freezing for three months, reaching a minimum temperature of –23 centigrade in inland areas and taking more than twelve months to return to normal.[19]

In this dark Arctic climate, without sunlight for photosynthesis and with perpetual sub-zero temperatures, no crops would grow and livestock and humans would starve or freeze to death. The millions of tons of dangerous pyrotoxins such as sulphur dioxides, cyanides, vinyl chlorides, carbon monoxides, dioxins and furans would cause vast smogs and acid rains. They would contaminate water supplies, kill lakes and rivers and destroy forests, crops, farm animals and marine life. After twelve months of darkness and cold, as the dust settled and the smoke cleared from the atmosphere, the 'nuclear winter' would be followed by a 'nuclear summer' of intense ultraviolet sunshine which could last for several years.[20]

A 5,000 megaton war would emit sufficient quantities of nitrogen oxides to destroy a third of the protective ozone layer in the upper atmosphere which filters out many of the harmful ultraviolet rays from the sun.[21] As a result, these rays would penetrate straight to earth causing severe sunburn and blistering within a short period of exposure, suppression of the human immune system and even blindness in people and livestock over a longer span of time. The ultraviolet rays would also inhibit plant growth and destroy near-surface marine plankton which would have a major detrimental effect on the whole marine food chain.[22]

Particularly frightening is Sagan's conclusion that effects almost as severe as these would also result from a 'tiny' 100 megaton city attack in which just 0.05 per cent of the world's nuclear arsenals were fired.[23]

At the other end of the scale, Sagan calculated that a very large 10,000 megaton exchange in the northern hemisphere would send temperatures plunging to –43 centigrade for four months and to below –3 centigrade for a year. Sunlight would drop to little more than 1 per cent of its present level and take at least twelve months to return to normal. Subsequently, ultraviolet concentrations would rise to four times greater than average. Even in the southern hemisphere, light levels would fall to 10 per cent of their current ambience and temperatures would sink to –18 centigrade.[24]

The net effect of a nuclear holocaust followed by a 'nuclear winter' and a 'nuclear summer' would be the total annihilation of civilised life.

As Sagan concludes: 'In any large-scale nuclear exchange between the superpowers, global environmental changes sufficient to cause the extinction of a major fraction of the plant and animal species on the earth are likely. In that event, the possibility of the extinction of Homo Sapiens cannot be excluded.'[25]

Indeed, a full-scale nuclear war would almost certainly reduce our entire planet to a mass of rotting and stinking rubble populated by nothing more than bacteria, fungus and insects. With the whole evolutionary process turned back millions of years, ants and grasshoppers would inherit the earth. It would become their kingdom and they would have dominion over all things.

The Arguments for an Alternative

Given these cataclysmic consequences of nuclear war, the case for alternative defence seems self-evident. A non-nuclear strategy is the only sane and rational option. Even if the aftermath of a nuclear war is only half as bad as Sagan suggests, almost any alternative is preferable to our present high-risk nuclear policy which effectively gambles with the future of life on Earth.

The current period of heightened international tension and bellicose gesturing by the superpowers gives the quest for nuclear disarmament and non-nuclear alternatives an added urgency. Today we live in a more unstable and insecure world where the possibility of nuclear war, whether by design or accident, is growing more likely rather than less. Since the late 1970s, detente has collapsed, a second cold war has begun and disarmament talks between the USA and the USSR have broken down.

On the Russian side, there has been the invasion of Afghanistan, the imposition of martial law in Poland, the crushing of the free trade union Solidarnosc, the implacement of SS–20 missiles in Eastern Europe, and the persecution of human rights activists and unofficial peace groups throughout the Soviet bloc.

Conversely, the increasingly jingoistic and sabre-rattling governments of Britain and America have whipped up a strident anti-Sovietism, announced vast increases in armaments expenditure and new offensive weapon systems, and – through the creation of rapid deployment forces – have shown themselves ready, if not eager, to protect their global interests by armed force everywhere from the Lebanon to Grenada, Central America to the Gulf.

But the most serious escalation of all has been the US decision to station low-flying hard-to-detect Cruise missiles and super-fast Pershing II missiles in Western Europe. This decision has made our countries prime targets in the event of war and has already provoked the Soviets to respond with retaliatory measures. It has led 65 per cent of people interviewed in a *Guardian* Marplan poll to conclude that the Americans and the Russians are both *equally* to blame for the current level and growth of nuclear weapons;[26] and 51 per cent to believe that the prospects for world peace are getting *worse*.[27]

The case for an alternative defence policy is also strengthened by the failure of the peace movement to win majority support for unilateralism *despite* thirty years of a nuclear disarmament campaign; *despite* the recent huge upsurge in peace camps, marches, books and films on the subject; and *despite* more widespread knowledge of the truly exterminist consequences of a nuclear conflagration.

Despite all this, public opinion polls indicate that support for unilateralism is no longer on the increase. In fact, it has been fairly static for the last three years. Currently a mere 30 per cent of the electorate support a policy of Britain unilaterally renouncing nuclear weapons. Regrettably, more than twice as many people want us to retain our nuclear capability. Equally grim, well over 70 per cent of the population want Britain to remain part of the NATO nuclear alliance. Less than 10 per cent support us pulling out.[28]

No one seriously committed to peace and disarmament can evade the facts: we may have won new converts, but not enough to win the unilateralist debate. The great mass of the British people are unconvinced and support for unilateralism remains a distinctly minority point of view.

This depressing reality does not mean that we ought to give up and capitulate to the sirens of 'multilateralism' and rearmament. It does mean, however, that if all the traditional pro-unilateralist arguments have failed to win the day, then we have to try new approaches. In particular, we need to understand the reason why a lot of sincere people feel unable to support out-and-out unilateralism and how they could potentially be won over. Many of them are genuinely concerned that so long as there are nations in arms, war is always a possibility.

Rightly or wrongly, they worry that Britain's security could be threatened if we were to give up the Bomb. They share a lingering doubt about Soviet intentions towards Western Europe and fear that without nuclear weapons Britain would be vulnerable to aggression – either now or in years to come.

To many supporters of unilateralism, these doubts and fears are baseless. But that is not the point. *We* may believe that the Russians have no desire or capacity to invade us, but millions of others do not. However unfounded their fears may be, they are real and tangible fears which constitute a major obstacle to winning people to the unilateralist banner.

It is this anxiety that Britain would be left defenceless without the Bomb which is the lynchpin of the pro-nuclear case. To win majority support for unilateralism we therefore need to offer a credible *non-nuclear* defence strategy – a strategy which can both allay people's fears by providing a militarily effective substitute for nuclear weapons and, at the same time, remain *non-provocative* and make a positive contribution to the de-escalation of militarism.

A further factor in favour of alternative defence is that by extending our concern beyond the limited scope of nuclear weapons, it opens up the prospect of a far wider critique of current defence policy and a far more radical reform of the armed forces. For over thirty years, the defence debate has revolved around the simple 'two option' choice of either retaining or rejecting the Bomb. But why should the left and the peace movement restrict their criticism to nuclear weapons? Surely, instead of just opposing Britain's atomic arsenal, which is only one aspect of defence policy, we ought to be challenging the whole range of traditional defence thinking and practice, both nuclear and conventional?

Unfortunately, apart from unilateralism and cuts in defence expenditure, most of the non-nuclear aspects of defence policy seem to have been taken for granted. We cannot afford to be so complacent: our armed forces are highly undemocratic, substantially offensive in character, excessively dependent on the United States' military umbrella, and more geared to both external foreign objectives and internal civilian repression than to the self-defence of Britain. It is to these broader issues, in addition to nuclear disarmament, that we ought to address ourselves by looking seriously at an alternative *non-provocative* and *de-escalatory* strategy of territorial defence. Based on a radically democratised and civilianised citizen's army and augmented by forms of non-violent civilian resistance, this method of defence is explicitly non-nuclear and non-imperialist, as well as being self-reliant, genuinely democratic and unambiguously defensive.

Such a strategy is not, of course, the optimal disarmament measure, even if it is organised on an overtly non-aggressive basis. Ultimately, we must aim for the abolition of all armies, weapons and wars. But demands for immediate and total disarmament, however laudable, have never won majority backing in any society at any point in history.

At the moment, the number one priority is not the long term goal of generalised disarmament, but the removal by *whatever means possible* of the principal danger to the survival of the human race – nuclear weapons and the threat of nuclear war. However imperfect and short of our ideal, by arguing for nuclear disarmament in tandem with support for *non-threatening* conventional defences, we are more likely to win majority support and thereby avert this danger.

Such ideas are bound to be controversial on the left. Some critics who insist on a purist demand for unilateralism or nothing will argue that it is not the task of the peace movement to come up with alternatives. Certainly, it would be much easier for the movement to play a strictly negative oppositional role. But this would also be an abdication of responsibility. If we really do take the threat of nuclear holocaust seriously, we have a moral duty to offer a constructive alternative which can command popular endorsement.

Others may say it is not our business to advise and reform a militaristic capitalist state. Yet these same critics already seek to reform the state by campaigning for the dismantlement of its nuclear arsenal. Why not take this a stage further? Most of these people readily support legislative reforms to repeal racist immigration laws, promote women's equality and protect trade union rights. If these reformist measures are acceptable, why are alternatives designed to reduce militarism so objectionable?

Finally, there are some critics who will dismiss both nuclear and non-nuclear defences as equally evil. But whilst all weapons *are* horrendous, some weapons are more horrendous than others: there is a world of difference between a hand grenade which can kill a few people and an atomic bomb which can kill millions, yet again a full-scale nuclear war which could obliterate human civilisation. Whatever the imperfections and weaknesses of an alternative defence strategy, it is infinitely preferable to such a monstrous fate. There is no point in even beginning to think about socialism or any other humanitarian ideal if we are denied a world in which to create it.

Chapter Two:

What is There to Defend?

Our Right to Self-Defence and Self-Determination

War always involves terrible suffering, cruelty and inhumanity. Ultimately, we must aim to abolish it and thereby remove the necessity for any kind of defence policy. However, whilst all war is immoral and all military expenditure is a waste of resources, so long as some nations possess arms and are prepared to use military force as a method of resolving international disputes, war always remains a possibility and there will always be a demand that our country is defended against potential aggressors – real or imagined, present or future. Pacifist-inspired total disarmament, no matter how honourable and principled, never has and never will win majority support. Though most people would agree that war is abhorrent, they also believe that in certain exceptional circumstances it is justified to prevent even greater evils such as the barbarity of fascism which threatened Britain forty-odd years ago. Faced with the Nazi policies of concentration camps, gas chambers and genocide against the Jews and other minorities, millions of British people who deeply loathed the prospect of war (including many who had previously expressed pacifist sentiments), eventually felt obliged to support military resistance to fascism.

If Britain was ever threatened with invasion again, just as in 1939–45, there would be overwhelming support for a war of *self-defence* to preserve our right to self-determination and to protect the civil liberties and trade union freedoms which have been hard won by the struggles of working people over the last two centuries.

This widespread popular belief in the justice of self-defence against aggression is mirrored in civilian society. Women demand defence against rapists. Homosexuals band together to defend each other from queerbashers. Elderly folk call for protection against muggers. Black people declare that self-defence in the face of racist attacks is 'no offence'. Animal rights campaigners even seek to defend other species from the tortures of vivisectionists.

At a broader level, whole communities unite to defend themselves from destruction by encroaching motorways and speculative office development, or against the dangers posed by nuclear missile installations, atomic power stations and the dumping of toxic chemical wastes.

Whether it be the defence of one's race, sexuality or neighbourhood, most people believe that there are certain things in life which are worth defending and that no one else has the right to violate or destroy these. Essentially the same reasoning underlies self-defence at national level – the idea that there are aspects of our culture and way of life which we value and the loss of which would restrict our liberty and even cause us great suffering, e.g. freedom of speech and the press, democratic elections, the right to strike, trial by jury, etc. There is a world of difference between a relatively democratic state such as Britain (however right-wing and unjust) and the naked dictatorship and brutality of fascist rule and imperialist occupation. It is a difference which is worth defending, as anyone who has lived in Czechoslovakia, South Africa, Chile or Turkey will know.

But more important than any specific set of values or institutions is the defence of our right to shape our own future free from foreign diktat. This is not just our right. All nations have the right to self-determination, and none has the right to impose its will on another. If we premise our defence on this universal and internationalist principle which applies equally to all nations and peoples, then we minimise the danger of defence being associated with nationalism and jingoism. At the same time, this principle does imply that the British people have as much right to forge their own destiny free from external interference as the peoples of Nicaragua, Eritrea, Namibia, Czechoslovakia or Afghanistan. As Mao Zedong argued during the Chinese war of resistance against Japan: 'We cannot even speak of socialism if we are robbed of a country in which to practise it.'

At the outbreak of the Second World War, however, sections of the British left took quite a different view. Ignoring the will of working people to defend the freedoms and social advances they had won over the years, the Independent Labour Party and the Communist Party respectively took pacifist and revolutionary defeatist lines, denouncing the conflict with the Nazis as just another 'imperialist war'. After years of condemning fascism as a mortal threat to peace and liberty and defending the democratic Spanish republic, such political somersaults earned the left a period of sadly deserved ridicule and rejection. We cannot afford to make the same mistake today. A failure to recognise that there are certain circumstances when defence *is* legitimate would again result in the disastrous political isolation of socialists and the marginalisation of the ideas we represent. What is required is a clear distinction to be drawn between a just war of self-defence such as fought by the British in 1939–45 or by the American independence movement in the late eighteenth century; and an unjust war of imperialist aggression such as waged by the British against the Maoris in the middle of the last century or by the US against Vietnam in the 1960s.

At present, Britain obviously faces no immediate military threat. If, however, at some point in the future we were threatened with invasion, it would be quite indefensible for us not to resist – particularly, if there was any chance that the occupying army might impose martial law and censorship, ban political parties and trade unions, outlaw elections and strikes, and cart off Jews, blacks, homosexuals, socialists, pacifists, trade unionists and other 'dissidents' to concentration camps and torture chambers. The successful imposition of such a regime would be a catastrophic defeat for all progressive forces and it would therefore have to be resisted, however reluctantly, by all available methods including armed force. Even many fervent anti-militarists would find it hard to abstain from violent resistance in a situation where a conquering army was pursuing a policy of genocide against sections of the population and where their own family, neighbours and work colleagues were suddenly disappearing or being incarcerated in forced labour camps.

Whilst accepting the legitimacy of self-defence and being prepared to fight a war of resistance for the sake of self-determination, we could not, however, legitimate it in the name of defending a reactionary government and increasingly authoritarian state – let alone justify defence for the purpose of maintaining Britain's privileged position in the world economy or the class system which still deeply divides our society.

Britain is one of the richest industrial nations. We benefit enormously from the unequal international free market economy which condemns two-thirds of the world's population to live in a state of chronic underdevelopment, poverty and starvation. Every single day, 90,000 people die from hunger in the Third World. Another 1,000 million are permanently undernourished – half of them children. Each year, a further 300,000 youngsters go blind through a lack of vitamin A; though this blindness could be prevented at the cost of 2p (the price of a carrot) per child per year.

The money spent on just one Trident nuclear submarine would be enough to feed 100 million starving children for a year. Instead, a third of all the babies born in the world are left to die from malnutrition and disease before the age of five, and in 30 countries the average life expectancy is less than 50 years (compared to 73 in the UK). For people living in the poorest countries, their income is as little as £70 a year. On British-owned tea estates in Malawi, for example, the typical wage of tea pickers is a mere 20p per day.

Certainly defence cannot legitimately be about protecting British economic interests which perpetuate such gross international suffering and inequality. Nor can it justifiably be about the preservation of the class divisions between rich and poor in Britain. Though we may be one of the richest countries in the world, not everyone shares that wealth equally. There are over three million people officially unemployed and the TUC estimates the real figure is closer to five million, given the large numbers who do not bother to sign on and the government's exclusion from the figures of all those on training and temporary employment schemes. Amongst the unemployed are 3,000 doctors, 10,000 nurses and 400,000 building workers who could be caring for the sick and building new houses for the homeless.

According to a study in *New Society* by Martyn Harris, the average income of the unemployed is less than a third of those in work and this means they are generally 'unable to afford trips to the pub, cinema, relations or friends and unable even to phone them'. The children of the unemployed are more subject to child abuse, and are more likely to have literacy problems and miss school because of ill-health. Amongst those who have been jobless for over a year, the suicide rate is 19 times higher than average. Harris also found that 40 per cent of all defendants in English courts are on the dole.[1]

While the unemployed struggle to make ends meet on subsistence benefits, in 1982 Britain's top 28 company directors earned salaries of more than £125,000 each and the Conservative government's reduction in the tax rates for the super-rich since 1979 has put an extra million pounds in their pockets.[2]

In tandem with mass unemployment, the Thatcher government has also pursued a policy of massive cuts in public expenditure. This has meant that in real terms spending on housing has been cut since 1979 by 55 per cent, overseas aid by 20 per cent, welfare benefits by 9 per cent and education by 6 per cent, while defence spending has been *increased* by 23 per cent.[3]

Overall, between May 1979 and June 1983, each day of Tory rule meant 1,395 jobs lost, 28 fewer teachers, 1,806 more people on Supplementary Benefit, 5 less National Health Service beds and 312 fewer houses built.[4]

In terms of practical effects, these cuts have hit the poor hardest and have exacerbated the cleavage of our society into 'two nations'. There are now 80,000 families and 100,000 single people homeless. One million families are living in severe overcrowding. Two million households are forced to share with others because they have no home of their own. Two million people also live in dwellings which are officially declared unfit for human habitation or which lack basic amenities such as baths and hot water. 1.2 million are on council house waiting lists with little hope of ever getting a home.[5]

Simultaneously, million-pound mansions and penthouse apartments are being built for speculative profit, and hundreds of thousands of dwellings are standing empty either because they are the second and third homes of the very rich, or because cuts in central government housing finance are denying local authorities the funds they need to refurbish them.

In the health service, at least 1,000 kidney patients – including about 30 children – die unnecessarily every year because the government refuses to put extra money into the NHS to pay for the operations they need.[6] For the same reason, many heart patients have also been turned away to die by doctors at major hospitals such as Guy's in South London, and the huge increase in hospital waiting lists resulting from government-imposed cuts in the NHS has needlessly prolonged the pain of patients requiring new hip joints, cancer surgery, etc.[7] Of course, it is only the poor who suffer and die. The rich simply jump the waiting lists by paying for private medical treatment in the growing number of private hospitals which have sprung up following the total or partial closure of over 100 NHS hospitals since the Thatcher government first came to power.

To cope with the social unrest provoked by its divisive policies, the government has launched one of the most sustained assaults on civil liberties since the Napoleonic Wars. Even the *Guardian* was moved to state in its editorial of 8 March 1984: 'It's not McCarthyism, but it's beginning to look like a British equivalent – a steady, surreptitious and insidious encroachment upon fundamental liberties.'

The Prior and Tebbit Employment Acts, and the 1984 Trade Union Act, have variously restricted trade union rights which in some cases stretch back nearly 200 years. Severely curtailed are the rights of unions to freely and independently organise their own internal affairs and to strike, picket, maintain political funds and take sympathy action in solidarity with other workers. The most extreme abrogation of union rights, the government's decision to outlaw union membership completely at the Cheltenham General Communication Headquarters, has been condemned by the International Labour Organisation as a violation of Convention 87 which was ratified by Britain in 1948. The government's union ban also contravenes Article 23 of the *United Nations Covenant on Civil and Political Rights* which states that 'everyone shall have the right to freedom of association with others, including the right to form and join trade unions for the protection of his interests'.

The Tory government's workplace legislation has also

weakened protection against unfair dismissal and the enforcement of health and safety regulations. Women's maternity rights and benefits during illness have been eroded. The Fair Wages Resolution has been abolished and the powers of Wages Councils and Inspectorates to defend the interests of the low paid have been undermined.

During the 1984 miners' strike the police virtually sealed off whole counties, setting up roadblocks and turning back miners who sought to exercise their legal right to picket peacefully. Even 150 miles away from the disputed coalfields, Kent miners were stopped by the police at the Dartford and Blackwall tunnels and threatened with arrest if they persisted in 'travelling in a northerly direction'. In the same dispute, the police infiltrated picket lines with undercover agents, mounted baton-wielding 'Cossack' cavalry charges against demonstrating miners, tapped union telephones, invoked the ancient crimes of 'conspiracy' and 'riot', held arrested miners for up to 13 days without bail, imposed bail conditions tantamount to house arrest and interrogated miners about which party they voted for in the 1983 general election.

Since the union ban at GCHQ and the ban on civil servants attending the House of Commons Select Committee looking into affairs at Cheltenham, the government has begun a much more wide-ranging policy of harassment and intimidation against public sector trade unionists. It has, for example, instructed all civil service department heads to 'challenge and deter union activities within the civil service which tend to undermine support for the government's political objectives'. As a consequence, an increasing number of union activists have been officially warned that their criticisms of government policy in internal union bulletins and letters to their MPs are 'unacceptable' and a 'breach of conduct'. In the case of a Manpower Services Commission union branch newsletter which was critical of the Youth Training Scheme, the entire editorial board was threatened with dismissal for 'disloyalty'.[8]

In an unprecedented attack on local democracy, the Conservative government has announced plans to abolish the Labour-controlled Greater London Council and the six metropolitan county councils, despite overwhelming public hostility. This will destroy a tier of elected local government representing a third of the British electorate. It is a decision calculated to remove a major source of opposition to the government. In place of these councils, Mrs Thatcher proposes to substitute a 'remote controlled' democracy of unelected quangos and joint boards which will in many cases transfer political power to Tory majorities without an election. For the surviving local authorities, government rate-capping will dictate their finances from Whitehall. This will remove the right of councils to fix their own rates which they have enjoyed for nearly 400 years.

A whole host of other measures have seriously curtailed individual civil liberties and shifted the balance of law in favour of an increasingly authoritarian, centralised and secretive state. The government and police continue to permit phone tapping despite the declaration of the European Commission of Human Rights that it is an unjustified invasion of personal privacy. Though only 2 per cent of those arrested under the Prevention of Terrorism Act have ever been charged with an offence, the Tory government has enshrined this emergency legislation, which authorises a system of 'internal exile', as a permanent police power. The Police and Criminal Evidence Bill gives the police the right to use 'reasonable force' in the execution of their duties, maintain indefinite roadblocks, enter premises without warrants in certain circumstances, search the houses of people not suspected of a crime to look for evidence of a serious offence, arrest persons on the grounds that they *might* commit an affront to public decency, conduct forcible intimate inspections of a suspect's mouth, anus or vagina, and detain people in a police station for up to four days without charge (which removes the right to justice without delay as enshrined in Article 40 of the Magna Carta of 1215 and in the 1679 Habeas Corpus Act).

The Thatcher government has also pursued a set of policies which have progressively whittled away minority rights. In particular, the 1981 Nationality Act removed a right which had existed for nearly 1,000 years, namely that anyone born in the UK was entitled to British citizenship. This Act and the tightening up of immigration regulations have blatantly discriminated against black Britons and their dependants – even to the extent of separating parents from their children. To hunt down illegal immigrants, the police have mounted military-style raids against whole factories, DHSS offices and housing estates; and in a disturbing number of cases, black Britons have been required to produce their passports when seeking NHS treatment and council housing.

This abrogation of minority rights and civil liberties, and the class division between rich and poor, is inimical to the interests of genuine national self-defence. Indeed, the greater the degree of social injustice and inequality, the more people will feel that they have nothing worth defending. As in the First World War, they will increasingly and quite rightly ask why they should be prepared to risk life and limb to defend a society which robs them of all dignity and many of the elementary decencies of life. What is the use of people putting their lives on the line if, at the end of it all, their only reward is a return to the dole queues and the dereliction of our inner cities?

Likewise, as the government moves further and further in an authoritarian direction, many people who have been on the receiving end of the new Tory despotism will begin to wonder just how much democracy there is left to defend. With freedom already significantly constrained, would invasion and occupation really be that much worse? What is the point of fighting a war in the name of liberty if many of those liberties do not exist in the first place and would continue to be denied in the aftermath of victory?

Successful defence requires a unity of will and purpose in which the whole population backs the war effort. This cannot be achieved in a society riven by class privilege and the suppression of civil liberties. The abolition of class inequalities and the extension of democracy and individual rights to create a more egalitarian society is therefore an integral part of any truly effective defence policy.

The Rich Must Bear the Burden

Defence also costs money. Somebody has to pay for it, the question is who? In deciding who pays, account needs to be taken of the respective wealth and financial capabilities of different sections of the population: in the midst of Britain's so-called recession, and at a time when the government's pay norm was around 3 per cent, the FT share index hit a record high of 900-plus in the first half of 1984. This was nearly double what it had been in January 1982, implying an average 85 per cent rise in the wealth of equity holders in just over two years.

Even before this particular boom, the pre-tax profits of some of the biggest companies had reached staggering proportions – in 1981–82 British Petroleum reaped £4,274 million and Shell £10,284 million. In the manufacturing sector, 1982–83 saw pre-tax profits of £856 million for BAT Industries (up 25.1 per cent on the previous year), £725 million for Unilever (up 2.3 per cent) and £670 million for the General Electric Company (up 14.7 per cent).[9] Although these are pre-tax profit figures, the Labour Research Department revealed that in 1981–82 half of all British companies, including 14 of our 20 largest corporations, paid no tax at all due to over-generous tax allowances and well-developed tax avoidance schemes. The tax payments of the other six amounted to only 4½ per cent of their profits.[10] Among the prominent firms paying no tax were ICI, Esso, Bowater, GKN, Ford, Grand Metropolitan and Reed International. The government has estimated that accumulated tax losses due to big business avoidance schemes totalled £30,000 million in 1982 and that the figure is increasing at the rate of £5,000 million a year.

In 1982, share dividends totalling £4.7 million were paid to David Sainsbury. Tiny Rowland received a dividend of £3.9 million. In the same year, Britain's highest paid company director, Dick Giordano of BOC, was given a rise of £2,000 a week bringing his annual salary to £579,000. Similarly, Robert Wilmot, the managing director of ICL, took a 100 per cent pay rise of £76,000, whilst his employees received only a 9 per cent increase. Sir Lawrie Barratt of Barratt Developments was awarded a 39 per cent rise worth £35,766 whereas his workforce had to make do with a 7 per cent wage settlement.

Britain's richest man is the Duke of Westminster. His fortune is reputed to be in excess of £2,000 million. Following the 1984 budget which slashed the rate of Capital Transfer Tax from 50 to 30 per cent, his family is likely to be £300 million better off. Providing the duke and his wife pass on most of their wealth at least three years before each of them dies, the Inland Revenue will now only be entitled to £450 million instead of the £750 million which would have been taken in tax before the budget.

Expressed in national terms: in 1980, the richest 1 per cent of the population owned 23 per cent (£566,000 million) of total marketable wealth, and the richest 10 per cent owned 58 per cent. Conversely, the poorest 50 per cent of the population owned only 6 per cent of all marketable wealth. In other words, whilst the poorest half of the population had private assets amounting to a mere £1,600 each, the richest 1 per cent possessed over £300,000 per person.[11]

Under the Tory government, these enormous disparities have been considerably widened and the long-term trend towards narrowing the gap between the rich and the poor has been reversed. Within two years of Thatcher coming to power, the richest 5 per cent of the population had increased their share of the national wealth from 43 to 45 per cent. During the same period, the richest 25 per cent pushed up their share from 81 to 84 per cent.[12]

As for the plight of the poor: by 1984, 7.5 million people were claiming or dependent on Supplementary Benefit – the state's traditional definition of the poverty line. This 70 per cent increase from 4.4 million claimants in May 1979 represents an explosion of poverty which is unprecedented since the late 1920s. In addition, there are nearly 1.5 million others living below the Supplementary Benefit level but not claiming benefit, out of pride or ignorance of their entitlement. This includes 800,000 pensioners, 100,000 sick and disabled persons, 400,000 unemployed workers and 50,000 one-parent families. It raises the total numbers living on or below the Supplementary Benefit poverty line to nearly 9 million or one sixth of the population.

Such poverty is not confined to people on benefits. In 1983, the

Low Pay Unit reported that a third of Britain's adult workforce – six million employees – earned wages below the official definition of low pay. In fact, it found that the gap between the better paid and worse paid workers is now greater than it was nearly 100 years ago. In 1886, the poorest 10 per cent of male manual workers earned 68.6 per cent of the average male wage; but by 1982 they earned only 68.3 per cent of the average.

Quite clearly, the mass of the working classes are currently suffering very real poverty and hardship. They are in no position to bear the brunt of funding Britain's defences and cannot be reasonably expected to do so. Given the extravagant wealth of the super-rich, the burden of defence taxes on the poor is not only unjust, it further alienates working people from a commitment to defend the society which is responsible for their impoverishment.

There are, however, a substantial number of immensely wealthy people and corporations in a far better position to financially underwrite the bulk of Britain's defence effort. To ensure this, they ought to be subject to steeply progressive and escape-proof taxation on their company profits, personal incomes and inherited wealth. And why shouldn't they forego some luxuries, instead of the poor being forced to forego essentials? It is the rich who so often talk about patriotism. Well, if they *are* truly patriotic and genuinely concerned about the defence of democracy, rather than the defence of their own class privileges, they should put their money where their principles are.

Whilst we may all have a common interest in defending our right to self-determination and therefore all have a responsibility to make some sacrifices, fairness dictates that those with greater resources should make correspondingly greater sacrifices. So long as the rich refuse to carry a more reasonable share of the defence burden, they reveal themselves for what they really are – paper-thin patriots who would rather defend their own wealth than defend their country, its people and its liberties.

Threats – The Soviet Union and Others

In terms of what we are defending ourselves against, the Soviet Union is generally held to be the main contemporary threat to our security. Whilst popular fears concerning the 'Russian threat' embody more myths than realities, it is certainly true that the USSR is a harsh totalitarian state and that the imposition of its regime on our society would reverse many of the democratic freedoms won by working people over the last 200 years.

There is little doubt that the Soviet government originally began in 1917 with noble and humanitarian ideals – the overthrow of Tsarist tyranny, an end to the 1914-18 war, 'bread and land' to the impoverished working class and peasantry, direct democracy through workers' and soldiers' councils, women's emancipation and the collective ownership of industry and agriculture for the benefit of the common people.

There is also little doubt that, despite Western encirclement and embargoes for over 60 years, the USSR has made enormous strides in transforming one of the poorest and most under-developed nations into the world's second greatest industrial, scientific and military superpower. Though there are continuing consumer shortages, these advances mean that for the average Soviet citizen rents, public transport and entertainment are incredibly cheap; education and sports facilities are the envy of most of the world; there is comparatively little unemployment and inflation; and the inequalities between rich and poor are far narrower than in the West.

However, all this has been achieved at a terrible cost in human suffering and the denial of liberty. Opposition political parties, independent trade unions and unofficial peace groups are banned. Strikes are outlawed and censorship is pervasive. Freedom of speech, assembly and religion is severely curtailed. To criticise the Soviet system is a criminal offence of 'slander against the Soviet state'. Under this law and other blanket charges such as 'anti-Soviet agitation and propaganda', nationalists, political dissidents, free trade unionists and autonomous peace activists are savagely suppressed by internal exile in remote and inhospit-able parts of the country and imprisonment in the 'gulag' of forced labour camps. Amnesty International estimates that around 10,000 political prisoners are held in these camps under a harsh regime in which food and medical treatment is limited and visits and letters are frequently denied. Other dissidents are certified as mentally insane and incarcerated in psychiatric hospitals on the grounds that they are suffering from 'reconstruc-tional delusions'. The Russians describe this as a form of schizophrenic fantasy in which individuals imagine they can change society. The 'treatment' consists of forcible injections with sulphur drugs which induce agonising pain, fevers, body swelling and convulsions.

Examples of Soviet repression are legion: a group of left-wing dissidents led by former Red Army general, Pyotr Grigorenko, were imprisoned and tortured after they staged a demonstration outside the Kremlin in 1968 to protest against the Soviet invasion of Czechoslovakia. Since the mid 1970s, members of the Keblanov group of free trade unionists and the Free Inter-Professional Association of Workers (SMOT) have been persis-tently harassed by the KGB, dismissed from their jobs and sentenced to prolonged forced labour. After complaining about the appalling conditions in the Donbas mines and attempting to set up an independent union, Aleksei Nikitin was confined to a mental hospital. The same fate befell the invalided Aleksandr Vorona when he began campaigning for the rights of the disabled and signed a peace appeal in 1983.

Perhaps the most damning critique of Soviet society comes from the last of the Old Bolsheviks, Ernest Kolman. Whilst remaining committed to Marxism and the communist ideal, in 1976 Kolman wrote an *Open Letter to L.I. Brezhnev, General Secretary of the CPSU:*[13]

> I wish to inform you that I am leaving the Soviet Communist Party. I am 84 and have been a Party member for 58 years. I joined its ranks in order to fight for social justice, for a happy future for mankind. Now, after long and painful reflection, I have come to this difficult decision . . .
>
> As a Red Army soldier, I fought on four fronts for the establishment of Soviet power. In the 1920s I worked illegally in Germany, and was a member of the Central Committee of the German Communist Party. I was sentenced to five years' hard labour, but after half a year's solitary I was freed in an exchange.
>
> Afterwards I held responsible ideological posts in the Comintern, in the Moscow Party committee and in the Soviet Academy of Sciences. I was also elected member of the Moscow Party control commission and the Moscow Party district commission. I knew Lenin personally, worked with Krupskaya, Khrushchev and many others . . .
>
> After Khrushchev's revelations about the bloody crimes of Stalin, euphemistically described as 'the personality cult', I began to understand how deeply distorted the Soviet Communist Party and Soviet power had become, and that I, as a Party member, must bear my share of responsibility for this. However 1968 was the real turning-point for me, when I had occasion to observe the 'Prague spring' and see with my own eyes with what enthusiasm the united people of Czechoslovakia backed the strivings of the Party to rekindle the socialist ideals and the fight for socialism with a human face.
>
> When your tanks and armies occupied Czechoslovakia, subjecting it to your political diktat and merciless economic exploitation – in short turning it into your colony – I lost any illusions I may have had about the nature of your regime . . .
>
> And in any case, what sort of socialism can one talk about in the Soviet Union, when the place of the former capitalist and landlord has been taken by the privileged castes of the Party and state bureaucracies? They are drowning in wealth,

live isolated from the people, above them, and contemptuous of ordinary folk, not wishing to and incapable of understanding their needs and sufferings.

What sort of socialism can one talk of when you are continuing Stalin's totalitarian dictatorship within the country and a great power policy abroad?

The Soviet Union lacks the most elementary democratic rights; instead of free elections there is voting for candidates imposed from above; there is no public political life; strikes are forbidden and the trade unions are subservient to state interests; political discussions are forbidden and everything is covered by universal censorship; information is subject to the interests of lying propaganda.

Basic human rights are crudely trampled on in the Soviet Union: dissidents are harshly persecuted, tens of thousands of them are languishing in jails, concentration camps and psychiatric hospitals, many being punished for their religious beliefs only. In the sixtieth year of Soviet power there are no elementary intellectual freedoms and there is no freedom for the creative artists . . .

A human being must be able to say aloud what he thinks, write down what he thinks, read what takes his fancy, choose his place of abode freely and go wherever he wants to go. But we are once again afraid, just as under Stalin, we hide our manuscripts, stop trusting one another, write meaningless letters for fear of the censors, and sever links with friends . . .

Isn't it inhuman to take away children from parents, block the reunion of families, deny exit visas to visit relations abroad and to deny the families of political prisoners the right to see their loved ones for years and even to write to each other? Can one live amid such conditions? And how long can one live like this? I can no longer go on living like this.

My decision to leave the Communist Party does in no way mean that I will be abandoning the ideals of socialism, with which I became acquainted in 1910 and which have since constituted the main substance of my long life.

On the contrary, I have come to the firm conclusion that my staying in the ranks of the Soviet Communist Party would amount to a betrayal of the ideals of social justice, humanism and the building of a new and more humane society, for the attainment of which I have strived, despite my mistakes and the errors of my ways, and shall go on striving to the end of my days.

Signed: Academician Ernest Kolman

It is quite evident that the Soviet system today represents the exact opposite of almost everything that the left in the West is striving for – obsessive state secrecy rather than freedom of information, centralised bureaucratic control instead of devolved decision making and public accountability, total state power over the individual as opposed to inalienable civil liberties, authoritarian economic management rather than trade union freedom and industrial democracy, and a government-manipulated media instead of greater diversity and choice in news and information sources.

So far as the absence of democracy is concerned, the USSR is not unlike many of the pro-Western dictatorships which anti-Soviet right-wingers tolerate in silence and which the left so roundly condemns – such as Paraguay, Zaire, Philippines, Guatemala, Indonesia, not to mention Turkey, a NATO member – except that in the Soviet Union there is less resort to torture and political executions.

But undesirable as the Russian system may be, and however much its imposition on our society would be a major defeat for democracy and social progress, do the Soviets actually have the desire or capacity to invade the West? Not according to Enoch Powell. He refers to 'the misunderstanding of Soviet Russia as an aggressive power militaristically and ideologically bent upon world domination . . . The notion has no basis in fact; it exists wholly in the realm of imagination. While the United States, often with some of its allies, has fought two major wars in Asia and intervened with military force in Central America and the Middle East, no Russian soldier stands today an inch beyond where Russian soldiers stood in 1948, with the one solitary exception that proves the rule – Afghanistan, where a backyard war is being fought with the same motives and the same prospects of failure as it was twice fought by the British Empire in India.'[14]

A similar critique of the exaggerated 'Soviet threat' was expressed by Brian May in a *Guardian* article on 6 February 1984: 'The Russians have shown no desire to expand beyond the buffer they set up after the war to protect themselves from the American-led West. This is in line with the traditional Tsarist reluctance to wage offensive war in Western Europe – a policy that may arise from recognition of a wide cultural gap, which would make government from Moscow impossible. If they had had more far-reaching aims they would have long ago gobbled up Finland, which gave them a pretext by fighting on the German side, and seized its forests – a valuable source of hard currency. They would have also remained in Austria, instead of leaving it in 1955, and they would at least have tried to annex Yugoslavia.'

The truth is that contemporary Soviet military policy is very much conditioned by a sense of vulnerability which is rooted in Russia's long history of repeated foreign encirclement and subjugation going back to the thirteenth-century Mongol invasion which dominated the country for 250 years. Twice since Napoleon razed Moscow to the ground in 1812 the Russians have come close to being conquered by invading armies. The first was shortly after the Bolshevik Revolution when the new Soviet state was subject to a war of intervention waged by a dozen foreign powers, including Britain and the USA. The second and most devastating occasion was the Second World War, when 40 per cent of the country was laid waste by the Nazis. Soviet losses and suffering were greater than those experienced by any other nation. Over 25 per cent of all property and material wealth was destroyed – 6 million houses, 32,000 factories, 40,000 hospitals, 43,000 libraries, 84,000 schools, 96,000 collective farms, 70,000 villages and 1,700 towns and cities were bombed and burnt to rubble.[15] By the end of the war, 20 million Soviet citizens had been killed and 30 million wounded, so that total casualties amounted to nearly a third of the entire Soviet population.

Since 1945, the USSR has seen itself subject to renewed encirclement by NATO to the west, China to the east, Islamic fundamentalists to the south and by the USA to the north across the pole. The Americans have nearly 400 major military bases and 2,000 auxiliary installations in 30 different countries which surround the Soviet Union on all sides of the globe. They additionally outflank the USSR with their 2nd Fleet in the North Atlantic, their 6th Fleet in the Mediterranean and their 3rd Fleet in the North Pacific; plus 336,000 US troops, 754 US combat aircraft and 9,000 US tactical nuclear weapons which are permanently stationed in Western Europe and which point directly eastwards. No wonder the Soviets feel threatened.

It is more a sense of vulnerability to attack, rather than great power expansionism, which motivates the Kremlin's 'overinsurance' defence policy. With memories of the terrible devastation wrought by the Nazis, the Soviets are determined that such a fate will never befall their country again. To this end, and fearful of a US first strike, the Russians have sought military parity with the West and the creation of a buffer zone of communist states in Eastern Europe to shield them from NATO and act as a forward line of defence. But however understandable, this can never justify the invasions of Czechoslovakia and Afghanistan; nor can it explain the extent of Soviet overreaction in its build-up of offensive-inclined weapons such as 1,398 inter-continental ballistic missiles, 59,000 tanks, 62,000 armoured vehicles, 22,000 pieces of heavy artillery, 10,400 combat aircraft, 239 attack submarines and an indeterminable stockpile of chemical warheads. These are hardly the kind of weapons to inspire confidence in the Kremlin's professed peaceful intentions.

Whatever the current state of affairs, the blame for first beginning to carve the world up into military blocs rests squarely with the USA. Between 1947 and 1954, it concluded military pacts with groups of nations surrounding the USSR on all sides – the Western Hemisphere Defence Treaty Organisation (1947), North Atlantic Treaty Organisation (1947), Australia, New Zealand and United States Treaty (1951), and South East Asian Treaty Organisation (1954). It was not until 1955 that the Russians retaliated by forming the Warsaw Treaty Organisation.

Likewise, it has nearly always been the US which has accelerated the arms race by developing new weapons of aggression and mass destruction. In 1945, the US became the first country to acquire nuclear weapons and the only country ever to use them. The USSR did not succeed in manufacturing its own atomic bomb till 1949. The Americans were also the first to deploy intercontinental long-range bombers in 1948 (USSR 1955), the H-bomb in 1954 (USSR 1955), submarine-launched ballistic missiles in 1960 (USSR 1968), multiple warhead missiles in 1966 (USSR 1968), multiple independently retargetable warheads in 1970 (USSR 1975), long-range Cruise missiles in 1982 (USSR none), and the neutron bomb in 1983 (USSR none). Currently, the US is further escalating the arms race with its plans for 'killer satellites' in outer space and its proposed deployment of 7,414 sea and air launched Cruise missiles in the North Atlantic over the next ten years.

In contrast to the popular view of the Soviet Union as an aggressive and expansionist superpower, Enoch Powell is forced to conclude: 'If Russia is bent on world conquest, she has been remarkably slothful and remarkably unsuccessful. Even her much feared influence in other continents through money, arms and propaganda has spluttered out more ignominiously than the influence which the West sought to acquire by similar means.'[16] Indeed, of the 155 countries in the world, the USSR has significant influence in only about 20. Of the 125 wars since 1945, the US and NATO have been responsible for 79 per cent of all foreign interventions, Third World nations for 15 per cent and the USSR and Warsaw Pact for only 6 per cent.[17] Unlike the 2,400 US bases and installations scattered all over the world, the Soviet bases are almost exclusively within the USSR and bordering states and are much more evidently for the purpose of buffer defence against invasion – 79 per cent of Soviet ground forces are stationed inside the USSR; 16 per cent in East Germany, Poland, Czechoslovakia and Hungary; 3 per cent in Mongolia and 2 per cent in Afghanistan. The Russian air force is based almost entirely within the USSR and the Warsaw Pact, the only exceptions being Afghanistan and reconnaissance planes operating out of Vietnam, Ethiopia, Cuba and Angola.[18]

NATO war planners constantly, but quite falsely, allege vast Soviet military superiority over the West. In *some* weapon categories, whilst the USSR does have more nuclear delivery systems and missiles than our side, many of its missiles are outdated and carry only one or two warheads. By contrast, the US and NATO may have fewer delivery systems and missiles, but each missile carries many more warheads of much greater accuracy. Since the advent of multiple independently retargetable warheads, it is the number of warheads, rather than delivery systems and missiles, which is crucial. The total number of long, medium and short-range nuclear warheads deployed in the European theatre by NATO in 1980 was 7,668 (including 6,000 short-range weapons kept in West Germany, of which a large proportion can hit targets in Eastern Europe), compared with only 2,509 by the Warsaw Pact (excluding 3,500 short-range warheads which are kept in the Soviet Union and cannot hit targets in Western Europe).[19]

It is true that by 1982 the USSR had a lead in intercontinental ballistic missiles of 5,500 warheads to the USA's 2,100. But fixed ICBM launch pads are extremely vulnerable to attack. Much less vulnerable are the hide-and-seek submarine-launched ballistic missiles. Their mobility makes them difficult to detect and destroy, and this gives SLBMs a 'secure retaliatory capacity'. In 1982, the US had an overwhelming superiority in SLBMs with 576 missiles carrying 4,700 independently retargetable warheads; whereas the USSR had a mere 1,900 warheads carried by 989 missiles. Indeed, at any single moment the Russians can only launch 150 SLBM warheads. The Americans, however, can fire 3,200 simultaneously. Furthermore, 55 per cent of all US nuclear submarines are combat ready at all times, compared with only 15 per cent of Soviet submarines.[20]

Former US admiral Gene LaRoque summed up American naval supremacy over the Russians:

> The United States Navy today has 550,000 men. The Soviet Navy has 450,000 men; that is, the United States has 100,000 more men than the Soviets. In addition, the United States has a Coast Guard; the Soviet Union does not. The United States also has 185,000 marines; the Soviet Union has 16,000 marines. The United States has more marines than all the countries in the world put together, including the Soviet Union. The United States Navy has about 3,000 active aircraft. The Soviet Union has 1,500 active aircraft. The United States Navy is younger than the Soviet Navy when you compare the age of all our ships and all the Soviet ships. Our Navy is more modern and physically younger by

> actual measure of years of operation. We have 44 naval bases around the world. The Soviet Union has six major naval bases and no naval bases outside of its territory. None. And of the six naval bases the Soviets have, four of them freeze up in winter. In one of them you have to pass under a Turkish bridge in order to get into the Mediterranean; that is the naval base in Sevastopol in the Black Sea. So the whole fleet in the Black Sea must pass under the bridge that connects European and Asian Turkey. The Soviet Union has a hundred fewer submarines today than it had ten years ago . . .
>
> Many of the Soviet submarines, for example, are also very short-range. They have to stay in their own coastal waters. Again, theirs is a defensive navy. The Soviets have almost no logistics capability.[21]

The Western alliance also comes out on top in terms of member states and military personnel. The seven nations of the Warsaw Pact are outnumbered by the sixteen countries which comprise NATO. The latter have nearly twice the population and a huge lead in industrial output and scientific-technological knowhow.

Soviet ground, sea and air forces in 1981 amounted to 3.7 million. The combined Warsaw Pact forces totalled 4.8 million. NATO forces also numbered 4.8 million. If, however, the 500,000 French troops are added to the NATO side, the Warsaw Pact is outnumbered by half a million troops on its western flank alone. But to the east the USSR also faces a military force of 4.7 million Chinese, bringing the total anti-Soviet armies to 10 million. Thus, the USSR and its allies are outnumbered by 5.2 million soldiers.[22]

Another false charge levelled against the USSR is that it outstrips the West's military expenditure. This is based on a tabulation of total Soviet weaponry and personnel and the estimation of how much it would cost in US dollars for the Americans to build the same weapons in the USA and to employ the same number of troops at US rates of pay. However, taking into account the actual rouble cost of the Soviet armaments and wages bill, the US Arms Control and Disarmament Agency found that between 1970 and 1979 NATO outspent the Warsaw Pact by $207 billion – a total of $1,946.6 billion spent by NATO compared to $1,739.6 billion by the Warsaw Pact. As Garrison and Shivpuri conclude in their study *The Russian Threat*, the USSR is 'out-spent, out-gunned and out-numbered'.[23]

Such realities have forced the former US ambassador to Moscow and long-time hawk, George Kennan, to conclude that: 'The Soviet leadership has no intention, and never has had any intention, of attacking Western Europe.'[24] It is a view which has also come to be shared by Admiral Gene La Roque: 'Our fear of the Soviets is based on a lack of information and total absence of factual data. If you look at the success of the Soviets as imperialists, they are flops. They are not strong around the world . . . I just can't get excited about the Soviet military threat.'[25]

Even if the Russians *did* have territorial ambitions in Western Europe, their capacity to realise them is highly doubtful. Already, they have great difficulty in containing their existing sphere of influence in Eastern Europe and the destabilising Islamic revival in their own Central Asian republics. The Cominform, established in 1947 to unite the European Communist parties, has long ago collapsed. The Soviet monolith has fractured and fissured with Yugoslavia, Albania and Romania successively gaining a significant degree of independence from Moscow, as have the breakaway Eurocommunist parties. There have been major rebellions in East Germany (1953), Hungary (1956), Czechoslovakia (1968) and Poland (1970, 1976 and 1981-83). Currently, despite repression, unrest remains widespread in Poland, Czechoslovakia and East Germany – where Solidarnosc, Charter '77 and a church-sponsored peace movement form in each case a continuing focus of dissent. The USSR remains bogged down in an unwinnable guerrilla war in Afghanistan, and at a considerable drain on its own economy it is financially committed to bailing out Cuba, Poland and a host of national liberation movements. This is despite the fact that the Soviet and East European economies remain sluggish, with low output and growth, and excessive dependence on Western imports. These are hardly favourable circumstances for the USSR to launch a war. In any case, why would the Kremlin want to go to war when it can acquire most of the Western grain and 'hi-tech' products it needs by trade and peaceful coexistence?

The Soviet Union has every reason to desire peace and stability, if only to preserve its existing bloc of buffer states. To this end, in recent years the USSR has undertaken a number of disarmament initiatives. As an act of good faith to encourage Washington to ratify the SALT II treaty, President Brezhnev withdrew 20,000 Soviet troops and 1,000 tanks from East Germany in 1980. The American response was to bombastically accuse the Russians of 'fraud' and 'propaganda'. A year later the Soviet foreign minister, Andrei Gromyko, proposed at the UN that all the nuclear powers should sign an agreement to renounce the first use of nuclear weapons. Both the UK and the US rejected the Soviet proposal with scorn and derision. When the USSR *unilaterally* renounced the first use of nuclear weapons at the 1982 UN Special Session on Disarmament, the Americans and the British reacted by provocatively emphasising NATO's continuing commitment to a first strike option. Early in 1984, the Warsaw Pact collectively called on NATO to conclude an East-West non-aggression treaty and agree to a freeze on military expenditure leading to a phased reduction in all defence budgets. Once again, the Soviet initiatives were ridiculed and rejected out of hand.

Whilst the traditional view is that we need to defend ourselves against the Russians, there are other potential threats as well. At some point in the future, if Britain elected a radical left-wing government which proceeded to expel US troops and military bases and expropriate American multinational corporations, we might end up having to defend a socialist Britain against the USA. Unlikely as this may seem at the moment, in changed circumstances it is not an impossible scenario. After all, whenever America's economic and strategic interests have been threatened, the US has never baulked at the use of direct military force – as for example in Korea, Vietnam, the Dominican Republic, Lebanon and Grenada. Nor has Washington been reluctant to topple democratically elected governments such as the Arbenz administration in Guatemala in 1954 and the Chilean presidency of Salvador Allende in 1973. Closer to home, the US has defended its own national self-interest by indirectly helping to sustain pro-American dictatorships against the forces of democracy in the Portugal of Salazar and Caetano, Franco's Spain and Greece under the colonels. In the mid 1970s, when the fortunes of the Italian Communist Party were rapidly rising, covert US aid was channelled to the right-wing parties and there were dark mutterings that Washington would not stand idly by and allow Italy to 'go Red'.

Another possible source of future military conflicts and threats is the looming ecological crisis. The history of human society on our planet spans well over 10,000 years. Yet in the last 200 years alone – a mere fraction of human existence – capitalist industrialisation by a handful of countries in Western Europe and North America has brought the whole world to the brink of devastating resource scarcity and environmental pollution. The capitalist form of expansionist production and consumption has rapaciously exploited the earth's finite and irreplaceable raw materials, rapidly using up deposits of minerals and other natural resources which took millions of years to form and accumulate. Given the massive depletion of scarce resources which has already occurred in the wake of industrialisation in a few pockets of our planet, imagine what will happen as more and more Third World countries industrialise in pursuit of economic development and a standard of living equal to ours in the West. Such an explosion of demand would place an intolerable strain on the earth's finite supplies of many basic raw materials. At current rates of expanding consumption, in 40 or 50 years time as many of these resources such as oil begin to run out, become excessively costly to extract, or simply cannot be produced in sufficient quantities to meet rising demand, our economies and cultures will face potential collapse. This prospect of being unable to sustain an accustomed level of economic activity and prosperity will precipitate fierce competition for control of diminishing resources. With the survival of huge manufacturing monopolies and multinationals under threat, whole national economies in jeopardy and the future of the Western way of life at stake, the rich industrial states are likely to become increasingly desperate in a bid to preserve their privileged access to the raw materials which form the basis of our civilisation. This brings with it the possibility of a fascist resurgence and a new round of inter-imperialist wars, both East-West and North-South, for the control of declining resources. In such a context, British raw materials such as coal, oil, gas or fish might be a target for acquisition by force of arms and Britain may need to defend itself against other predatory industrial states.

In addition to these scenarios, many other new and unforeseen threats may arise in years to come: a wider conflict spreading from a localised war between Greece and Turkey, Iran and Iraq, or Israel and the Arab states; superpower confrontation over Middle East oil supplies; American intervention to prevent German reunification and neutralism; or Soviet 'fraternal assistance' to a beleaguered left government threatened by the fascist right and a military coup. Since no one can know what the future holds, history and common sense tell us that so long as war remains a possibility we ought to have at least some capacity for self-defence.

Chapter Three:

What's Wrong With Britain's Defence Policy?

External Objectives – Unprepared for Self-Defence

To a large extent, Britain's nuclear weapons policy is merely an extension of the older imperialist tactic of strategic bombing whereby the great powers sought to force rival states to submit to their will. Indeed, our contemporary nuclear strategy entirely accords with the whole history of the British armed forces which is predominantly one of imperial conquest rather than self-defence. Even today, the character of our military services is still very substantially marked by their traditional imperial role of subjugating other nations, garrisoning the annexed colonies and maintaining a global navy and an interventionist capacity to safeguard British spheres of economic and political influence. From the late seventeenth century, our armed forces evolved predominantly to meet these predatory requirements of the British Empire and, as a consequence, became explicitly geared to an expansionist and external function of conquering other nations, instead of defending our own.

For centuries, as an island state, Britain was relatively secure against invasion. Prior to the late 1600s, our defence was traditionally based on the navy, with the army existing as a mere appendage and consisting solely of locally raised part-time militias. However, the defeat of the Spanish Armada in 1588 bought about a major change in defence policy. In establishing British naval supremacy, it laid the basis for a new era of imperial rivalry and colonial expansion lasting for 350 years.

From this time on, Britain's military power grew steadily less concerned with self-defence and more with foreign conquest and the defence of British interests overseas. The huge expansion of the armed forces and their changing character, including the creation of the first permanent standing army, was very substantially influenced by ensuing events – a series of European and colonial wars against rival imperial powers such as France, Spain and the Netherlands; the seizure and maintenance of order in the new colonies; and the suppression of colonial rebellions and indigenous races such as the native Americans and Australian aborigines.

This dominant external function of the British armed forces is highlighted by the Pax Britannica which they eventually imposed on a quarter of the world's population. From the early seventeenth century Britain began to colonise India, North America and the West Indies. In the late 1600s, following wars with the Netherlands, the Dutch were ousted from their eastern seaboard settlements in the Americas and a new wave of English colonies were established. Around the same time, Anglo-French rivalry culminated in the British conquest of Gibraltar and several West Indian islands. From the mid eighteenth century, the French were also successively pushed out of Canada, Florida and India. By the 1790s, British forces had pacified most of the Indian subcontinent and laid claim, in the name of the Crown, to the new-found territory of Australia.

There followed a massive growth in the standing army during the Revolutionary and Napoleonic Wars with France from 1793 to 1815. These wars led His Majesty's Government to extend its dominion over the Cape Colony, Ceylon, Malta, Tobago, St Lucia, British Honduras, British Guiana and Mauritius. In the first half of the nineteenth century, the navy ran up the Union Jack over Singapore, Malaya, Aden and New Zealand. From 1850, British military expeditions in East and West Africa resulted in the acquisition of substantial new colonies such as Nigeria and Rhodesia. During the reign of Queen Victoria, the army fought nearly forty wars in China, India, Burma, Afghanistan, Persia, Abyssinia, Sudan and Egypt.

But it was not always a case of bloody conquest followed by the deferential loyalty of the conquered peoples to the British monarch. The armed forces also had to deal with a series of colonial rebellions – the 1775–83 American War of Independence, an attempted revolution by the United Irishmen in 1795–98, the Anti-Colonial Revolt in Canada in 1837, the Maori Land Wars of 1846 and 1861–64, the uprising in India during 1857, the Ashanti War of 1874, the 1879 Zulu War, the Mashonaland Rising of 1896, the 1900–01 Boxer insurrection, the Fenian and Easter rebellions in Ireland in 1867 and 1916 and the Irish War of Independence between 1918 and 1922.

Because of this centuries-old bias towards the imperial objective of foreign conquest, the chiefs of staff were quite unprepared for a war of self-defence when Britain faced the prospect of Nazi invasion in 1940. Right up to the eve of the Second World War, the armed forces were blinded to the task of national defence by their dominant colonial role and the innate conservatism of their officer corps. Military thinking was strongly influenced by the 'blimps' and an aristocratic officer caste of traditional military families, which virtually inherited their rank from one generation to the next.

The 'Charge of the Light Brigade' mentality was still deeply entrenched. As late as 1937, the British Army's manual for *Cavalry Training (Horsed)* included a section entitled 'The Use of the Sword in War'. It instructed troopers as follows: 'In the charge against both cavalry and infantry, each man will ride at his opponent with the fixed determination of running him through and killing him.' The same manual contained 23 pages of sword and lance exercises with 22 illustrations, plus a further twelve drawings on drill, three detailing formations in action and only one concerning the firing of rifles.

Published simultaneously was the *Cavalry Training (Mechanised) Pamphlet Number One* for tank crews. It advised: 'The principles and system of training will be as laid down in Cavalry Training (Horsed) with certain modifications . . . It is of the greatest importance that all leaders should be trained: 1) To act quickly and make rapid decisions; with this object, officers will be encouraged to hunt and ride across country.' As Tom Wintringham, the left's leading military critic, sarcastically remarked at the time, the pamphlet omitted to state how many lumps of sugar officers should give their tanks after a good gallop!

Amongst the horse cavalry, whose officers were substantially drawn from the landed aristocracy, there was still great resistance, even in the late 1930s, to the introduction of mechanised divisions and considerable scepticism about the value of tanks in battle. The infantry was hardly more enlightened. Of a recruit's first three months training, nearly half the time was spent on square-bashing, physical jerks, guard duty and the performance of domestic services for senior officers.

The military traditionalists who oversaw this antiquated system constituted a very substantial stratum of the higher officer corps. They were unready and ill-suited for the threat of Nazi invasion and the modern technological warfare of dive bombers and armoured blitzkreig. As officers and gentlemen of empire, they were more attuned to policing the British Raj and quelling Indian 'mutinies' than to the defence of their homeland against fascist aggression. Steeped in the glory of an imperial history in which Britain had held unquestioned naval supremacy for 350 years and had never been conquered since 1066, the military chiefs were absurdly overconfident and complacent.

As a result, when the possibility of a German invasion was on the cards in mid 1940, they were caught unprepared with no clear strategy for dealing with it, and a corps structure and weapons inventory which was quite inadequate for a war of resistance to occupation. Fortunately for Britain, instead of sweeping across the Channel the Nazis turned east to Russia, which gave us the breathing space to modernise and adapt to the German threat. After the Second World War, and the momentary aberration of fighting for the self-defence of Britain, the armed forces reverted to their dominant imperial function abroad, being involved in over fifty military operations in all corners of the globe.

Even before the end of the war, the British army was used against our former allies in the partisan resistance movements in Italy and Greece and against the Anti-Japanese peasant armies in Burma, Indonesia and Malaya. Since then, there have been large-scale British military campaigns against national liberation movements in Malaya (1948–60), Kenya (1952–55), Cyprus (1954–58), Oman (1957–59) and Aden (1963–68).

The army was heavily involved in major military action in Korea (1950–55), Suez (1956), Malaysia (1963–66) and the Falklands (1982). It undertook smaller counter-insurgency and internal security operations in India (1945–47), Vietnam (1945), Palestine (1946–48), Aden (1947), Ethiopia (1948–51), British Honduras (1948, 1957 and since 1962), Singapore (1950), Akaba (1951), British Guiana (1953 and 1962–64), Oman (1955 and since 1965), Bahrain (1956), Hong Kong (1956, 1962 and 1966–67), Togoland (1957), Aden, Jordan, Nassau and Ghana (each in 1958), Gan (1959), Cameroons and Jamaica (each in 1960), Kuwait (1961), Zanzibar (1961 and 1963), Brunei (1962), Cyprus (since 1963), Swaziland (1963), Uganda, Kenya and Tanganyika (1964), Mauritius and Das Island (1966), Anguilla (1969), Ireland (since 1969), Zimbabwe (1980) and Lebanon (1983). Additionally, the army was used to break strikes in the Gold Coast and British Guiana in 1948, Nigeria in 1949 and Kenya and Tanganyika in 1950.

Even today, despite the continued decline of empire, our armed forces are overwhelmingly geared to external foreign objectives rather than a home-based defensive role. Their primary commitments are Ireland, the Falklands, and NATO support in West Germany. Secondary deployments take place in fifteen other parts of the world – Hong Kong, Belize, Gibraltar, Ascension Island, Diego Garcia, Brunei, Lebanon and Cyprus, together with a naval presence in the Indian and Pacific Oceans, the Caribbean, the English Channel, the Western and Eastern Atlantic and the North Sea. Furthermore, there are 660 British military advisers in 26 countries. The total number of British service personnel stationed overseas in 1982 amounted to 109,000 – a third of the total enlistment.[1]

As long ago as 1957, in the Defence White Paper of that year, the British government made clear its intention to continue neglecting home defence in favour of offensive strategic capabilities. In August 1957, the then Minister of Defence, Duncan Sandys, declared: 'We have taken a very bold step in deciding not to do the impossible. We decided not to defend the whole country, but to defend only our bomber bases.'[2]

The policy remains broadly the same today, with the government spending more on the air defence of the fleet than on the whole of mainland Britain. In 1983–84, the Ministry of Defence allocated £1,700 million to the British Army of the Rhine and only £703 million to home forces.[3] This inverted set of priorities seemed confirmed by the minister's 1983 *Statement on the Defence Estimates* where the section headed *Defence of the United Kingdom Base* merited just half a page out of 116.

Britain's continued pretensions to superpower status, as exemplified by our overseas bases and global policing role, fundamentally distort and weaken our home defence effort by diverting money and resources away from genuine self-defence. The Fortress Falklands folly, for example, in 1984 alone swallowed nearly £600 million and siphoned off to the South Atlantic 4,000 army and RAF personnel, several squadrons of Phantom and Harrier jets and Rapier air defences, plus a substantial fleet of Royal Navy submarines, destroyers, frigates and auxiliary vessels.

The Falklands and our other overseas commitments combine to create a situation not unlike the late 1930s. Our generals are so preoccupied with the legacies of the colonial era and NATO's strategy for continental Europe that they have no comprehensive plans for the defence of our own island against aggression. To the chiefs of staff basking in the last rays of Britain as an imperial great power, the military occupation of our country by a foreign army is unthinkable and, therefore, unplanned for. Their complacency is rooted in the history of empire and the history of their own regiments: Britain has never been subjugated for a thousand years and during more than three centuries of colonialism we were always the occupying power and never the occupied nation. This imperial history of fighting our wars on other peoples' territory is reflected today in the government's strategy of 'forward defence' in which the defence of Britain is seen as beginning on the Rhine. But what happens if that bulwark is breached? Or if an enemy attack does not proceed to the anticipated pattern of a single westward invasion across the north German plain? Where are the plans for the actual self-defence of the British mainland? There are none. No such plans exist. The British armed forces have neither the plans, corps structure nor weapon systems required for national self-defence against direct attack and invasion.

Armed for Offence and Civil Repression

Britain's preoccupation with the defence of its overseas interests inevitably means that much of our armoury is made to measure for that role and is therefore ill-suited for a strictly self-defensive task.

Consequently, in both our nuclear and conventional arsenals there is a bias towards weapon systems with an offensive and invasive capacity: submarine-launched nuclear missiles, long-range strategic bombers, hunter-killer submarines, aircraft carriers and armoured tank divisions. These are not the weapons of pure self-defence, but more the instruments of external aggression for theatres of war thousands of miles beyond the British Isles.

A detailed examination of the 1983 *Statement on the Defence Estimates* reveals a significant aggressive and interventionist capability. In late 1982, the government announced plans for an American-style rapid deployment force able to mount trouble-shooting missions at short notice in any part of the world. The Army's 5th Brigade is to be equipped to air-drop two battalions of the parachute regiment and reinforced with a helicopter squadron, engineers and an armoured reconnaissance regiment. The character of the army's 12 engineering and 19 armoured regiments is fairly ambiguous. Their firepower, speed and construction abilities make them highly suited for offensive operations and the surmounting of natural obstacles such as rivers and manmade fortified defensive positions which would typically be encountered in the invasion of another nation's territory. The army's inventory of 1,200 tanks and 5,500 armoured cars, with another 1,900 mechanised infantry combat vehicles on order, is arguably much more than we need for exclusively defensive purposes. So, too, is the equipment of increasing numbers of army units with nuclear-capable Lance missiles and M–109 and M–110 howitzers.

The Royal Navy's more provocative-inclined units include 31 submarines (four of them Polaris nuclear missile carriers), 5 aircraft carriers and assault ships, 47 frigates and 13 guided-missile destroyers. Deployed with these vessels are Sea Harrier aircraft which can carry free-fall nuclear bombs and Sea King, Wessex, Wasp and Lynx helicopters which can deliver anti-submarine nuclear depth charges. There is also a substantial Fleet Auxiliary Service of 14 tankers, 4 replenishment ships and 6 landing vessels which give the navy the ability to mount long-range operations way beyond our maritime defensive waters. The total expenditure on these aggressive-tending naval units in 1983–84 amounted to £1,430 million, i.e. 67 per cent of the entire Royal Navy budget.[4]

Dominating the air force are the 12 offensive squadrons of bomber, strike and reconnaissance aircraft, and 5 offensive support squadrons which include nuclear-capable Jaguars, Buccaneers, Tornados and Harriers; plus 11 long-range air transport and tanker squadrons. These units enable the RAF to land troops and bomb targets deep inside an enemy's heartland. In 1983–84 expenditure on these aircraft cost £1,399 million; nearly 44 per cent of the total RAF financial allocation and more than double the £579 million spent on interceptor planes and air defences.[5] The RAF is to further enhance its offensive capacity with the purchase of 220 nuclear-capable GR1 Tornado bombers, 60 nuclear-capable Harrier GR5 V/STOL strike aircraft and 6 Tristar long-range transporters.

Though the armed forces have been predominantly concerned with defending Britain's overseas interests since the 1600s, a subordinate function, equally removed from the self-defence of Britain, has been their role as agents of civil repression.

From the late eighteenth century, in response to a rising tide of agitation by food rioters, strikers, luddites and republicans, the government decided to expand the army, adapt it to an internal security role and station troops in barracks throughout the industrial districts of working-class discontent. Proposing the new policy for the first time in 1793, Prime Minister Pitt argued: 'The circumstances of the country, coupled with the general state of affairs, rendered it advisable to provide barracks in other parts of the kingdom. A spirit has appeared in some of the manufacturing towns which make it necessary that troops should be kept near them.'[6] By 1815, the government had built 155 barracks and many of the big factory towns came to resemble a nation under military occupation. Throughout the nineteenth century, the suppression of strikers and political protesters was a regular feature of army duties. Eleven people were killed and 400 injured in the Peterloo massacre when the army was used in 1819 to disperse suffrage demonstrators in Manchester. In 1839, as John Frost led 3,000 Chartist miners into Newport, soldiers shot dead ten marchers and wounded 50 others. Later, at the greatest of all Chartist mass meetings, held on Kennington Common in 1848, troops were put on standby to prevent the Chartists from marching into central London. Dozens of protesters were wounded when the cavalry were called out to put down the 1848 bread riots in Glasgow, and hundreds were injured in Whitehall on Bloody Sunday in 1887 when the Grenadier Guards attacked demonstrators protesting against unemployment and British colonial rule in Ireland.

Even in this century, the military has been used against the civilian population to quell trade union and political agitation. In 1911, the army brutally suppressed striking South Wales miners, particularly at Tonypandy. Eight years later, tanks and troops were ordered onto the streets to crush the 'Red Clyde' rebellion and the Limehouse riots.

During the 1926 General Strike, the navy was sent to garrison the London docks and armoured cars escorted the convoys of blacklegs. Since 1945, the armed forces have been used as strikebreakers against dockers (1948, 1949, 1970 and 1972), railway workers (1955), miners (1970, 1972, 1973 and 1974), dust collectors (1975) and firefighters (1977-78).

Today, the army is increasingly being adapted for an internal security responsibility within mainland Britain. The shape of things to come was set out by Brigadier Frank Kitson in his book *Low Intensity Operations*, published in 1971: 'The purpose of this book is to draw attention to the steps which should be taken now in order to make the army ready to deal with subversion, insurrection and peace-keeping operations.'[7] Kitson defined subversion as: 'all illegal measures short of the use of armed force taken by one section of the people of a country to overthrow those governing the country at the time, or to force them to do things which they do not want to do. It can involve the use of political and economic pressure, strikes, protest marches and propaganda.'[8] Kitson seems to be implying that any political action which seeks to force the resignation of a government or pressure it to alter its policies is illegitimate. Even traditional methods of political protest such as boycotts, industrial action and demonstrations are classified by Kitson as potentially 'illegal' measures which the army ought to be ready to 'deal with'.

Kitson's book is merely a public statement of ideas which are now fairly commonplace amongst senior military staff and which have long been incorporated into the army's official *Land Operations Manual*. Volume 3, on Counter-Revolutionary Operations, defines the army's enemies as not only 'guerrillas' and 'terrorists', but even mere 'dissidents'. The subversion which the army is supposed to counter is described as any 'action taken to undermine the military, economic, psychological, morale or political strength of a nation and the loyalty of the subjects'.[9]

The section of the *Manual* detailing the army's internal security role sets out its basic aims thus: 'to give general guidance on the conduct of counter-revolutionary operations, whether they are concerned with civil disturbances, terrorism or insurgency'.[10] Under the heading 'Types of Operations', it states that the function of internal security is anti-terrorism, peacekeeping and 'dealing with civil disturbances resulting from labour disputes, racial and religious antagonism and tension or social unrest'.[11]

Citing the types of disturbances the army might need to take action against, the *Manual* lists 'unlawful assemblies, strikes and picketing, civil disobedience, riots, arson and looting'.[12]

To cope with eventualities such as these during a period of political upheaval, the British army is now increasingly committed to highly sophisticated counter-insurgency techniques which have been tried and tested in the north of Ireland: news and information control, covert surveillance and computerised intelligence files, SAS-style infiltration and undercover operations, as well as psychological warfare methods, including 'dirty tricks' and 'black' propaganda, to discredit opponents and split their supporters.

A substantial proportion of an army recruit's total training time is now allocated to rehearsing an internal security role applicable to the urban areas of northern Ireland and mainland Britain. According to former Royal Marine commando Ian Phillips: 'Each company took it in turns to be "rioters" and "terrorists" one day, and the security forces the next . . . Within the barracks there is a mock town consisting of several streets and alleyways, generally resembling any ordinary working-class district. Practical training is given in riot control, house searching, interrogation techniques, sniper positioning, setting up secret observation posts, etc.'[13]

There is also growing cooperation between the armed forces and the civil authorities, particularly the police, in joint exercises such as the blockade of Heathrow and Stansted airports in 1974, nuclear war planning and civil defence, the guarding of Cruise missile bases and launcher convoys, and the establishment of joint training and secondment programmes.

Clearly this internal security function has nothing to do with the defence of Britain against foreign aggression. It is actually a damaging diversion from national self-defence and it fundamentally threatens the democratic rights and civil liberties which the armed forces supposedly exist to defend.

Dependence on the Americans

The preponderant alignment of our armed forces towards overseas commitments and an internal security role at home leaves Britain ultimately – and unhealthily – dependent on the US military umbrella. As the price of this American protection, Britain has steadily and stealthily been converted into the United States' forward base for a European war against the Russians. Our island has become America's flagship in the North Atlantic – an unsinkable aircraft carrier for the launching of US military operations into Europe.

In June 1980 the defence minister, Francis Pym, reluctantly admitted that there were 12 American military bases in Britain. Within two months, he was forced to revise this implausible figure and confirm the existence of 56 US installations. By April 1983, the Ministry of Defence had made further adjustments and came up with a total of 64 American bases manned by 27,000 US service personnel.

Since then, new investigations by journalists such as Duncan Campbell have put the true figure at more than 150 US military installations and depots staffed by nearly 40,000 American military and civilian personnel. The largest of these include 21 military bases, 9 transportation facilities, 17 weapon storage sites, 38 communication centres and 10 intelligence gathering stations. The best known of these are the Cruise missile bases at Greenham Common and Molesworth, plus the nuclear submarine base at Holy Loch and the air force bases at Upper Heyford and Lakenheath. The latter is the largest USAF base in Europe with 96 nuclear bombers in a constant state of readiness for war.

Less well known are the US National Security Agency station at Mentwith Hill which, among other tasks, monitors overseas telephone calls. Boscombe Down, Chicksands and Morewenstow operate as key American listening posts. Sited at Brawdy in south-west Wales is the biggest US submarine surveillance station anywhere in the world. The Edzell, Thurso and Croughton bases are key links in the Pentagon's Defence Satellite Communications System. Between them, the American storage depots at Welford and Mildenhall contain the largest concentration of nuclear weapons in Europe. Mildenhall also doubles as a secret US spy plane base and home of the specially adapted Boeing 707 'flying command centres' from which American commanders would direct military operations in Europe during a time of war.

At no point has the establishment of these American bases been the subject of parliamentary debate or approval. Instead, they have been secretly authorised by successive prime ministers and specialist cabinet committees, often without the knowledge of the full cabinet, let alone parliament and the British people.

None of these bases is strictly speaking for the defence of Britain. They primarily exist to back up the United States' European and global rivalry with the Soviet Union. Despite claims that these bases are part of NATO and for our own self-defence, the US military authorities retain their own independent lines of communication, command and control. The installations are frequently used by the Americans for purposes which are clearly outside NATO's direct remit of defending Western Europe. During the 1973 Middle East war and the attempt to free the American hostages in Iran in 1980, the Pentagon repeatedly made use of British-based installations without notifying either our government or NATO.

This lack of consultation is just one aspect of a growing rift between Washington and Western Europe which gives our dependence on the American military umbrella an increasing number of drawbacks. The vast array of US bases dotted across our countryside may be advantageous to the Pentagon strategists who want a forward base to counter the Soviets and maintain their star-spangled sphere of influence in Europe. But from a British perspective, these bases make our country a prime target in the event of war. Far from enhancing our survivability, they actually make it more likely that, if war broke out, our island would be a major battleground and a target for full-scale obliteration. In any war, the Kremlin would very probably ignore countries like Sweden and Portugal which possess little or no belligerent ability. But because Britain has an offensive, retaliatory strike capacity and is the heart and brains of US military operations in Europe, we are highly likely to be number one on the Soviet hit list.

Another area of divergent interests is the overall American military strategy of confining any war with the Russians to the European continent so as to avoid damage to the US home base. In the words of US Admiral Gene LaRoque: 'We fought World War I in Europe, we fought World War II in Europe, and if you dummies let us, we'll fight World War III in Europe.'[14] But Washington would not only rather fight its wars on our territory, in so doing it is prepared to unleash ghastly weapons of mass destruction which would devastate our countries. This White House strategy of containing a Soviet-American war within Europe has been the driving rationale behind the development of smaller-scale tactical nuclear weapons. Instead of a full-scale intercontinental ballistic holocaust in which the principal targets and annihilated nations would be the USA and the USSR, the Americans have sought to limit the size of a nuclear exchange and restrict it to the European theatre in the hope that the US mainland will emerge unscathed.

It is in this context of establishing Europe as the first line of American defence that the White House pushed ahead with the siting of the first Cruise and Pershing missiles in our countries in late 1983. In the scenario leading up to the emplacement of the missiles, there was one very sinister and still unexplained factor: the shooting down of the Korean airliner KAL 007 by the Soviet Union on 1 September 1983. In the immediate aftershock, public opinion polls in Britain which had previously been running at nearly 2 to 1 against Cruise suddenly registered a dramatic increase in support for the missiles. How convenient for Mrs Thatcher and President Reagan! What good fortune that the airliner strayed hundreds of miles off course into prohibited Soviet airspace for nearly two hours and just happened to fly over two top secret Russian military bases at Kamchatka and Sakhalin! And on the very night that the Soviets were planning to test their new PL-5 missile. Curious how KAL 007 radioed back to base that it was on its normal legitimate flight path and that it failed to readjust its route even after it crossed the Soviet radio beacons at Kabaru, Kokutan and Lopatka which would have clearly identified its true position. Strange how the Korean airliner was shadowed by an RC-135 US spy plane which made no attempt to intercept it and put it back on course, and no attempt to inform Washington or Moscow. Even stranger that KAL 007's radio, computer and radar all suddenly and simultaneously broke down and that the radio miraculously repaired itself just in time for the pilot to report that the plane had been hit by the Russians. Equally odd, why did the Korean airliner make no response at all throughout the entire 75 minutes that Soviet MIG-23 and SU-15 jets buzzed it, sent radio messages, fired warning cannon across its path and made visual signals such as close passes with the undercarriage down? Particularly suggestive of something sinister was the way in which the US initially issued official versions of the tragedy which later turned out to be quite untrue, including doctored transcripts of Soviet fighter pilot conversations. The American explanation appears to have been deliberately intended to cover up all the inconsistencies and contradictions surrounding the disaster.

It has since been confirmed that KAL airliners fitted with special cameras and electronic devices are regularly used by the CIA to overfly Russian airspace to gather military intelligence. This makes it very likely that KAL 007 *was* on a spy mission and that the Americans quite consciously put the airliner in a high-risk situation in the knowledge that if it was shot down the tragedy could be turned into a major propaganda victory against the Soviets and the peace movements in the West during the crucial period before Cruise missiles were due to arrive in Europe. And that is exactly what happened.[15]

However fantastic such a theory may sound, it seems highly probable. After all, in recent years it has been revealed that the CIA set up the Gulf of Tonkin incident in 1963 to provide the pretext for a massive increase in American troops and military aid to South Vietnam. If the CIA was prepared to go to such lengths to win public and Congressional support for greater intervention in Vietnam, it might very well have been equally willing to risk a civilian airliner to secure public backing for Cruise missiles in Europe.

Whatever the precise truth about KAL 007, the disaster certainly gave President Reagan the perfect excuse he needed for his nuclear rearmament programme. It certainly gave the flagging pro-Cruise lobby a major injection of new support. But most importantly, it also revealed the darker side of American politics and, together with the Grenada invasion, raised fresh doubts about the extent to which we can trust the United States.

The British government's agreement to accept the American-controlled missiles in late 1983 added a further chapter to a long line of decisions which have bit by bit surrendered our sovereignty and effectively given an American president, whom we did not elect and cannot remove, the right to decide whether Britain lives in peace or declares war. It is surely the ultimate irony that Mrs Thatcher has argued that we need Cruise missiles to defend our sovereignty, yet because they are under American control, their emplacement on our soil actually involves a loss of sovereignty by the British people. Indeed, we are now so overwhelmingly dependent on the United States in all military matters as to place serious constraints on our ability to pursue any kind of genuinely independent defence, foreign or economic policy.

Resentment at this surreptitious loss of independence, fear of America's nuclear war-fighting strategy for Europe and recognition of conflicting interests between ourselves and the US is reflected in Britain by a 55 per cent opposition to the stationing of the new American missiles in our country[16] and a 66 per cent distrust of the US commitment to consult the British government before firing them.[17] As many as 37 per cent of the electorate believe that Britain is 'too closely' aligned to American foreign policy,[18] and following the US landings on Grenada, 59 per cent feel that the invasion has made them 'less likely' to trust the US government.[19]

In other West European countries, the feelings are similar, if not stronger. Amongst the Dutch, 63 per cent of the population oppose the deployment of Cruise, including 45 per cent of Christian Democrat supporters.[20] Coinciding with the arrival of the first missiles in late 1983, there were unprecedented anti-Cruise demonstrations of over a million people throughout West Germany and hundreds of thousands in London, Rome and Paris. In The Hague alone, 550,000 people attended a rally addressed by the Dutch queen's sister, Princess Irene.

Apart from Cruise missiles, the widening rift with the Americans has manifested itself in other ways too. Following the Soviet invasion of Afghanistan and the imposition of martial law in Poland, Britain and Western Europe refused to comply with the US demand for a boycott of the Moscow Olympics and trade sanctions against the Russians. American opinion was further disregarded with the export of arms to Iran and high-technology equipment to the USSR, as well as the decision of the West German government to build the Russian gas pipeline and buy large quantities of Soviet natural gas. The clash of interests has also been evidenced by the way in which American protectionism, high interest rates and an over-strong dollar have damaged the West European economies. In recent years, the governments on our side of the Atlantic have been increasingly critical of US policies in Central America, the Middle East and southern Africa. Following the Pentagon's latest proposal for 'star wars' killer satellites, even the conservative Bonn government has castigated the Americans for a dangerous and destabilising escalation of the arms race.

In view of this more critical West European attitude towards the US and a growing divergence of interests, are we wise to depend on the Americans to defend us? Can we be so sure that the USA would be willing to risk the nuclear incineration of its own cities to defend an increasingly independent-minded Western Europe? It seems more and more doubtful. The determining factor in American foreign and defence policy is self-interest. Indeed, this has always been the case. Even during the First and Second World Wars, self-interest initially kept the USA out of both conflicts. That traditional American isolationism towards Europe seems to be resurfacing again. Over the last year, a number of prominent US politicians have questioned the present American commitment to Europe.

Early in 1984, Dr Henry Kissinger and Lawrence Eagleburger, the US Under-Secretary of State, repeatedly emphasised the growing differences between the American and West European governments on a whole range of issues. Eagleburger suggested that if the Europeans did not adopt greater self-reliance in defence matters, Washington might react by downplaying its commitment to the NATO alliance in favour of the Pacific and the Far East. Kissinger proposed that the US should withdraw nearly half of its 336,000 troops from Europe. This creeping isolationism is also reflected in public opinion where a clear majority of Americans no longer believe that Europe should be defended by US nuclear weapons – 54 per cent are opposed to their government using nuclear weapons to halt a Russian attack on Europe with only 34 per cent in favour.[21] According to Democratic Senator Sam Nunn, in the not too distant future the President and Congress are likely to be forced by the pressure of public opinion to downgrade their support for NATO unless Europe assumes a greater responsibility for its own defence. Indeed, Nunn's legislative proposals to this effect were only narrowly defeated in the Senate in June 1984. Whatever may have been true in the past, we can certainly no longer take the American military umbrella for granted. Dependence on the US is becoming both increasingly implausible and undesirable.

Nuclear Weapons – Unusable and Counter-Productive

In addition to our dependence on the Americans, the other delusory pillar of our defence policy is dependence on nuclear weapons. The government claims these weapons exist purely as a deterrent. If that were true, however, we would only need a few. Indeed, the former US Defence Secretary, Robert MacNamara, suggested in the early days of the arms race that 300 nuclear warheads were sufficient for deterrence. Now, of course, NATO has many thousands of strategic and tactical weapons and the Americans alone are planning to deploy 17,000 new nuclear warheads in the period 1983–92.

Clearly, these vast numbers of atomic weapons greatly exceed what is required for deterrence. They are part of an increasingly offensive US-NATO strategy for waging and winning a nuclear war with first, second and third strikes. Such a strategy is envisaged by the new American doctrine of 'Airland Battle' which was officially adopted by the US Army in 1982 and – according to Defence Secretary Caspar Weinberger – was first tested out during NATO's 'Reforger' exercise in the same year. It has since been strenuously impressed on all NATO chiefs of staff even to the extent that West German commanders have already put their signatures to some Airland Battle documents. But with or without written West European endorsement, given that the Americans dominate NATO, the US commitment to apply Airland Battle to the defence of Europe is, for all practical purposes, tantamount to NATO's unofficial acceptance.

Airland Battle and the related Field Manual 100/5 which constitutes an operational order, confirm the shift away from deterrence towards a more aggressive strategy of fighting to win a protracted nuclear war 'limited' to tactical weapons and the European theatre. It has four main elements. First, going on the offensive with nuclear and chemical weapons right from the outset of any conflict. Second, speed and manoeuvrability to exploit the rapid changes in battle situations. Third, deep strikes into the USSR and Eastern Europe to knock out the Soviet second and third echelon back-up forces. Fourth, an integrated and flexible battlefield which includes fighting with a mixture of conventional, nuclear and chemical weapons. The proposed use of such weapons in both rear *and forward* battle areas has quite lethal implications for the civilian populations of Western Europe.

Even before the adoption of Airland Battle, the amassing of huge nuclear arsenals of high-speed missiles with pinpoint accuracy was greatly increasing the pressure to use them and the danger of a war by accident.

As more and more nuclear warheads are stockpiled and deployed, the number of military personnel with access to them grows. So does the risk of human error. Over 700 American fighting units and 150 NATO units, totalling several thousand servicemen and women, supervise or have access to atomic weapons. It is only natural that amongst all these personnel some are occasionally prone to mental and emotional instability and susceptible to the influences of drugs, alcohol, blackmail or bribery. According to a US Congressional inquiry, 3,647 personnel with access to nuclear weapons were removed from their jobs in a single year because of mental illness, drug abuse, alcoholism and indiscipline. Whilst drunkenness is the big problem amongst British troops, the US inquiry found that drug-taking is the major issue of concern in the American forces. During 1980, 50 per cent of all servicemen aged between 18 and 25 admitted taking drugs in the previous year, and 17 per cent admitted taking cocaine. More than a third of all US military personnel of all ages admitted to using drugs regularly and the figure was even higher in the navy.[22] In February 1984, Dr James Thompson of Middlesex Hospital, London, confirmed he had studied the documents of an American serviceman who had remained in his job guarding nuclear weapons in Britain for several months despite a drug addiction that rendered him incapacitated from time to time.[23]

The other great danger of war by accident or the pressure of events arises from the speed and accuracy of the new generation of nuclear missiles. The pinpoint precision of the new weapons enables each side to target exactly on the other's missile silos and thereby destroy their ability to strike back. This capacity is now encouraging a pre-emptive first-strike 'use them or lose them' philosophy amongst military planners. Each side is afraid that in a crisis situation, if they don't fire their nuclear weapons first, the other side will, destroying their launching pads and missiles before they can even be used. Thus the winner of any conflict will be the side that strikes first. With this prospect in mind, since 1981 the US has adopted a pre-emptive nuclear strike as one of its war-fighting options.

A further dangerous escalation of the arms race is the rapid flight-time of Pershing II missiles. They would take only 6–8 minutes to reach their targets in the USSR. Such speed dramatically reduces Soviet advance warning of an impending missile attack and lessens its opportunity to verify and negotiate with the USA. This puts pressure on the Kremlin to adopt a launch-on-warning nuclear retaliatory strategy as implied by Marshal Ustinov in May 1984; i.e. immediately after being alerted to an incoming missile attack, the Russians would automatically fire their missiles in a counter-attack. Obviously, everything depends on the accuracy of the Soviet computers and their correct identification of belligerent missiles. But what happens if the computers malfunction and cause a false alarm which triggers a retaliatory strike in error? It is not impossible. NATO's early warning computers have set off over 140 false nuclear alerts in the last few years, and by 1983 the rate of malfunctions had reached an average of two false alarms of impending nuclear war every three days.

But the most damning military argument of all against our dependence on nuclear weapons is the fact that once the bluff and rhetoric of deterrence is swept away, they are largely incapable of providing any practical defence against actual attack and invasion. In the words of Robert MacNamara: 'Nuclear weapons serve no military purpose whatsoever.' In a similar vein, the ex-deputy chief of the French air force, General Etienne Copel, has criticised dependence on nuclear weapons as a dangerous 'illusion' because it diverts resources away from 'real' defence against possible invasion.

Though Britain had nuclear weapons and sent them to the South Atlantic in 1982, this did not stop Argentina from invading the Falklands/Malvinas or force it to withdraw. Nor would our possession of nuclear weapons necessarily deter a Chinese invasion of Hong Kong, a Spanish invasion of Gibraltar or a Guatemalan invasion of Belize – let alone a Soviet invasion of Britain (on the questionable assumption that this is what the Russians plan).

In the scenario of a Soviet conventional attack on Britain and Western Europe, the Kremlin knows that NATO would be most reluctant and unlikely to use even small-scale nuclear missiles against its forces for fear of provoking an horrendous and irreversible escalation of the conflict.

It is true that NATO is publicly committed and militarily prepared to mount a nuclear first strike and fight a 'limited' nuclear war using tactical nuclear weapons against a Soviet conventional attack. The US ex-Secretary of State, General Haig, has also admitted that there are precise NATO contingency plans to 'fire a nuclear warning shot for demonstrative purposes, to demonstrate to the other side that they are exceeding the limits of toleration in the conventional weapons area'.[24]

However, behind the public rhetoric of commitment to first use and tactical weapons, NATO's response in practice to a conventional Russian invasion is much less certain. Our chiefs of staff are aware that if they did use nuclear weapons to repel the Soviets, the Kremlin could not afford to stand idly by. If the Russians failed to retaliate in kind, their nuclear weapons would be revealed as pure bluff and this would give the US the signal to walk all over them. For this reason alone, the Soviets would be forced into immediate nuclear retaliation in order to maintain the obscene rationality of nuclear deterrence. Once these initial tactical nuclear exchanges got under way, they would almost certainly escalate out of control into a full-scale nuclear apocalypse in which there would be no winners, only losers. As Plato once wrote: 'Many a victory has been and will be suicidal to the victors.'

Whilst NATO military doctrine maintains the possibility of a 'limited' nuclear war, as long ago as 1960 the military strategist and historian, Basil Liddell-Hart, argued that the use of tactical nuclear weapons would most likely precipitate 'illimitable and suicidal H-bomb devastation of countries and cities'.[25] His view was echoed by Lord Mountbatten in 1979 when he stated that the suggestion that nuclear weapons 'could be used in warfare without triggering an all-out nuclear exchange leading to the final holocaust . . . is more and more incredible'.[26] The same fear of a virtually inevitable escalation from tactical to strategic nuclear war is shared by Field-Marshal Lord Carver and by NATO's Supreme Commander, General Bernard Rogers, who was quoted in 1981 as saying: 'The use of theatre nuclear weapons would in fact escalate to the strategic level, and very quickly.'[27]

Whether large or small, *any* nuclear exchange is bound to destroy the very things we are seeking to defend. Even in the unlikely event that the USSR did not retaliate, NATO's planned use of tactical nuclear weapons to halt a Russian invasion into Western Europe implies that these weapons would be detonated on NATO territory against advance Soviet forces which had already breached the West German border. Such a plan, as conceived in Airland Battle, would spell disaster for the populations of Western Europe. Writing in 1962, the future Bonn Chancellor, Helmut Schmidt, said the use of 'tactical nuclear weapons . . . would most probably mean the extensive destruction of Europe and, at all events, of Germany'.[28] The former US Assistant Secretary of Defence, Alan Enthoven, came to the same conclusion: 'Tactical nuclear weapons cannot defend Europe; they can only destroy it.'[29] This is precisely the reason France rejected an American proposal to use nuclear weapons against the Vietnamese during the seige of Dien Bien Phu in 1954. In response to John Foster Dulles' offer of two atomic bombs, the French foreign minister, Georges Bidault, replied: 'If those bombs are dropped near Dien Bien Phu, our side will suffer as much as the enemy. If we drop them on the supply lines from China, we will be risking a world war.'[30]

Thus our dependence on nuclear weapons leaves Britain in a Catch-22 situation: in the face of a conventional Soviet invasion we either refuse to use our nuclear weapons because of the catastrophic consequences, in which case they are exposed as a toothless bluff; or we go ahead and use them, and in the process obliterate everything we wanted to defend and possibly even precipitate the end of the world as we know it. Whatever our response, nuclear weapons would be shown up as either completely unusable or totally counterproductive. In both cases, nuclear defence is no real defence at all.

This ultimate ineffectiveness and irrationality of nuclear weapons as a method of defence is now increasingly being recognised by the most senior military officers. The former chief of the defence staff, Lord Carver, has identified himself with the 'no first use' lobby, opposition to the deployment of Cruise and Pershing missiles in Europe and the call for NATO to unilaterally withdraw all short-range battlefield nuclear artillery shells. General Sir David Fraser recently argued that NATO has unnecessarily large numbers of nuclear weapons, and that far from achieving any rational objectives in war, their use would end up destroying Europe in order to save it.[31]

Prior to the Second World War, the unpredictability and nightmarish consequences of gas and chemical weapons led to them being virtually abandoned. A similar dilemma is facing the defence chiefs today as they contemplate the 'mutually assured destruction' which would result from a nuclear war. This has led the more liberal wing of the military establishment to start examining non-nuclear alternatives. On the civilian side, the former permanent secretary at the Ministry of Defence, Sir Frank Cooper, has suggested that Cruise missiles should be made non-nuclear and all battlefield nuclear weapons should be abolished to 'enhance our safety and reduce the risk of nuclear exchange'.[32] Amongst military men, NATO's Supreme Commander, General Bernard Rogers, has argued for the development of a non-nuclear defence plan to give Europe the option of defending itself without recourse to nuclear weapons.[33]

Accordingly, the US and the NATO countries have started to develop a new range of conventional weapon systems based on 'emerging technologies', otherwise known as ETs. These are 'hi-tech' precision-guided and robotic munitions equipped with mini-computers, electronic sensors and laser targeting. Often referred to as 'smart' weapons, they are able to independently identify and zero in on their targets – even to the extent of flying through dense fog, smoke and snow storms to hit a particular window in a multi-storey building hundreds of miles away. One example of these weapons is the Wasp sub-munition. These are remote-controlled midget missiles released in clusters from air or land. When they approach their target, they turn on their own radars and rocket motors to home in with deadly accuracy.

However, the problem with many of the new precision-guided munition systems is that whilst they are non-nuclear, they still have the same offensive deep-strike capability as their atomic counterparts, i.e. the composition of the weapons has changed, but their provocative capacity and purpose has not. NATO, for example, plans to use the new 'smart' munitions as part of its offensive strategy of Airland Battle. Thus, far from reducing international tension, the offensive character and use of many of the ET weapons threatens to further destabilise the military balance and provoke an escalating conventional arms race.

The rivalry to take the lead in microelectronic weaponry has already sent military expenditure soaring, and at current rates of growth it will eventually cripple our economies. The Tornado aircraft programme, for instance, will cost £11,300 million. Each Tornado multi-role combat aircraft is priced at £20 million, compared with just £6,000 for a Spitfire airframe in 1945. The 385 Tornadoes being built for the RAF will cost 40 times more than all of the Spitfires built during the Second World War.[34] According to US Senator Proxmire, the funds that would have purchased 100,000 fighter planes in 1945, after adjusting for inflation, would now purchase only 1,000 of the latest American strike aircraft. At the current rate of weapons cost-inflation, the expenditure of the entire 1981 UK defence budget of £12,600 million will only be sufficient to buy one warship in 30 years time and one aircraft in 52 years time.[35] This prohibitively expensive conventional arms race is clearly not the kind of non-nuclear defence system to which the Labour and peace movements ought to subscribe. Whilst we ought to take advantage of *some* of the new defensive ET 'anti-weapon' systems, these should be kept in proper perspective. Five simpler aircraft or ships stand a better chance of surviving and hitting their targets than one very sophisticated plane or vessel costing an equivalent price.

The Illegality of Nuclear War

As well as being ineffective and counter-productive, the government's nuclear weapons policy also appears to be contrary to the body of international law which has been enacted over the last one hundred years and to which Britain is a signatory.[36] These laws, which are binding on all nations, have consistently sought to ban military actions causing precisely the kind of consequences that would follow from a nuclear war: indiscriminate attacks, civilian deaths, mass destruction and excessive suffering.

The Declaration of St Petersburg in 1868 was a milestone in that it ruled that the right of a nation to injure an adversary is not unlimited. It specifically outlawed 'the employment of arms which uselessly aggravate the sufferings of disabled men or render their death inevitable'. This principle was enhanced by the Hague Declaration of 1899 which prohibited 'the use of projectiles, the sole object of which is the diffusion of asphyxiating and deleterious gases'.

The IVth Hague Convention of 1907 embodied several principles which nuclear weapons appear to contradict:

> *Article 22:* The right of belligerents to adopt means of injuring the enemy is not unlimited.
>
> *Article 23:* In addition to the prohibitions provided by Special Conventions, it is especially forbidden
>
> a) to employ poison or poisoned weapons;
> b) to kill or wound treacherously individuals belonging to the hostile state or army; . . .
> e) to employ arms, projectiles or material calculated to cause unnecessary suffering . . .
> g) to destroy or seize the enemy's property, unless such destruction or seizure be imperatively demanded by the necessities of war . . .
>
> *Article 25:* The attack or bombardment, by whatever means, of towns, villages, dwellings, or buildings which are undefended is prohibited . . .
>
> *Article 27:* In sieges and bombardments all necessary steps must be taken to spare, as far as possible, buildings dedicated to religion, art, science, or charitable purposes, historic monuments, hospitals and places where the sick and wounded are collected provided they are not being used at the time for military purposes.

But most important of all, this Convention inserted the 'Martens Clause' to cover future unforeseen developments in weapons technology:

> Until a more complete code of the laws of war has been issued, the high contracting parties deem it expedient to declare that, in cases not included in the Regulations adopted by them, the inhabitants and the belligerents remain under the protection and the rule of the principles of the law of nations, as they result from *the usages established among civilised peoples, from the laws of humanity, and the dictates of the public conscience.* (My emphasis: P.T.)

Many years later, after the Second World War, the Nuremburg Military Tribunal confirmed its continued applicability to modern weapons and warfare when it referred to the 'Martens Clause' as:

> . . . much more than a pious declaration. It is a general

> clause, making the usages established among civilised nations, the laws of humanity, and the dictates of the public conscience into a legal yardstick to be applied if and when the specific provisions of the Hague Convention IV do not cover specific cases occurring in warfare or concomitant to warfare.

Nuclear weapons also violate a number of other conventions and protocols. The wind-borne dispersal of radiation into non-belligerent states after a nuclear war would seem to contravene the Vth Hague Convention of 1907 which ruled in its first article that 'the territory of neutral powers is inviolable'. The 1925 Geneva Gas Protocol banned the use of poisoned weapons:

> Whereas the use in war of asphyxiating, poisonous or other gases, and all analogous liquids, materials or devices, has been justly condemned by the general opinion of the civilised world; . . . this prohibition shall be universally accepted as part of International Law, binding alike the conscience and the practice of nations . . .

Since radiation sickness could be construed as a form of poison, nuclear weapons are almost certainly contrary to this protocol.

In September 1938, the League of Nations agreed a British resolution governing the rules of aerial bombardment which nuclear weapons would certainly breach:

1. The intentional bombing of civilian populations is illegal;
2. Objectives aimed at from the air must be legitimate military objectives and must be identifiable.
3. Any attack on legitimate military objectives must be carried out in such a way that civilian populations in the neighbourhood are not bombed through negligence.

Following the Nazis' attempt to exterminate the Jews during the last war, the Genocide Convention of 1948 enacted new prohibitions against the mass murder of civilian populations. All the indications are that the first three articles of this convention would render the use of nuclear weapons illegal:

> *Article 1:* The Contracting Parties confirm that genocide, whether committed in time of peace or in time of war, is a crime under international law which they undertake to prevent and to punish.
>
> *Article 2:* In the present Convention, genocide means any of the following acts committed with intent to destroy, in whole or in part, a national, ethnical, racial or religious group, as such:
>
> a) Killing members of the group . . .

Article 3: The following acts shall be punishable:
a) Genocide;
b) Conspiracy to commit genocide;
c) Direct and public incitement to commit genocide.

A year later, in 1949, the Geneva Convention sought to add new specific protection for civilians and wounded combatants in time of war. Article 18, for example, provides that civilian hospitals shall in no circumstances be the object of attack – something which the indiscriminate nature of nuclear weapons could never guarantee.

In 1950, the United Nations International Law Commission adopted the Principles of International Law which had been recognised at the Nuremburg Tribunal. The manufacture and use of nuclear weapons, and even the planning of nuclear war-fighting strategies, are arguably war crimes according to Principle VI:

The crimes hereinafter set out are punishable as crimes under international law:
a) *crimes against peace;*
(i) planning, preparation, initiation or waging of a war of aggression or a war in violation of international treaties, agreements or assurances;
(ii) participation in a common plan or conspiracy for the accomplishment of one of the acts mentioned under (i).
b) *war crimes;*
Violations of the laws or customs of war which include, but are not limited to, murder, illtreatment or deportation to slave labour or for any other purpose of civilian population of or in occupied territory, murder or illtreatment of prisoners of war or persons on the seas, killing of hostages, plunder of public or private property, wanton destruction of cities, towns or villages, or devastation not justified by military necessity.
c) *crimes against humanity;*
Murder, extermination, enslavement, deportation and other inhuman acts done against any civilian population, or persecution on political, racial or religious ground, when such acts are done or such persecutions are carried on in execution of or in connection with any crime against peace or any war crime.

The 1949 Geneva Convention was greatly strengthened by the Geneva Protocol I of 1977 which nuclear weapons explicitly contradict:

Article 35: Basic Rules
1. In any armed conflict, the right of the Parties to the

conflict to choose methods or means of warfare is not unlimited.

2. It is prohibited to employ weapons, projectiles and materials and methods of warfare of a nature to cause superfluous injury and unnecessary suffering.
3. It is prohibited to employ methods or means of warfare which are intended, or may be expected, to cause widespread long term and severe damage to the natural environment.

Article 36: New Weapons

In the study, development, acquisition or adoption of a new weapon, means or method of warfare, a High Contracting Party is under an obligation to determine whether its employment would, in some or all circumstances, be prohibited by this Protocol or by any other rule of international law . . .

Article 48: Basic Rules

In order to ensure respect for and protection of the civilian population and civilian objects, the Parties to the conflict shall at all times distinguish between the civilian population and combatants and between civilian objects and military objectives and accordingly shall direct their operations only against military objectives . . .

Article 51: Protection of the Civilian Population

2. The civilian population as such, as well as individual civilians, shall not be the object of attack. Acts or threats of violence the primary purpose of which is to spread terror among the civilian population are prohibited . . .
4. Indiscriminate attacks are prohibited. Indiscriminate attacks are:

   a) those which are not directed at a specific military objective;

   b) those which employ a method or means of combat which cannot be directed at a specific military objective; or

   c) those that employ a method or means of combat the effects of which cannot be limited as required by this Protocol;

   and consequently, in each case, are of a nature to strike military objectives and civilians or civilian objects without distinction.
5. Among others the following types of attacks are to be considered indiscriminate:

   a) an attack by bombardment by any means which treats as a single military objective a number of clearly

separated and distinct military objectives located in a city, town, village or other area containing a similar concentration of civilians or civilian objects; and
b) an attack which may be expected to cause incidental loss of civilian life, injury to civilians, damage to civilian objects, or a combination thereof, which would be excessive in relation to the concrete and direct military advantage anticipated.

6. Attacks against the civilian population or civilians by way of reprisals are prohibited . . .

Article 55: Protection of the Natural Environment

1. Care shall be taken in warfare to protect the natural environment against widespread, long-term and severe damage. This protection includes a prohibition of the use of methods or means of warfare which are intended or may be expected to cause such damage to the natural environment and thereby to prejudice the health or survival of the population.
2. Attacks against the natural environment by way of reprisals are prohibited.

Though the US and Britain signed the 1977 Geneva Protocol I, they declared that their signatures were subject to the understanding that the new rules 'are not intended to have any effect on, and do not regulate or prohibit, the use of nuclear weapons'. It is hard to see how the Protocol could possibly be observed if nuclear weapons were used, and if the use of such weapons does not violate the protocol, then what does?

After reviewing the body of international law, the organisation *Lawyers Versus the Bomb* concluded that nuclear weapons are illegal and their use would be a war crime for the following main reasons:

1. They do not distinguish between combatants and non-combatants;
2. They inflict unnecessary suffering upon civilians and militia alike out of all proportion to the object of war;
3. They infringe the Hague Convention and the Gas Protocol since they create radioactivity which is a poison;
4. The territory of neutral countries is violated, since, at the very least, they suffer the direct effects of fallout;
5. The fulfilment of the protection given by law to civilians and incapacitated combatants becomes impossible;
6. The legal provisions designed to protect property and buildings and undefended cities cannot be kept;
7. If the effects of nuclear bombardment cannot be limited

> in scope neither can they be limited in duration. The laying waste of great areas of land and the poisoning of the environment – all illegal – continues after hostilities have ceased. Civilian administration becomes impossible for any survivors there may be. Any legal safeguards for the aftermath of war become irrelevant.

The lawyers also agreed that there is prima facie evidence from the statutes of international law that the manufacture, possession, transportation and storage of nuclear weapons together with the drawing up of battle plans and training programmes for their deployment and use, constitutes conspiracy to commit a war crime on the part of Her Majesty's Government, the chiefs of staff and individual officers and men.

The British government, however, has consistently rejected the interpretation that international conventions outlaw the use of nuclear weapons. It argues that their legality has been established by 'custom and practice' and the de facto recognition of their existence which is implied by the Test Ban and Non-Proliferation Treaties. In the government's view, nuclear weapons are legal because there is no law which specifically bans them. This is a bit like saying that genocide by nerve gas is legal because the 1948 Genocide Convention does not explicitly name and forbid mass extermination by this method. A civilian comparison would be a murderer claiming in his defence that since there is no law which states that elderly people must not be beaten to death with iron bars, his actions were therefore perfectly lawful.

If nuclear war is a war crime, then any British government or military personnel who authorised, fired, aided or abetted the use of such weapons in any way would be guilty of a war crime or conspiracy to commit a war crime. This would include everyone from the prime minister, the entire cabinet (given the principle of 'collective responsibility'), senior Ministry of Defence officials and the chiefs of staff. It would also include the crews of Polaris nuclear submarines, sailors on warships carrying nuclear-armed planes and nuclear depth-charges, RAF nuclear bomber pilots and those who serviced their aircraft, and soldiers operating nuclear missiles and howitzers.

The London Agreement on War Criminals (1945) established that no one of whatever office or rank is above the jurisdiction of international law. All individuals are deemed to be personally responsible for their actions. They cannot plead in their defence that they were merely obeying orders, regardless of whether they are principals, accessories or abettors to a war crime. The Agreement is binding on all states and individuals, even when it conflicts with national law:

> *Article 6:* Leaders, organisers, instigators and accomplices

> participating in the formulation or execution of a common plan or conspiracy to commit any of the foregoing crimes (crimes against peace, war crimes, crimes against humanity) are responsible for all acts performed by any persons in execution of such plan.
>
> *Article 7:* The official position of defendants, whether as Heads of State or responsible officials in Government Departments, shall not be considered as freeing them from responsibility or mitigating punishment.
>
> *Article 8:* The fact that the Defendant acted pursuant to order of his Government or of a superior shall not free him from responsibility . . .

These articles of the London Agreement were reconfirmed as principles of international law at the Nuremburg Tribunal and by the 1950 UN International Law Commission which stated:

> *Principle 1:* Any person who commits an act which constitutes a crime under international law is responsible therefore and liable to punishment.
>
> *Principle 2:* The fact that internal law does not impose a penalty for an act which constitutes a crime under international law does not relieve the person who committed the act from responsibility under international law.

In 1957, the British government tacitly admitted that international law is universally binding when it passed the Geneva Convention Act which gave the 1949 Convention direct legal status in United Kingdom law. Under its provisions, serious breaches of the conventions committed anywhere in the world are triable in Britain and are punishable by a maximum sentence of life imprisonment.

The House of Commons also legislated the Genocide Act in 1969 which incorporated the 1948 Convention into British statutes. According to *Lawyers Versus the Bomb:*

> A person found guilty of such an offence is liable to be imprisoned for life if it is for a killing and for up to 14 years for any other case. It is an offence triable even if it is committed abroad by civilians or military personnel and those suspected may be extradited for trial to or from this country. Extradition can not be avoided on the ground that it is done for 'political' motives. Neither is it a defence for an accused to say that under the jurisdiction of the place where that person is arrested an act of genocide is not a crime. Neither is it a defence for persons otherwise guilty of genocide to establish that they were acting in self defence.

British service personnel are caught in the trap of being

required, under threat of discipline, to obey all commands from their superior officers, including those pertaining to the use of nuclear weapons. Yet they are also exhorted by military legal authorities to obey the international laws concerning warfare. At the Royal Military Academy at Sandhurst, lecture notes on the 'Law of Armed Conflict' state:

> A distinction must be drawn between combatants and non-combatants. The former are permitted to take part in hostilities, whereas the latter are not; the former may be attacked, while the latter are protected from attack . . .

Chapter 14 of the British Manual of Military Law further elaborates:

> 443: members of the armed forces are bound to obey lawful orders only, and they cannot escape liability if, in obedience to a command, they commit acts which both violate the unchallenged rules of warfare and outrage the general sentiment of humanity . . .
>
> 624: The term 'war crime' is the technical expression for violations of the laws of warfare, whether committed by members of armed forces or by civilians . . .
>
> 627: Obedience to the order of a government or of a superior, whether military or civil, or to a national law or regulation, affords no defence to a charge of committing a war crime but may be considered in mitigation of punishment . . .
>
> 632: Heads of States and their ministers enjoy no immunity from prosecution and punishment for war crimes . . .
>
> 638: All war crimes are punishable by death, but a more lenient penalty may be pronounced.

The government's blatant disregard for the international laws related to nuclear weapons was evidenced during the Falklands war when nuclear weapons were taken to the South Atlantic in clear contravention of the 1967 Treaty of Tlatelolco which has legally established Latin America as a nuclear-free zone.

A similar attitude has been evidenced by the British government's response to disarmament initiatives at the United Nations. During the last session of the UN General Assembly in late 1983, Britain voted in favour of just eight out of nearly seventy resolutions calling for various forms of multilateral disarmament. Our representative voted against 21 separate resolutions proposing policies such as a freeze on nuclear weapons, a 'no first use' declaration, a ban on further test explosions of nuclear warheads and the condemnation of nuclear war as a 'monstrous crime' which is 'contrary to human conscience and reason'. Britain abstained on the votes calling for cooperation with the UN World Disarmament Campaign, the prevention of an arms race in outer space and the prohibition of new chemical and bacteriological weapons of mass destruction. Most of these resolutions were carried by the votes of more than 100 countries (including the Soviet Union), with less than 20 governments lining up with Britain and the US to oppose them.

Chapter Four:

An Anti-Democratic Army

Mindless 'Bull' and Petty Regulations

Although our armed forces purportedly exist to defend our democratic way of life, they are probably the most undemocratic institutions in our society. Service personnel are arbitrarily denied many of the fundamental freedoms and liberties which they supposedly exist to defend. The excessively conservative, elitist, authoritarian and even brutal character of the military attracts a very narrow range of recruits and this makes it quite unrepresentative of society as a whole.

The army's unwritten training philosophy is that 'to make a soldier, you first have to break the man'. Years ago, the forces openly admitted such a policy. Brigadier-General F.P. Crozier, for example, in 1915 described his battalion's training programme as follows:

> I, for my part, do what I can to alter completely the outlook, bearing and mentality of over 1000 men . . . Blood lust is taught for the purpose of war, in bayonet fighting itself and by doping their minds with all propagandic poison. The German atrocities (many of which I doubt in secret), the employment of gas in action, the violation of French women, the 'official murder' of Nurse Cavell, all help to bring out the brute-like bestiality which is necessary for victory. The process of 'seeing red' which has to be carefully cultured if the effect is to be lasting, is elaborately grafted into the make-up of even the meek and mild . . . The Christian churches are the finest 'blood lust' creators which we have, and of them we must make full use.[1]

The British soldier,' Crozier concludes, 'is a kindly fellow . . . it is necessary to corrode his mentality.'

Nowadays, the army is more conscious of its public image, though its practices remain much the same. There is no military necessity for the extraordinary amount of time squaddies spend on drill and square-bashing, the 'bulling' of kit and barrack room 'spit and polish'. Their purpose is simply to destroy all individuality and create a regimented, blindly obedient soldier.

To this end, the armed forces enforce an absurdly strict code of otherwise quite petty and useless regulations. These vary slightly between the different services and, though there may be considerable liberalisation amongst some 'combat ready' units, throughout the training regiments the regulations are harshly enforced. For barrack-room inspections, sheets and pillow-cases have to be starched and ironed and all beds made exactly according to the official stipulation, right down to the top sheet being folded back precisely to within quarter of an inch. Even inside the privacy of a soldier's own locker, all kit and personal effects have to be meticulously laid out according to army regulations. The finer details include vests and shirts having to be wrapped around sheets of A4 paper to ensure their uniform size and immaculate appearance. Bootlaces have to be coiled to the official size and shape, loose coins kept in a neat stack and the soles of casual 'civvy' shoes scrubbed clean and placed in the regulation position within the locker.

It is still commonplace for kit to be 'bulled' so that all metal and leather shine like mirrors. New recruits waste about 20 hours 'bulling' a pair of best boots. Using a hot spoon or knife, they have to iron out any wrinkles and then apply layers and layers of polish in regulation 'small circular motions' till the boots shine like patent leather. In some units, leather laces have to be 'bulled' as well and the plastic coating has to be scraped off boot eyelets so that the brass underneath can also be 'bulled' to a brilliant gloss. A similar high standard has to be achieved on all uniforms – from the buttons, buckles, corps insignia and pips, to the split pins under the uniform which hold them on, but which, of course, are never seen. Perhaps the most absurd example of army 'bull' is the issuing of ties which are narrower than the regulation width. Soldiers therefore have to spend hours stretching them to the correct size, within a tenth of an inch.

At the time of major administrative inspections, 'bulling' can be carried as far as picking out dust from between the floorboards, polishing the tops of doors and dismantling wall radiators to clean the wall behind them. It sometimes also involves repainting all barracks, including the floors. They may not need it, but repainting ensures that they look their best. Such extravagance costs the taxpayer a small fortune.

All this mindless 'bull' is irrelevant to military efficiency. Its function is purely to accustom troops to obeying even the most irrational orders so that in battle they will follow commands without regard to the morality of an order or their own personal safety.

Much the same logic is behind the otherwise senseless practice of square-bashing – marching around the parade ground for hours on end. During training up to 50 per cent of a new recruit's time is spent on square-bashing and other forms of drill. If the squaddies do not achieve absolute perfection in the allocated time, it is quite normal for them to be forced to practise drill in their off-duty hours – till as late as ten o'clock at night and beginning as early as five in the morning.

The Class Division between Officers and Lower Ranks

Apart from their own initial training at Sandhurst, officers are subjected to few of these privations and indignities. Within the military there is a class division between officers and lower ranks which is far more extreme than in civilian society. It is reinforced daily by the 'forelock touching' ritual that all officers are saluted and addressed as 'Sir' (or 'Ma'am') rather than simply by rank or name. Harking back to a semi-feudal era, in some units the main entrances to buildings are reserved for officers only, with other ranks being expected to use the 'tradesmen's entrance' at the rear. Just to emphasise the hierarchy, officers' uniforms are always made of better quality material and are much more finely tailored. In many cases, officers have their uniforms made to measure at private tailors in Savile Row which specialise in military attire. This reflects the military view that officers are first and foremost 'gentlemen', and to this end their training at Sandhurst places great stress on 'social graces', 'espirit de corps', 'honour', 'chivalry' and 'bravery'. The land-owning aristocratic tradition of some cavalry regiments is reinforced even today by the continuing expectation that officers maintain a polo pony and a ceremonial charger.

Whilst only 5 per cent of school-age children attend public schools, 55 per cent of the army's commissioned officers in 1977–78 came from the private education sector. Within the forces, they live quite a segregated and privileged life. The officers' mess is usually the largest and most impressive building in any military camp. Surrounded by its own lawns, flower beds, fountains, fishponds and tennis courts, it has the appearance of a well kept stately home. Inside, there is the atmosphere of an exclusive gentlemen's club with thick pile carpets, leather-bound chairs, and silver trophies and battle honours adorning the walls. At regimental headquarters such as the Royal Artillery at Woolwich, the officers' mess contains a vast display of immensely valuable silver and gold plates, candlesticks and statuettes, most of which have been looted from conquered nations over the centuries. In the library, intricately carved timber shelves are well stocked with classical literature, imperial history, military theory and cold war academia. The newspapers available tend to be the most convervative – the *Daily Mail, Express* and *Telegraph* – with rarely even the *Guardian*, let alone the *Morning Star*.

The officers' mess often includes a very impressive bridge room, smoking lounge, billiard hall and ballroom. However, the dining room is always the grandest of all. It typically consists of a huge mahogany table graced by silver candelabras and exquisitely engraved cutlery, and is overhung by a massive crystal chandelier. Around the table, on the polished parquet floor, are elaborately carved antique chairs. On the surrounding walls hang ornate gold-framed oil portraits of distinguished regimental officers. The cuisine is equal to a five-star restaurant, with wine on every menu and privates and corporals providing a waiter service at the table.

By comparison, the other ranks' mess is more like a cheap cafeteria. It serves three meals a day to several hundred troops in a vast fluorescent-lit building laid out with dozens of fixed laminex-topped tables and tubular steel chairs. Whilst some of the smaller messes offer fairly good food, at larger army bases and training establishments the meals provided still leave a lot to be desired. The food is frequently lukewarm and badly cooked. The choice of menu is often limited and repetitive, the staple course on offer being chips or mashed potatoes, fried eggs or sausages and processed peas with baked beans.

The same class inequality is evidenced in the different standards of accommodation. Married service personnel of all ranks can live out of camp. Many live on nearby council house-style army estates. Whilst the majority of single soldiers live in barracks on their base, far more single officers are accorded the privilege of living off-base on army estates or in their own private accommodation. In 1980, 65 per cent of all army officers owned their own houses, but only 14 per cent of lower ranks (mainly sergeants and warrant officers).[2] The ordinary rank service personnel who live in barracks or on army estates are caught up in a system of 'tied housing'. Their accommodation goes with the job and the loss of a job means the loss of a home.

All officers living in barracks have their own private rooms. Their quarters usually have no showers, only baths. This quaint snobbery arises because officers are supposed to be 'gentlemen' and it is thought that they ought to be able to enjoy the luxury of a leisurely bath. The lower ranks, however, are assumed to only have time for a quick shower, so their barracks tend to be equipped solely with showers and rarely with baths. Instead of private rooms, the average soldier sleeps in an impersonal dormitory, ranging in size from 20-30 troops to a room down to 2 or 3. A typical dormitory sleeps six men and consists of a linoleum or bare wooden floor, fluorescent lighting, steel-framed beds and metal lockers. This system of compulsory barracks not only denies soldiers the right to choose where they live and who they live with, it also represents a total denial of all privacy. A large barrack block might house 120 personnel sharing communal showers and toilets. If extra troops are posted to a unit, a dormitory which is meant to sleep 20 might end up accommodating 30. Even though they have less space and might be grossly overcrowded, each soldier will have to pay the same rent as before when only 20 shared the room.

Though officers tend to 'muck in' with their men and share the same standard C-rations in army 'war games' and combat situations, during ordinary field camps many of the disparities between officers and lower ranks are faithfully reproduced, even to the extent of setting up separate toilets for the officers. Whilst the ordinary soldiers are issued with groundsheets and sleeping bags and live six to a tent, officers sleep one or two to a tent the same size on specially provided camp beds. The most senior officers convert supply vehicles into their own private 'caravans' complete with proper mattresses, wash-basins and electric lights. The officers' mess tent is laid out with carpets and armchairs. The tables are spread with white linen tablecloths and the mess silverware. Lower ranks act as waiters and wear freshly pressed crisp white shirts and best dress trousers to serve aperitifs to the officer class. Whilst these officers might dine on pheasant soup with croutons, the ordinary soldiers will typically queue (possibly in the pouring rain) for a mess tin of stew and two slices of bread which they will have to eat sitting on the ground or standing up (depending on the weather).

Probably the most offensive aspect of the Army's class system is the officers' exploitation of ordinary soldiers as butlers, valets and personal domestic servants – at the taxpayers' expense. Apart from being assigned to serve afternoon tea and wait on tables in the officers' mess, in the more traditional regiments the junior ranks are still used to make the officers' beds, polish their kit and clean their baths, toilets and private rooms. Sometimes this batman system is even carried as far as soldiers being required to wake their officers with a personal alarm call and a cup of tea first thing every morning.

Sexual and Racial Discrimination

Another aspect of reaction which pervades the armed forces is the institutionalisation of sexism and racism. This makes the sexual and racial composition of the military quite unreflective of the surrounding community and contradicts its claim to exist for the defence of the democratic rights of all citizens.

In 1983, there were only 15,400 women in the army, navy and air force, representing a mere 5 per cent of the total service enlistment. The military is specifically excluded from the provisions of the Equal Pay Act 1970 and the Sex Discrimination Act 1975. Women do, however, now receive the same pay as men, though they are still excluded from some jobs. None of them serve in combat roles and very few are senior officers. They are signed up and trained in completely segregated all-female corps such as the Women's Royal Army Corps.

It was not until 1983 that the first women officers were admitted for training at the former all-male preserve of Sandhurst; even so, during the actual training programme there is still considerable separation of male and female cadets. In addition, there is also a WRAC College at Camberley where women spend eight months learning to be officers and 'ladies'. According to Major Joan Roulstone: 'Quite a lot of what we do comes under the heading of polishing up the social graces – things like passing the salt.'[3]

The basic function of most ordinary women soldiers is to perform an auxiliary role in support of the front-line male units. In many cases, their 'Florence Nightingale' roles are an extension of women's traditional domestic labour as mothers and housewives: nursing, catering, cleaning, driving, secretarial and administrative jobs are fairly typical. Women mechanics and tank instructors are considerably rarer.

Even where women personnel are making inroads into the 'action' arms of the forces, it is strictly in a back-up role. In the Army Air Corps, for instance, whilst the men have the glamour of flying helicopters, the women are confined to the routine of pulling them in and out of the hangars and fuelling and cleaning the choppers so that the male pilots don't have to waste their time on mundane tasks or get their hands dirty. An American woman officer on an exchange programme at the Royal School of Artillery, Captain Barbara Kent, summed up her attitude to the British women's forces: 'I don't see any reason why we can't do everything the men do . . . To tell the truth, I don't think much of the WRACs. They are too worried about preserving their femininity, having guys open the doors for them, all that sort of garbage. At Camberley, if you can believe it, cadets get taught things like flower arrangement.'[4]

So far as homosexuality is concerned: the armed forces have an obsessive fear and loathing of same-sex relationships and these are treated as violations of the military discipline Acts – even when the homosexual relationship is with a civilian and is limited to off-base liaisons in off-duty hours. Though male homosexuality has been legal in civilian society between consenting men over the age of 21 since the 1967 Sexual Offences Act, that legislation specifically excluded members of the armed forces. Gay personnel are frequently charged, imprisoned and dismissed under the catch-all Section 69 of the Queen's Regulations which forbids 'conduct prejudicial to good order and military discipline'. Lesbianism has never been an offence under civil law and, as with male homosexuality, there is no military regulation explicitly banning it. Nevertheless, what is perfectly legal in civilian society is treated as a crime under military law. According to an internal memo, *Female Homosexuality in the Army,* lesbianism is punishable by dismissal on the grounds that it is 'unacceptable' and 'detrimental to unit discipline and morale'.

Though a few individual liberal-minded officers may turn a blind eye to discreet gay personnel, usually the slightest hint of either male or female homosexuality is sufficient to launch widespread investigations, interrogations and purges by the Special Investigation Branch of the Military Police. These can include the raiding of personal lockers (no search warrants required), interception of mail and telephone calls, covert surveillance of off-duty suspects, interviews by psychiatrists, strip searches and intimate body inspections. Any soldier discovered to be gay is put under very strong pressure to identify others, including civilians whose names are often handed over to the police for filing or prosecution. This pressure sometimes involves virtual blackmail, whereby military investigators offer an administrative discharge in exchange for the names of sexual partners (instead of a court-martial and prison sentence).

Between 1976 and 1980, 200 gay service personnel were dismissed from the army and RAF following a court-martial. More than half of them served a military prison sentence before discharge. A further 500 homosexuals were dismissed administratively without court-martial and ended up on the dole queue.[5]

In addition to sexual discrimination, racism is also rife throughout the forces – even though most senior ranks would personally disapprove of it. There are, for instance, very few black officers and only a handful of black senior NCOs. In some elite regiments such as the Guards, there are virtually no black soldiers, and in others, black troops are unofficially segregated from white ones by putting all the blacks together in the same platoon. More commonly, they are simply singled out to do the dirtiest jobs and receive harsher punishments for breaches of discipline than white squaddies. According to a West Indian ex-military bandsman, Lloyd Hayes: 'The NCOs always seemed biassed against us, we were always more severely punished than the others.'[6] On duty in northern Ireland, Hayes says that black troops were often given the most dangerous jobs: 'We were being used for night foot patrols while the whites would do the cushy vehicle patrols.'[7] In a particularly extreme case, during the mid 1970s, a very senior officer in the Royal Green Jackets had such a pathological hatred of black people that he was determined to force all blacks out of his regiment. He therefore instructed the NCOs to give black recruits a very hard time so they would be persuaded to resign, and if that failed, to get them dismissed under Section 69.

Racism against black soldiers is only paralleled by hatred of Catholics and the Irish. A former Royal Marine Commando, Brian Moran, summed up the attitude amongst British troops during his posting in Ireland: 'We were supposed to be there to keep the peace, but I found a lot of prejudice in the Marines against ordinary Catholics. They gave people a lot of public abuse on the streets.'[8] Another ex-soldier who served in Belfast recalls: 'They think that the Catholic community is the enemy and should be treated as such. How often I heard remarks from troops about the "Fenian B's" and "Papist B's"; never would one hear anything about the "Prod B's" . . . Part of my duties consisted of being at the reception centres at Holywood and Curdwood barracks. Here I saw many young men brought in by the army, frightened and bewildered, and as far as I could see, their only crime being that they were males aged between 15 and 50, lived in a certain area and were of a certain religion.'[9]

On tours of duty in the north of Ireland, Orange Order and Ulster Volunteer Force newspapers openly circulate amongst British troops. In British barracks, National Front literature is more common and there is rarely any attempt by officers to discourage it.

The Denial of Civil, Political and Trade-Union Rights

Unlike the civilian population, service personnel are subject to very major restrictions on their civil, political and trade union rights. Though soldiers are officially permitted to join any political party, they are not allowed to be actively involved in its affairs. However, even mere membership of a radical left-wing organisation such as the Socialist Workers Party would normally be construed as a threat to security and discipline and therefore be grounds for dismissal. Likewise, simply discussing left-wing politics is open to interpretation as a disciplinary offence under Section 69 or the regulations covering sedition and incitement to disaffection. In 1980, a soldier in the British Army of the Rhine was imprisoned after being caught in possession of an anarchist newspaper. In the early 1960s, RAF members who wrote to the pacifist periodical *Peace News* were court-martialled and gaoled for eighteen months after requesting information on how to set up a Campaign for Nuclear Disarmament branch.

As well as being denied the right to freely participate in political parties, join left-wing groups or even discuss radical politics, no member of the armed forces is permitted to engage in any form of public debate concerning politically controversial topics unless, exceptionally, they are given prior authority to do so. This stipulation effectively muzzles the lower ranks because such authorisation is normally granted only to senior officers.

Many soldiers are unable to vote in elections. Being posted from place to place, they often do not qualify to vote where they are stationed. For those who want to vote in their home constituencies, there is the difficulty of getting their names on the electoral register. Even if their name is included, they frequently have considerable problems in securing proxy or postal voting forms and some units do very little to encourage or assist them to exercise their democratic rights. Whilst an officers' mess may include a display of election procedures, party manifestoes and voting forms, these are rarely provided for the lower ranks which include a higher proportion of Labour voters.

As if all this was not bad enough, early in 1984 the government announced major new restrictions on soldiers' political liberties. Amendments to paragraph J5:581 of the Queen's Regulations have made it an offence for service personnel to take an active part, not only in political parties, but also political 'movements' such as CND, Greenpeace or Animal Aid. They are also now forbidden to 'participate in political marches or demonstrations' of any description, whether in or out of uniform. Whilst the new regulations do not issue a blanket ban on attendance at political meetings, they do specify that soldiers can only attend providing 'uniform is not worn, service duties are not impeded and no action is taken which could bring the service into disrepute'. These provisos are another catch-all clause like Section 69, and are open to such wide interpretation that they could effectively be used to ban attendance at all political meetings.

Recently, the Ministry of Defence has also investigated ways of dealing with members of the armed forces who, whilst not being 'extremists', belong to or sympathise with organisations promoting policies contrary to those of the government. It has already been mooted that forces personnel should be more closely politically vetted with a view to banning those who support the Labour and Alliance parties from holding sensitive positions and having access to classified material.

The denial of more general civil liberties begins from the very moment a new recruit signs on to join the services. Unlike civilian employees, soldiers cannot just hand in their notice and quit their job. They are bound by a fixed long-term contract of three to 22 years which treats them as a form of indentured labour. After the first three years, troops can 'buy' themselves out at eighteen months notice; though this is purely at the discretion of officers. If an individual's skills are in short supply, there might be a 'trade restriction' on discharge by purchase which would substantially delay his or her release. Particularly in the RAF, the 'controlled exit' system often means a long wait for discharge. In the case of servicewomen, pregnancy is a terminal 'offence'. There is no maternity leave. Any woman who becomes pregnant is automatically discharged from the forces with no right of return.

If civilian employees absent themselves from work, the worst that can happen is that they are sacked. For a soldier, however, Absence Without Leave or desertion are serious disciplinary offences usually punishable by detention in the guardroom, or even imprisonment.

There is no overtime pay in the armed forces. This means that when privates do a tour of duty in Ireland and put in as much as 90 hours per week, their average rate of pay works out at less than 60p per hour after stoppages for food and rent.

Service personnel are bound by military law which is quite separate from civilian legislation. They are required to observe the Queen's Regulations and the three service discipline acts – the Army Act 1955, the Air Force Act 1955 and the Naval Discipline Act 1957. The armed forces operate a system of total discipline in which the military act as police, judge, jury and gaoler. There are five main stages of discipline: platoon commander, company commander, commanding officer, district court-martial and general court-martial. As well as dealing with military offences, a commanding officer and court-martial can also try civilian crimes like theft, drunken driving, fraud and murder. If a soldier commits a military offence such as insubordination or failing to salute an officer, either a platoon commander, company commander or commanding officer can invoke their personal powers of summary and arbitrary discipline to judge and sentence the offender. There is no jury, though a soldier does have a right of appeal against their decision. Both platoon and company commanders can hand out fines. Whilst a platoon commander is only empowered to order a restriction of privileges which includes things like confining a soldier to base, a company commander can authorise detention in the guardroom for a maximum of 28 days. In addition to fines and up to 60 days in the guardroom, the commanding officer can in very exceptional circumstances pronounce a military prison sentence. Court-martials try the most serious offences. At a district level, they are presided over by three officers and at a general court-martial by five. Despite the absence of a proper jury, a court-martial can mete out sentences just as severe as a civilian court. After being confirmed by a regional commander, the court-martial's decision is final. There is no appeal.

So far as sentences are concerned, even quite petty misdemeanours like failing to have a haircut or being late on parade can result in a fine amounting to more than half a soldier's weekly wages. Detention in the guardroom is an even worse fate. The regime there typically consists of three or four cells, each about 7 feet by 5 and furnished only with a bed and a chair. While locked in the guardroom, often from 6 pm till 6 am, prisoners have no rights at all. They may be denied all visits and communication with the external world, apart from that involved in their forced daytime labour. Any concession, such as a visit from a fellow soldier or a close relative, is purely discretionary and can be denied. Prisoners are usually forced to wear a boiler-suit with no hat or belt and boots without socks or laces. During the day, they are normally assigned to do the most menial jobs such as cleaning toilets, drains and greased-up pans in the cookhouse. Perhaps the worst aspect of detention in the guardroom is that prisoners are guarded by their own units, and in the case of unpopular prisoners, this often leads to the settling of old scores and personal grudges. The fouling of food and being beaten and kept awake at night are fairly routine.

In military prisons such as Colchester, the regime is even harsher. Soldiers are sometimes denied mattresses on their beds, which forces them to sleep either on the bare wires or on the floor. Everything is done 'on the double'. It is not uncommon to get only 15 minutes for a meal break or be forced to run at double-time on the spot while showering and going to the toilet. Deliberately degrading punishments include tasks like detailing prisoners to wash the ceilings and the undersides of dining-room tables with tiny pieces of sponge. If the guards want to be difficult or have a grudge against a particular prisoner, they might foul the freshly washed surfaces and make the prisoners clean them all over again. Even more humiliating treatment is meted out to homosexuals and conscientious objectors. In the worst cases, they may be ordered to scrub the toilets with their bare hands or sweep the corridors with a toothbrush. As with guardrooms, in military prisons beatings are fairly regular, sometimes resulting in cracked ribs, broken arms and fractured skulls.

Discipline is also enforced in an unofficial way. A soldier can be victimised and punished by an officer without ever being put on a charge. This can be done by officers allocating dirty jobs and extra duties to a particular individual for days and even weeks on end. Refusal to obey such orders would be 'disobedience'. To argue with the officer would be 'insubordination'. And failure to do the job properly would be 'conduct prejudicial to good order and military discipline' – all chargeable offences. In theory, a serviceman or woman could protest against such treatment; but most are afraid to do so because they know it would only result in further and even worse victimisation.

Another form of unofficial punishment is drill, e.g. sending an individual or a whole platoon out square-bashing all night till 4 am under the guise of preparing them for a ceremonial regimental day parade. Rifle drill is also used for similar disciplinary purposes. Soldiers might be stood at attention or made to present arms for hours in all weathers while holding a heavy twelve pound rifle. In 'pokey' drill, on the pretext of improving fitness, troops are made to run around the square with rifles held above their heads and their packs full of bricks until they drop. In addition to these unofficial punishments, there is also the outright brutality of soldiers being beaten up in the showers, their heads forced down lavatories, and being stripped naked, tied to flagpoles and hosed down with icy water in the middle of winter. Those who don't fit in with the army's macho, beer-drinking, right-wing image are the most common victims – blacks, homosexuals, loners and anyone with unorthodox views or habits. Whilst many officers disapprove of such ill-treatment, it still goes on behind their backs and very few of them take positive steps to root it out.

In the case of a gay private in the Corps of Drums, James Darkin, this bullying was so bad that he was driven to suicide in 1980. Darkin had been dipped in a duck pond, kicked, forcibly bathed, urinated over and scrubbed down with scouring powder. His pubic hair had been shaved off and his shirt smeared with boot polish. Despite his repeated complaints to senior officers, they took no action and told him that he should 'stand up and take it like a man'.[10]

A rare case of soldiers being disciplined for brutality occurred in 1984 when four Royal Marine instructors were reprimanded and fined for ill-treating recruits at Lympstone, Devon. They were accused of stinging trainees with nettles, squirting shaving cream into their mouths, pouring rifle oil over their heads, wiping a brush soaked in urine across their faces and beating them as they slept in their beds at night.[11]

It is true that the internal regime of the armed forces is slowly being liberalised and changed for the better. In the late 1970s, the Ministry of Defence finally lifted the ban on service personnel writing to their MPs without the prior permission of their commanding officer. Nevertheless, soldiers still have to get authorisation from a sergeant before they can visit the doctor, and despite their Hippocratic oath, most military doctors have no hesitation in breaching confidentiality to report evidence of homosexuality, venereal disease or drug-taking to the commanding officer and Military Police. The regulation haircut is still short-back-and-sides, and the Royal Navy still forbids its sailors to wear moustaches (though they can grow full beards).

Perhaps some of these more inexplicable petty regulations would disappear if the trade unionisation of service personnel was permitted. Currently, though technically soldiers can join a union, they are strictly forbidden from taking any part in union affairs and the union is forbidden from representing them in any official capacity. Normally, only personnel planning to leave the forces are actually encouraged to join a trade union; this being solely in order to improve their chances of finding civilian employment in jobs where a closed shop might operate. However, even during the final stages of their enlistment, apart from paying their union subscription, troops are banned from participating in branch activities. Even merely discussing trade unionisation with fellow troops could technically be construed as mutiny, incitement and a violation of Section 69.

Responding to an initiative from John Cousins of the Transport and General Workers Union in July 1969, Roy Hattersley replied on behalf of the Labour government that trade unionism in the forces would be 'unacceptable' because it would 'imply the recognition of the union principles of collective bargaining and the right to withdraw labour . . . A serviceman who withdrew his labour could be charged with failure to obey a lawful command. A group of men who took strike action might be charged with mutiny.'[12]

The armed forces have always been explicitly excluded from any new rights granted to employees under legislation such as the Trade Union and Labour Relations Act 1974, the Employment Protection Act 1975 and successive Health and Safety regulations. The latter exclusion has resulted in deaths and illness amongst servicemen involved in atomic tests in Australia during the 1950s. Under official regulations, they are denied the right to sue the Ministry of Defence for negligence. Thus soldiers have no effective means of either individually or collectively pursuing grievances over wages, food, accommodation, brutality, negligence, unfair punishments, demotion or discharge. They are entirely at the whim and mercy of their officers with no practical means of redressing abuses.

The weakness of democratic liberties and ideals within the forces is also manifest in other ways: new recruits, for example, are required to swear personal allegiance to Her Majesty the Queen, rather than to Parliament and the democratically elected government. The hereditary monarch, and not the prime minister, is commander-in-chief of Britain's armed forces. The contempt held for elementary democratic principles by some sections of the military is evidenced by their talk of 'intervention' during the political crisis surrounding the miners' strike of 1974. There was widespread alarm amongst some officers at the prospect of a radical left-wing Labour government being elected to power that year, and a fear that it might proceed to abolish the House of Lords and nationalise large sectors of industry. Field-Marshal Lord Carver has since confirmed that 'fairly senior' officers had suggested that if the political situation got out of hand, 'the army would have to do something about it'. He stressed that he 'took action to make certain that nobody was so stupid as to go around saying those things'.

In a similar vein, the September 1984 issue of *New Socialist* revealed details of a conspiracy by the military top brass to sabotage Labour's non-nuclear defence policy. In 1981 they drew up contingency plans to petition the Queen to sack a future Labour government if it attempted to implement a policy of unilateral nuclear disarmament.

A commitment to defend our democratic way of life hardly seems compatible with the Army Staff College and the Royal College of Defence Studies helping to train officers on secondment from fascist regimes and military dictatorships in Turkey, Indonesia, South Korea, Oman, Chile, Pakistan, etc. The Ministry of Defence also sends a substantial number of military advisers overseas to train troops in similarly repressive states.

Even here in Britain, an authoritarian mentality is actively encouraged by the army's training and education programmes. Soldiers are instructed rather than educated. They are taught the establishment's justification of the status quo and an imperial view of history in which Britain's past and continuing global military role is taken for granted as a natural right. There is no attempt to develop independent critical thought or encourage the asking of questions. This anti-intellectual streak and the constraints of repetitive routine, strict regulations and harsh discipline, combine together to discourage innovative and imaginative ideas and produce an extremely conservative and traditional outlook amongst military personnel. The emphasis on stability, order, hierarchy, authority and conformity means that soldiers with controversial views are unpopular and run the risk of being denied promotion and being reassigned or dismissed. Orthodoxy is the watchword because discharge would not only mean the loss of a job, but also the loss of everything else the forces provide, including accommodation, pensions and children's education. It's a powerful incentive to toe the line.

But the most disturbing aspect of the army's training programme is the way in which new recruits are given an implicitly suspicious, conspiratorial and negative view of democratic protest. This is depicted as being largely engineered by outside agitators and usually escalating to violence. This in turn is used to justify the army's preparedness for its role of military aid to the civil power during periods of social and industrial unrest. An ex-member of the Royal Artillery remembers what riot training was like: 'One half of us pretended to be Irish or the miners – or whoever was on strike at the time – and the other half would just charge into them. We'd think "today we'll really get those strikers, or those Irish". We really thought like that.'[13]

This view of democratic protest as being of doubtful legitimacy, and hence a justifiable target for military surveillance and suppression, is based on the presumption that the armed forces have a duty, and even a destiny, to defend our traditional institutions and values against external and internal foes. This presumption is certainly shared by many senior officers. They take the extraordinary view that almost all radical social change is illegitimate and that the Army would have an obligation to intervene against any protests which threatened to bring down the government or fundamentally alter the balance of wealth and power in society – even if such changes were made by the democratic methods of peaceful protest and the ballot box with majority support.

Brutality, Torture, and the Suppression of Freedom

A similar anti-democratic philosophy was used to justify the armed forces' post-war role in suppressing the independence movements in Britain's colonies, often with great ferocity and brutality.

During the Malayan counter-insurgency of 1948-60, the army interned without trial 34,000 opponents of British rule and forcibly uprooted tens of thousands of villagers from their land to rehouse them in barbed-wire encampments euphemistically known as 'new villages'.[14]

On 24 April 1954, in the war against the Kenyan nationalists, the British security forces mounted 'Operation Anvil' to screen the entire African population of Nairobi in a dragnet for supporters of the Land Freedom Army. On that one day, over 16,000 suspects were carted off to prison camps; a further 62,000 were detained without trial at various points during the war. Conditions in the camps were appalling – 350 prisoners died from maltreatment in 1954 alone. Hard labour, severe beatings, long spells in solitary confinement and darkness and deprivation of food, water and medical attention were commonplace. At the notorious Hola Camp, 11 detainees were beaten to death by prison officers in 1959 after refusing to do forced labour in protest at the barbaric conditions.[15]

Throughout the Cyprus 'emergency' of 1954–58, torture techniques were widely used by the British army. These included beating suspects on the stomach with a flat board, twisting the testicles, suffocation with a wet cloth and burning with cigarettes. In 1957, Britain was brought before the Council of Europe accused of 49 specific cases of torture in Cyprus; however a secret deal between the British and Greek governments got the cases dropped.[16]

From 1963 to 1968, during the agitation of the South Yemenis for self-rule, even worse tortures were employed by the British forces. In early 1981, the Scottish *Sunday Mail* reprinted parts of a dossier by an ex-member of the Argyll and Sutherland Highlanders containing information on 40 murders committed by the regiment in Aden.[17] Its publication provoked further ghastly revelations by other soldiers who were stationed there. Many of them attested to the abuse of the 'yellow card' instructions on the circumstances in which they could open fire. To detain an Arab suspect, soldiers were supposed to shout 'waqaf' (pronounced 'wakeef' and meaning 'halt'). If three warnings were ignored, the soldiers were then entitled to shoot. Some troops treated this as a joke and shouted 'corned beef'. When the Arabs did not understand this warning and failed to stop, they were gunned down.[18]

Ex-soldiers from Aden also told of heavy machine-guns being indiscriminately fired into shanty towns after an incident, the torture and murder of Arab detainees and the random killing of civilians at military checkpoints and in alleyways by troops on patrol. Some officers positively encouraged the killing of Arabs by awarding a Robertson's jam 'golliwog' sticker to units for every Arab they murdered. 'At one stage,' said a former soldier, 'my platoon had notched up 13 kills and another platoon were one kill behind . . . Their corporal even told the privates to use their bayonets, for it was to be that kind of killing. They went into an alley and killed a young Arab who was out after curfew.'[19]

An NCO who had been posted in Aden recalls that on arrival his unit was instructed that 'Arabs were to be roughed up when searched in roadblocks so they could be shown who was boss.'[20] The same serviceman also cited phosphorous smoke-screen shells being used as anti-personnel weapons against guerrillas and civilians to cause hideous skin burns.

Covert assassination by the British security forces was also widespread in the Aden war. According to George Lennox who was a corporal in the Royal Army Ordnance Corps based in Aden in 1964: 'I know that the Special Air Service were called into Aden to act undercover; covertly to act in an overtly provocative role. The SAS and other volunteers who were stationed inside Aden and who could speak the language were dressed up as

Adenis with chocolate colour on their faces. They went out into the streets and they had names of suspected 'terrorists' and those who were heading the then illegal political opposition groups. They had instructions to search them out and to assassinate them, to kill them.'[21]

Within Aden, the two main anti-colonial movements were the nationalist Front for the Liberation of South Yemen and the more Marxist-inclined National Liberation Front. Lennox describes the tactics used against them by the SAS as follows: 'The SAS's role inside Aden was to create confusion within both political organisations. They would go out and bump off a couple of the FLOSY guys and in turn this would be put out by the army press as being an inter-group fight. And, of course, this would make the FLOSY group take on a retaliatory role and go and seek out the NLF to take revenge and bump off a couple of their people.'[22]

The use of torture in Aden was systematic at the Fort Morbut Interrogation Centre and at Al Mansoura prison. Detainees were viciously beaten, interrogated naked, refused toilet visits and deprived of food and sleep. In 1964, the International Red Cross was refused permission to visit Aden to investigate torture allegations. A year later, they were reluctantly allowed in, but they were not allowed to see any prisoners. The same fate befell an Amnesty International emissary in 1966.[23]

To avoid the outcry which accompanied the army's use of torture in Cyprus and Aden, in northern Ireland more sophisticated and subtle techniques have been used – sensory deprivation, long-term exposure to freezing temperatures, solitary confinement, etc. Largely at military insistence, internment without trial was introduced in August 1971. Two years later, trial by jury was abolished for terrorist suspects and the rules of evidence were altered so that confessions could be used by the prosecution even if they had been obtained by the threat of force. Later, in the early 1980s, these rules were further amended to allow the uncorroborated statements of 'supergrasses' to be admitted as evidence against a defendant.

In 1971, the British government was forced to set up the Compton Committee to investigate allegations of army brutality against internees and republican sympathisers. The Committee concluded that electric shocks, hooding, loud noise, and sleep and light deprivation had been used by the security forces and that these methods constituted 'physical ill-treatment'.

Following its own separate inquiry, Amnesty International reported: 'It is a form of torture to force a man to stand at the wall in the posture described for many hours in succession, in some cases for days on end, progressively exhausted and driven literally out of his mind by being subjected to continuing noise, and being deprived of food, sleep and even light.'

In 1976, the European Commission on Human Rights declared that the British government and army were guilty of 'torture, inhuman and degrading treatment' in Ireland and that such practices were institutionalised and officially condoned.

The day to day brutality and harassment meted out by the British army in Ireland is exemplified by the following eye-witness account from an ex-member of the Royal Green Jackets, W. Sellick: 'My first encounter with army brutality was when an army patrol came under nail bomb attack, and the patrol lifted a man they thought *might* have been the thrower. I was watching the company TV when he was dragged into camp. He was shown to all the others in the TV room. He was then taken into the passageway and repeatedly hit in the stomach and balls with rifle butts. Then the rest of the soldiers joined in with their fists and boots. He then had his fingers broken by a corporal who jumped on them while two others held his arms out.'[24] In another incident, Sellick recalls: 'A boy of sixteen was stopped in an alleyway by an NCO who was pointing his rifle at him and telling the boy he was going to kill him. He kept asking the boy – who by this time had a dark patch down his jeans and was shaking a lot – what it felt like to know that you are going to die any moment.'[25]

A former Royal Marine Commando, Ian Phillips, gives a similar picture: 'My room where I slept was right next door to the interrogation room and every night you'd hear people coming in and getting roughed up, their heads being banged against the walls, screaming and everything . . . there was a little room called "The Box". It was about 10 feet by 10 feet with a table and chair in it – and it was covered with blood. Other blokes said: "It's just from blokes who get a working over". There were pictures in the Intelligence Room of blokes propped up between two marines, really smashed to pulp. There wasn't a day went by when you didn't witness some incident of brutality, whether it was someone dragged through the corridor by his hair or some woman who was smashed in the gob.'[26] Phillips also recollects his unit's searches of Crumlin Road prison: 'There was one guy in particular, everyone made a bee-line for his cell. He was stripped and given a hiding. You could hear the bloody screams all over the prison.'[27]

In addition to such ill-treatment, there is also the niggling army harassment described by a Welsh ex-officer: 'It is the simple things that upset people most. Like the Landrover patrol that takes an air rifle and fires pellets at people in Catholic areas deliberately to provoke an angry response. Or the house search where furniture is deliberately wrecked, "to teach these micks a lesson"; the householder being forced to sign a disclaimer saying that the troops have been courteous and polite, on pain of having his home wrecked again. Or the spot vehicle search in which a car's tyres are let down miles from anywhere in the dead of night with the owner left to cope as best he can.'[28]

In addition to intimidation and torture, a substantial number of innocent people have been murdered by the British army in northern Ireland. The most notorious of these killings was the murder of thirteen unarmed Catholic demonstrators in Derry by members of the Parachute Regiment on 'Bloody Sunday' in January 1972 – most of the victims having been shot in the back.

As in Aden, many other murders have been perpetrated by the use of undercover assassination squads. Ian Phillips gives the following account of his discovery of these methods while he was on duty in Belfast: 'In the Orderly Room of Tactical Headquarters was kept all day by day records of the unit's operations in the area. Whilst working as a general dogsbody in there, I was able to take in the full extent of *official* repression of the Catholics in Northern Ireland. I remember, in particular, the Sniper Files which documented the hits and misses of the unit snipers. The shooting of unarmed suspects by army snipers was carried out with the full knowledge of commanding officers.'[29]

The employment of such methods seems to be confirmed by incidents which the army was unable to hush up. One such incident occured on 11 July 1978 when an unarmed 16 year old youth, John Boyle, was shot in the back and killed by a covert SAS team in a cemetery in Dunloy, County Antrim.

More overt army murders have also taken place: twelve year old Magella O'Hare was walking to church near Whitecross, South Armagh, on 14 August 1976, when she was shot twice in the back by soldiers and later died. At first the army claimed that she was caught in crossfire between themselves and the IRA. But on 26 September the *Sunday Times* alleged: 'The police, however, are now certain that Magella was hit by two bullets fired by a soldier of the 3rd Parachute Regiment. The police have no evidence that any other shots were fired.'

In a rare case of army murderers being brought to justice, in 1980 two sergeants from the Argyll and Sutherland Highlanders were tried and gaoled for life for the murder of two Catholic farmers in County Fermanagh in 1972. One farmer had been stabbed 17 times and the other 13 times in the chest and heart.

Between 1972 and 1981, ten people were killed by the army's rubber and plastic bullets, including five children. Hundreds of others have suffered terrible injuries such as partial paralysis, multiple fractures, smashed hands, eviscerated eyes and flesh wounds requiring dozens of stitches. On 4 November 1971, Emma Groves was inside her own home in Andersonstown when she was shot in the face with a rubber bullet. It had been fired by a British soldier through her open window at a range of eight yards. As a result, both her eyes had to be removed. The soldier responsible was never charged.

Peter Doherty was standing in the kitchen of his first floor Divis flat on 24 July 1981 when a Royal Marine Commando in the street below shot him in the head with a plastic bullet, killing him instantly.

Ten year old Richard Moore was returning home from primary school in the Creggan area on 4 May 1972 when he was hit in the face by a rubber bullet fired from an army patrol. He was blinded in both eyes and his head wounds required 54 stitches.

Four Belfast surgeons based at the Royal Victoria Hospital studied 90 patients who had needed medical treatment after being hit by rubber bullets in 1970–72. They found that half had been shot from less than 15 yards, a third from less than five yards and 80 per cent of all victims had head injuries. In reply to a parliamentary question on 6 July 1981, the then Northern Ireland Secretary, Humphrey Atkins, stated that in the previous two months 110 people had been treated in hospitals for plastic bullet injuries. Of the 45 who were treated as in-patients, 31 had been shot in the head.[30]

Of all the units in the British army, the Ulster Defence Regiment probably has the worst record for brutality and slayings. In 1975, UDR members were convicted of the terrorist bombing of Biddy Mulligan's pub in Kilburn, London. In the same year, a UDR armourer was gaoled after admitting that weapons under his jurisdiction were used by the terrorist Ulster Volunteer Force and the gun parts switched around to avoid ballistic detection. The 'Miami Showband Massacre' on 31 July 1975, in which three members of the popular Irish musical group were gunned down dead, was perpetrated by serving or past members of the UDR. At the trial the following year, James McDowell and Raymond Crozier of Lurgan UDR were gaoled for 35 years for their part in the massacre. In 1979, Gerald McIlwaine, a member of the UDR and the notorious 'Shankill Butchers' gang, was convicted of the mass kidnapping and murder of Catholics. Quite clearly, this army tradition of colonial oppression, class privilege and the denial of civil liberties fundamentally conflicts with the democratic values which the military ostensibly exist to preserve. Far from defending democracy, an army which embodies such contradictions ultimately threatens it.

Chapter Five:

Democratic and Non-Nuclear Alternatives

Territorial Defence and Citizen Armies

Shaped by imperial history, and more recently by the American and nuclear-dominated Atlantic Alliance, Britain's current defence policy is still largely premised on a traditional great power strategy. Despite the decline of empire, it remains hidebound, conservative and cramped within the narrow definitions of conventional military wisdom. There is virtually no critical questioning of basic assumptions, very little innovation and rarely any serious examination of alternative ideas.

Radical and credible alternatives do, however, exist, and they have been applied with success in many other countries. The explicitly *non-provocative* defence policy of the Swedes, for example, is based on a very different military model. Their non-nuclear strategy of territorial defence by a large-scale citizen army includes provision for guerrilla warfare and non-violent civilian resistance in the event of invasion and occupation. This alternative strategy offers a much more democratic, self-reliant and non-provocative model of strict self-defence. It is not dependent on the US military umbrella, a suicidal and illegal reliance on nuclear weapons, or on undemocratic and offensive-oriented armed forces. Nor does it threaten other nations' security or add to the arms race.

The basic aim of territorial defence is to deter and, if necessary, defeat attack by making a country *hard to conquer* and ungovernable by a foreign power. Based on the resistance of the entire population, its rationale is to ensure that a nation is made so difficult to take over and pacify that any aggressor would sustain unacceptably high losses far outweighing any potential gains from conquest. It is an essentially decentralised and defensive military strategy in which the defence of a country's own territory is organised from within its own borders and based upon its own efforts.

Rather than being oriented towards a narrow linear or frontier defence, a territorial strategy is primarily based on a chequerboard defence 'in depth' in which thousands of localised units are spread out across the whole country. Their objectives are to deprive the enemy of any concentrated targets for attack, and to make the country impassable and uncontrollable by constantly harassing and attacking invading forces from all sides simultaneously, employing both conventional 'stand and fight' and guerrilla 'hit and run' methods of warfare.

Employing this *defensive deterrent* strategy, small and relatively weak nations such as Sweden, Switzerland and Yugoslavia have been able to preserve their independence and sovereignty against the expansionist ambitions of far stronger states without recourse to nuclear weapons, forward defence, global military bases or superpower alliances.

Complementary to a philosophy of empowerment – the right of people to bear arms in self-defence – a territorial model rejects dependence on an elite professional army in favour of placing the whole nation under arms through some form of mass militia or citizen army, thereby creating an army of the people rather than simply an army of the state.

Whilst being an effective defence and a potent deterrent to invasion, a territorial strategy is manifestly defensive and ill-suited to aggression or imperialist adventure. For this reason, it is not only non-imperialist; it is a specifically *anti-imperialist* policy. Furthermore, territorial defence offers the military and moral advantages of pure self-defence. Because it is dispersed in small units over the whole country, it presents no hard targets for attack. This absence of concentrated forces renders the use of nuclear weapons ineffective, so discouraging their use by would-be aggressor states. Since it poses no danger to the security of other states, a territorial policy is perfectly compatible with detente and disarmament. Indeed, because it is non-threatening, it can positively contribute to the reduction of international tension by encouraging other countries to withdraw from military pacts and de-escalate both the nuclear and conventional arms races. The civilianisation of the armed forces entailed by a militia or citizen army tends to facilitate greater popular control and accountability of military power. With the military having the character of 'citizens in uniform', the distinctions and potential antagonisms between the armed forces and the wider society are reduced. This lessens the possibility that the military could ever seize power in a coup or be used as an instrument of civil repression by a right-wing government.

The ideas of territorial defence and 'citizens in arms' stretch back at least two centuries and are rooted in democratic and socialist political theory. In the 1760s, Jean-Jacques Rousseau argued that citizenship involved both a duty and a right to bear arms in national defence and that the involvement of the whole population in military affairs – rather than leaving these to a select clique of full-time soldiers – was an essential prerequisite for democracy. At around the same time, though for more conservative reasons, the French military writer Guibert proposed the creation of armed nations in place of the armies of governments. He considered a militia system as being intrinsically more democratic, representative and efficient than the 'vilest and most wretched' professional and mercenary armies of eighteenth century Europe.

On the socialist side, Karl Marx viewed the arming of the people as a progressive demand and Frederick Engels envisaged that under socialism the repressive standing armies of the capitalist states, which were divorced from the general population, would be superceded by the 'self-acting armed organisation of the people'. The Paris Commune and the French and American Revolutions popularised the ideas of territorial defence and armed citizens as opposed to armed states. During the defence of Paris against the invading armies of England, Hanover, Hesse and Prussia in 1793, the entire population was mobilised for the war effort – either to bear arms or manufacture them. Every unmarried man aged 18–25 joined a column and each district raised a battalion to create an army 400,000 strong.

In 1880, the French revolutionary leader, Auguste Blanqui, drafted a bill to abolish conscription and the centralised standing army and replace it with a combination of volunteer regiments and locally based militias. Though critical of Blanqui, Gaston Moch's book *The Army of a Democracy* supported the principle of France adopting a Swiss-style militia system in order to establish a defensive posture which would not threaten other states. Moch felt this would encourage a mutual reduction in war preparations and defence expenditure, whilst also enhancing national security and safeguarding democracy against the militarism which he saw as being inherent in the professional army.

Similar ideas were expressed by the leader of the German Social-Democratic Workers' Party, August Bebel, who campaigned throughout the 1890s to democratise and civilianise military power by replacing the standing army with a people's militia. This proposition was later elaborated in greater detail by the founder of the French Socialist Party, Jean Jaurès. His commitment to military reforms grew out of a deep loathing of war and a fear that the French army, with its highly authoritarian officer class, could be used as an instrument of internal repression. In his book *The New Army*, which was published in 1911, Jaurès argued that the interests of democracy and peace would be mutually served by fusing the army and the people together in a new strictly self-defensive militia force where two-thirds of the officers and all the lower ranks were civilians.

In Soviet Russia in 1921, Leon Trotsky, who had been a great admirer of Jaurès' military writings, introduced a series of reforms which led to three-quarters of the Red Army being reorganised into territorial militia units; though this policy was later reversed by Stalin in the mid 1930s. Subsequently, Third World socialist leaders such as Mao Zedong and Ho Chi Minh revived the ideas of 'in depth' defence with their strategies of 'peoples' war'.

In recent years, new concepts of territorial defence have been developed by military writers and serving officers in a number of West European countries. Recognising that classical weapon platforms such as ships, aircraft and armoured vehicles are increasingly vulnerable to the new generation of precision-guided munitions, Horst Afheldt devised a territorial strategy for the defence of West Germany by a network of 'techno-commandos' armed with the latest 'smart' weapons. In his plan, the Federal Republic would be blanketed with 10,000 semi-autonomous commando units. Each would consist of 20–25 soldiers and be responsible for the defence of a specific 20 square kilometre area within which they would be stationed, hold regular exercises and prepare defensive positions. This would give the defenders the important military advantage of having an intimate knowledge of the area they were defending. Each unit would be divided into four smaller sub-groups armed with anti-tank guns, land mines and surface-to-air missiles. The rationale of this decentralised strategy is to disperse defence over a wide area so that an aggressor is offered no concentrated targets and instead gets bogged down in a never-ending series of attritional ambushes and small-scale battles. To augment the 'techno-commandos', Afheldt conceded the need for additional mobile units capable of blocking offensive thrusts, mounting counter-attacks and reinforcing local resistance in the face of heavy enemy assaults. He estimated that this strategy would require an armed force of 400,000 troops.

In almost every other country in Western Europe apart from Britain, ideas like these have generated considerable interest and even support among service personnel. In France, for example, Major Guy Brosselet proposed a fairly small hi-tech defence force of 80,000 'scientific guerrillas' covering the most strategic areas of France up to a total of 60,000 square kilometres.

Armed with 'emerging technology' weaponry, Brosselet's 'scientific guerrillas' would be formed into 2,500 light modules of up to 20 soldiers, with each module operating independently and covering a set area. These static light modules would be supplemented by 200 mobile heavy modules comprising three anti-tank helicopters, plus several extra heavy mobile armoured modules consisting of 54 tanks for the purpose of lightning strikes and defensive counter-thrusts.

The Austrian general Emil Spannocchi has argued for a dual system of border defence by a full-time regular army and in-depth territorial defence by a civilian militia. In the face of superior forces, Spannocchi suggests the avoidance of defensive concentrations and large set-piece battles which offer easy targets for sophisticated weapons and heavy firepower. Instead, defenders should seek to 'swallow' invading forces so they become stretched out over a large area and are forced to deploy their more vulnerable infantry. By this tactic, the initial strength of a more powerful aggressor is dissipated and dispersed, and territorial units are placed in a favourable position to progressively harass and wear down the invaders through a succession of demoralising and debilitating skirmishes.

Two West German commanders, Major-General Jochen Löser and General Franz Uhle-Wettler, have recently recommended that the Bundeswehr should put greater emphasis on its infantry strength and adopt a more territorial-inclined strategy. Löser advocates a zonal system of defence in which the frontier zone adjacent to the East German border is defended by precision-guided anti-aircraft and anti-tank missile units designed to incessantly pummel and shatter enemy air strikes and armoured columns. Behind this frontier zone, territorial forces would employ 'deep' defensive tactics to pin down the invaders. Uhle-Wettler calls for a decentralised defensive policy based on a large number of semi-independent fighting units scattered throughout the country. Equipped with the latest microelectronic 'anti-weapon' systems and entrusted with a high degree of devolved decision-making, these units would aim to cripple an aggressor through thousands of tiny punishing blows.

The ideas of territorial defence and citizen armies have now gained wide currency throughout Western Europe – forming the basis of several countries' defence policies. They have long been advocated in some form or another by most of the continental left.

For the last hundred years, however, most of the British labour movement has remained isolated in its uncritical acceptance of a professional standing army and its failure to advocate any form of military democratisation. Can it really be that we alone are right and the rest of the European left is wrong?

Such insular attitudes were not always the norm. Britain has a long militia tradition which was only finally eclipsed by a permanent standing army in the nineteenth century. The British militias date back to the fyrd of Anglo-Saxon times and the Welsh 'nation in arms' which rose up against the English in the reign of

Edward I. During the English Civil War, the Clubmen were formed as a mass organisation of peasants, initially with the purpose of defending their villages against the rival armies, though later, in 1645–46, they fought alongside the Parliamentary forces against the Royalists. In the first half of the 1800s, some of the Luddites and the revolutionary wing of the Chartist movement aspired to the formation of workers' militias and in some parts of the country they organised clandestine military drilling in fields and forests at night. In 1859, the threat of French invasion led to the formation of the Volunteer Rifle movement which Frederick Engels wrote for and endorsed. A later generation of British socialists, including Robert Blatchford and Victor Grayson, were strong advocates of citizen armies and soldiers' rights; and when Nazi occupation was a real possibility in 1940, it was left-wingers such as Tom Wintringham and George Orwell who revived the 'people's war' tradition and influenced the development of the Home Guard.

Whilst our own relatively recent militia history is largely forgotten, most other countries around the world have incorporated variants of territorial defence as part of their defence policies. The Swiss militia, Sweden's citizen army and 'People's Defence' in Yugoslavia are the obvious examples. But even within NATO member states, territorial ideas have taken root. Arising out of the Second World War resistance movements, both Norway and Denmark augment their regular forces with home guard units. These are organised on a part-time basis to perform local defence functions. The Norwegian home guard has a staff of only 300 full-time officers, yet it can mobilise 80,000 men within 24 hours. The West Germans have a partly territorial army, known as the Territorialheer. Though it has an impressive strength of 218,000, including 65,000 soldiers in the home defence forces, its territorial role is limited and it operates more as an auxiliary and rear-area support to the professional army. In France, the 200,000-strong Défense Opérationelle du Territoire is to some extent modelled on the Jacobin *milice populaire* and is intended to 'dissuade' invasion. Its remit is to 'oppose, throughout the country, all enemy forces, whether implanted, parachuted, brought in by sea or infiltrated'.[1]

Beyond Western Europe, Romania's fear of Soviet intervention led it to switch to a doctrine of 'territorial resistance' in 1972. Other socialist states – Cuba, Albania, North Korea, Vietnam and China – largely base their defence on a militia-backed strategy of 'people's war'. In the case of China, the militia system dates back before the 1949 revolution to the civil war against Chiang Kai-shek and the war of resistance against Japan. Since 1958, when the 'everyone a soldier' movement was launched, the militia has been steadily expanded. Now almost every factory, office and farming commune has its own units equipped with automatic weapons, anti-tank guns and small artillery.

China's low-technology and low-cost territorial strategy has been emulated by many newly emergent Third World states. They have found it a viable method of preserving their sovereignty without becoming dependent on superpower alliances or being crippled by the huge cost of traditional military strategies with their emphasis on highly sophisticated weaponry. Interest in territorial alternatives was also greatly stimulated by the Vietnamese victory over the United States. The late president of Pakistan, Zulfikar Ali Bhutto, observed:

> The Vietnam war has proved that a small nation can fight the most powerful nation in the world despite its inferiority in technique, wealth and numbers . . . For us the lesson of that war is that a people armed can resist any aggressor; for the great powers the lesson is not to get bogged down in such a quagmire. Pakistan's best deterrent would be a national militia, trained and led by professional soldiers, to support the standing forces in the event of total war . . . the prospect of a whole nation armed and trained is as powerful a deterrent as an underdeveloped country can hope to possess.[2]

Similar territorial ideas have been adopted with considerable success by the national liberation movements in Eritrea and the Western Sahara to secure the right of their peoples to self-determination; by the governments of Nicaragua and Angola to repel foreign aggression; and by the guerrilla armies in El Salvador and the Philippines to overthrow corrupt and dictatorial regimes. Many independent nation states such as Indonesia, Algeria, South Yemen and Mozambique owe their very existence to territorial strategies of resistance against occupying colonial powers.

During the Second World War, though badly equipped and poorly trained, the partisan resistance movements seriously hampered the Nazi war effort in France, Italy and Greece, and played a major role in the liberation of Yugoslavia, Albania and Bulgaria.

Thus far from being exceptional, or a fanciful daydream, territorial defence has a long history of practical and successful application in the preservation of sovereignty, the routing of invaders, the toppling of dictatorships and the securing of independence.

Sweden's Citizen Army and 'Total Defence'

It is worthwhile looking at the Swedish, Swiss and Yugoslav

defence policies in greater detail because they offer concrete examples of territorial defence in European countries not too unlike our own, with a significant degree of urbanisation and industrial development. They also happen to be countries which are much closer to the USSR and far more vulnerable to Soviet attack. Despite this, they have consciously rejected nuclear weapons in favour of a territorial strategy which has assured them long periods of peace and independence.

In the case of Sweden, a tiny population of 8.3 million is separated from 254 million Russians by only 250 kilometres of Finnish territory in the north and by less than 300 kilometres of Baltic sea in the south. Nevertheless, though Sweden has the technical ability to manufacture nuclear weapons, following debates in the 1950s and 1960s it decided against their acquisition. Instead, it has opted for a combination of armed neutrality, territorial defence and a citizen army which has protected the country from war, foreign occupation and military dictatorship for 170 years – a period of peace and democracy only paralleled by Switzerland.

Sweden's contemporary defence policy is premised on the concept of 'total defence', i.e. the involvement of the whole population and every social institution in the task of national self-defence. In the Swedish view, since war affects all members of society, everyone ought to contribute to the war effort, the success of which is deemed to be largely dependent on the determination of soldiers and civilians alike to resist.

A fundamental principle underlying Sweden's defence policy is to deter aggression by making it clear to a potential invader that any attack would be futile and self-destructive because it would result in more losses than gains: 'The defence has to be so strong that the costs to defeat Sweden are out of proportion as compared to the strategic advantages which an aggressor might gain.'[3] To meet this requirement, Sweden employs a combination of 'peripheral' frontier defence and 'inner' territorial defence, with the emphasis on the latter. Whereas the border defence is based on heavier mobile units equipped with high technology weaponry, including five armoured brigades, the 'in depth' defence is localised and static and relies on armaments which are simpler, cheaper and easier to repair and conceal. Sweden also attaches more importance to sustained defence than to a few decisive battles. According to the Report of the Commission on National Defence which was broadly accepted by the Riksdag in 1972: 'Total defence must take the form of a defence with staying power . . . capacity for stubborn and enduring defence is more important than great initial strength.'[4] Seeking a policy of minimal cost and maximal popular involvement, the Commission advocated: 'Priorities should be allocated . . . in accordance with the principle that it is better to obtain a larger number of technically less advanced weapon systems than a few technically very advanced ones.'[5] Sweden's military has subsequently become more army and infantry-oriented with more stress on savaging and shredding invading forces through both frontal assaults to push back aggressors and innumerable small-scale guerrilla attacks to wear down occupying forces.

To support this strategy, Sweden relies on universal male conscription. Lasting an average of eleven months, this is followed by periodic refresher courses till the age of 47 when reservists are demobilised. The strength of the regular armed forces stands at 65,000. This includes a cadre of 17,000 full-time professionals, all of whom are officers or NCOs, plus 47,000 conscripts who make up 50 per cent of the air force and navy and 80 per cent of the army. As well as the regular forces and reserves, there is also a home guard with an enlistment of 100,000 men under the age of 18 and over 47. Overall, the total mobilisable strength of the Swedish armed forces is 800,000 within three days, i.e. nearly 10 per cent of the entire population.

Because Sweden's deterrent is based on effective defence instead of retaliation, the navy and air force are equipped for home-base defence rather than a 'deep strike' retaliatory capacity. Accordingly, the air force has no long-range bombers. Its 430 combat aircraft are predominantly interceptor fighter planes for the defensive purpose of knocking out incoming enemy air strikes and assault ships; the rest being for reconnaissance and ground attack against invading armoured columns and infantry. Additionally, Sweden has strong anti-aircraft missile defences. The navy is geared to in-shore coastal defence to forestall seaborne invasion and bombardment. Its emphasis is on light, fast vessels armed with anti-ship torpedoes and missiles. These include 35 fast attack craft, plus numerous smaller coastal patrol boats and a substantial fleet of minelayers and minesweepers. In terms of larger warships, Sweden has only two destroyers and twelve submarines, big surface vessels being considered vulnerable to air or naval attack by Exocet-style missiles, particularly in the narrow confines of the Baltic.

This system of defence costs the Swedes about 3.1 per cent of their GNP – US $3,431 million a year or $412 per person in 1982 – compared with Britain's defence expenditure in 1981 of $24,223 million; this being the equivalent of $433 per person or 5.4 per cent of our GNP.

Besides the armed forces proper, Sweden also has plans for civil and economic defence and civilian resistance. The 230,000-strong civil defence force consists of women between the ages of 16 and 67 and men aged 16 to 18 and 47 to 67. Its function is to protect the civilian population and alleviate the consequences of attack through the preparation of shelters, provision of gas masks, evacuation of cities and the organisation of fire-fighting and rescue work. Planning for 'economic defence' includes the stockpiling of food, fuel and other essential materials and the indigenous manufacture of most of Sweden's key armaments to ensure a high degree of self-reliance in time of war. Widespread civilian resistance and non-cooperation with occupying forces is envisaged as an auxiliary method of defence. This is backed up by chapter 22 of the criminal code which allows for serious cases of collaboration with an invading army to be punished by long terms of imprisonment and by a system of war indemnity grants to compensate businesses for losses incurred as a result of their refusal to cooperate with the occupiers.

The Swiss Militia and Fortified Defence in Depth

Like Sweden, the armed neutrality and militia tradition of the Swiss has successfully deterred aggression for 170 years without the need for nuclear weapons. Though the possession of Switzerland would have been advantageous in the wars of 1870, 1914 and 1939, the belligerents on both sides were deterred by the prospect of Swiss obstruction and the consequently high cost of conquest.

Still today, Switzerland's defence is based on a strategy of 'dissuasion'. In contrast to NATO's emphasis on nuclear deterrence, the Swiss avoid war through *defensive preparedness*. This is achieved by a 'high entry price' policy of 'fortified defence in depth'. Its objective is to engage an aggressor as near to the frontier as possible in order to minimise armed incursions and exact a heavy toll on invading forces through a network of 'deep' defensive fortifications. These include heavy weapon emplacements and underground troop shelters, ammunition dumps, aircraft hangars, tank depots and weapon repair factories buried in the heart of the Swiss Alps. To effect a 'high cost of entry and presence', infantry units are dispersed to hold heavily defended key positions and destroy strategic bridges and mountain tunnels which are already primed for destruction. This combination of fortification and 'dispersion' reduces the concentration and vulnerability of targets presented to enemy forces and makes the use of nuclear weapons by an aggressor an ineffective proposition. As well as lightly armed static territorial units, the Swiss have highly sophisticated mobile mechanised forces to mount counterattacks; including 800 tanks and 330 combat aircraft which act in support of the ground defences. As a last resort, the Swiss are prepared to fall back to the alpine redoubts around St Maurice, Sargans and St Gotthard which constitute the most powerful artillery fortresses anywhere in the world. At this stage, the possibility of protracted guerrilla warfare and passive resistance by the civilian population is envisaged, though the Swiss have failed to undertake any detailed preparations for this eventuality.

General Frank Seethaler sums up the basic concepts of Swiss defence as follows:

> At the tactical level, the defensive action, 'defence' proper, finds its true expression in a *dynamic defence of territory.* The large number of available infantry units (some 40 per cent of the total manpower) hold key positions and vital zones of terrain. Mechanised combat units in company, battalion and regimental strength – depending on the importance of the zone or object to be held – in close combination carry out *counter-strokes.* In built-up, wooded or mountainous regions, *offensive action by infantry,* such as counter-attacks at night or raids, is also anticipated. Towed, mechanised and fortress artillery, as well as air power, conventionally support both the static troops and the mobile formations. On the other hand, there is no intention to wage wide-area offensive air warfare in the counter-air sense. The task of the air force is interception, local air superiority and ground support; in other words, it always operates in coordination with ground forces . . . A mechanised aggressor could not just move in Swiss territory. The transport infrastructure is disrupted in many places by the destruction of artificial passages. Countless numbers of natural obstacles and built-up areas, difficulty of finding one's way and the 'compartmentalisation' of the territory into confined spaces inhibit the momentum of a mechanised attack. In addition, conditions arise similar to those underlying the Finnish 'Motti tactic' in the 1939–40 winter war. On this territory, advantageous for the defender, but adverse to the aggressor, Switzerland's 12 divisions and 17 independent combat brigades are deployed in a chessboard pattern in their operative and tactical key zones. This not only results in a troop density unknown anywhere else in Europe, but also in a unique – in fact and historically – staggering in-depth ranging, for instance from Lake Geneva to the Lake of Constance. The mechanised aggressor has no choice other than to adapt his fighting doctrine to that of the defender: he is forced into a slow-motion battle on foot; his tank force, normally used to dictating the momentum of combat, is reduced to the role of fire support escort; flexibility provided in open spaces quickly turns into cumbersome awkwardness inside forced bottleneck passages . . . The *tactic of quick success* is no longer applicable; in its place comes the *painful toil of labouring through.*

> Sacrifices in material, time and prestige will be heavily felt and are in no reasonable relationship with the possible military gain. The adversary is forced into a *timely organised battle of attrition* with all its well-known feedback to dissuasion. The defensive battles throughout the entire territory, which will repeat themselves at every key position, are designed to consume the strength of the adversary. The anticipated *thrust tactic* on the part of an aggressor, then, is not met by the Swiss with a comparable type of warfare, as would be the case, for instance, in the mobile defence concept. 'Slowdown', 'defend' and 'counter-action' are the components that will be applied . . . The 'secret' for inflicting high loss quotas to the opponent largely lies in the operational dexterity of the defending troops . . . [in] delaying the presence of targets in the covered area through exploiting natural obstacles and setting up artificial ones; consistently staying behind hilltops, thereby remaining unnoticed until the moment of opening fire and ensuring a high first shot hit-probability; turning hard targets into soft ones for artillery and air power by forcing the enemy to use unarmoured combat engineering troops and dismounted infantry to clear obstacles; exploiting the channelling effect of the topography for surprise counter-attacks against the depth of the enemy's flanks.[6]

To effect this strategy of dissuasion, dispersal and fortification, the Swiss have a militia system of citizen-soldiers. Every man aged 20 is conscripted for four months basic military training. Much of this concentrates on partisan-style operations, sabotage and commando raids. After completing training, the recruits return to civilian life and take their rifles home with them. But thereafter they undertake refresher courses for three weeks each year for the following eight years out of twelve. From the age of 33, the citizen-soldier leaves the front-line mobile units and joins the territorial defence forces, the Landwehr, which train for two weeks every three years to defend their own local neighbourhood. At 43, militia members are transferred to the support arm, the Landsturm. There they train only once again before the age of 50 when they are finally discharged from the army for good.

The training is organised by a cadre of 5,000 instructors. These are the only permanent full-time soldiers in the Swiss army; all the rest, including senior officers, are either conscripts in training or civilian reservists. Out of a population of 6.4 million, Switzerland can mobilise 625,000 men within 48 hours. This militia system of defence costs the Swiss just 1.8 per cent of their GNP, i.e. a total of US $1,780 million or $281 per person in 1982. Though to some extent military service is a disruptive inconvenience for the young men called up and army exercises sometimes obstruct and delay everyday life, in a 1984 referendum the Swiss voted two to one in favour of keeping the conscript-militia system.

In addition to the armed forces, the Swiss have a comprehensive programme of civil defence which includes the provision of underground shelters for 80 per cent of the population. All men between the ages of 21 and 61 who are not assigned to the military are liable for civil protection duty. They are supplemented by women volunteers. A specialist section of the army, the Territorial Service, is responsible for air-raid warning and protection, guarding strategic installations, disseminating information and controlling vital elements of the war economy. There is considerable stockpiling of strategic materials and incentives are offered to farmers to encourage greater agricultural self-sufficiency so that the Swiss could survive a trade blockade during wartime.

Partisan Warfare and 'People's Defence' in Yugoslavia

Yugoslavia's defence policy has evolved out of the communist-led partisan resistance during the Second World War. The People's Liberation Army and the partisan detachments succeeded in inflicting heavy losses on the half a million pro-Axis troops stationed in Yugoslavia and by the end of the war they had liberated large areas of the country. Indeed, apart from Albania, Yugoslavia was the only nation in Europe which freed itself from Nazi occupation by its own efforts.

After the war, when Yugoslavia refused to accede to a Soviet model of socialist and military development, the Russians savagely denounced Tito as a 'fascist' and an 'agent of imperialism', and Yugoslavia was expelled from the Cominform in 1948. Nikita Krushchev recalled how Stalin boasted: 'I will shake my little finger and there will be no more Tito. He will fall.'[7] In this atmosphere of belligerence which prevailed between 1948 and 1953, Yugoslavia was extremely fearful of a Soviet invasion. Tito realised that his country would only be able to resist a major attack by the immense Cominform armies for a short period if it relied on traditional military methods. Accordingly, partisan units were formed during this period and large volumes of weapons were distributed and hidden in secret arms dumps all over the country. Plans were drawn up for protracted guerrilla war, the evacuation of territory and the relocation of government and industry in mountainous hideouts. These preparations are generally credited with discouraging a Soviet attack. Krushchev observed: 'But no matter how much or how little Stalin shook, not only his little finger, but everything else he could shake, Tito did not fall. Why? . . . Tito had behind him a state and a people who had gone through a severe school of fighting for liberty and independence.'[8]

By 1953, what had originally begun as hasty defensive preparations started to crystallise into a new strategic doctrine. Whilst the tactic of frontal defence was not abandoned, it was increasingly complemented by the concept of mobile 'territorial war'. This was conceived, not as a small-scale guerrilla war, but as a major form of warfare in its own right, centrally organised and involving the full use of tanks, planes and heavy artillery.

The 1958 National Defence Law elaborated these ideas a stage further by affirming the principle that all citizens had a duty to participate in the territorial defence of the country. This was incorporated into the programme of the Seventh Congress of the League of Communists of Yugoslavia in 1958 which stated that 'only through the organisation of *all-people's resistance* can they (the Yugoslav people) successfully defend their freedom and independence.'[9] This in turn led to the enunciation of the policy of 'total national defensive war' combining frontal and 'in depth' defence, regular and territorial forces and open and covert warfare.

But it was the Soviet invasion of Czechoslovakia in 1968, and the fear that Belgrade might suffer the same fate as Prague, which precipitated the complete reorganisation of the Yugoslav armed forces around the principles of 'general people's defence'. The 'Brezhnev doctrine' declared that the USSR and its allies had a right to militarily intervene in other socialist states whenever socialism was endangered and whenever 'the basis of our ties and the security of the commonwealth of our countries are threatened'. This doctrine, which implied the limited sovereignty of socialist states, was perceived by Yugoslavia as a direct threat to its independence.

To meet the danger of Soviet intervention, Yugoslavia did not turn to nuclear weapons, expanded conventional forces or an alliance with the other great superpower, the USA. Instead, convinced by the Vietnam war that it was possible for a small state to defeat a large one, the Yugoslavs promulgated a new National Defence Law in 1969. Based on the strategic concept of 'general people's defence', its introductory principles proclaimed: 'Socialist Yugoslavia recognises as justified only national liberation wars waged by oppressed peoples against invaders and occupiers, and defensive wars waged by attacked countries against aggressors. Defence against aggression and struggle against occupiers is the inalienable right of every nation and every country.'[10] 'General people's defence' was envisaged as having a dual function of both defence and deterrence. In his report to the Ninth Congress of the League of Communists of Yugoslavia in 1969, Tito stated: 'The system of nation-wide defence has the role of diverting the opponent from his intention of perpetrating aggression against this country. This means that the system is not simply an instrument for the successful waging of a defensive war in the event of attack, but is also a way of preserving peace, which is the fundamental purpose of our international policy.'

Under the 1969 Defence Law, the regular Yugoslav People's Army (YPA) and the locally-based Territorial Defence Forces were decreed to be co-equal partners in the defence of the country. Embodying a high degree of decentralisation, this law placed the national government in Belgrade in charge of the YPA and made the civilian authorities in the localities, provinces and six republics responsible for the territorial defence units and the direction of 'general people's resistance' in their districts.

The YPA is a unitary force which combines the army, navy and air force. It has 240,000 enlisted men – 200,000 in the army and 20,000 each in the navy and air force. Two-thirds of these personnel are conscripts. All men are obliged to do 15 months military training. After this initial service, 20 per cent of the conscripts are transferred to the 500,000-strong YPA reserve. The other 80 per cent are assigned to the Territorial Defence Forces which have a maximum strength of 3 million – half of whom can be mobilised within six hours and the rest within two days. Women are liable for service in the Territorial Defence Forces and those with specialist qualifications belong to the YPA reserve. All members of the territorial units and the YPA reserve are required to undertake regular refresher training up to the age of 55 for men and 45 for women. Furthermore, all schoolchildren receive military training, including weapons instruction, as part of their curriculum. All in all, the Yugoslavs can put 15 per cent of their population under arms and nearly 80 per cent of all citizens can be counted on to participate in some form of military or civilian resistance.

To back up the army, Yugoslavia has an air force of 400 combat planes explicitly geared to repulsing a frontal air attack and overland invasion. Having no long-range bomber capacity, the air force is based on 9 interceptor squadrons and 12 fighter-ground attack squadrons. Some of these are specifically for partisan-style warfare, being made up of very light aircraft capable of landing on grass and requiring only short take-off.

With 1,000 kilometres of coastline, Yugoslavia has also built up formidable coastal defences. Though these include 9 submarines and 3 corvettes, the mainstay are 44 fast attack craft – including 20 armed with guns, 10 with missiles and 10 with torpedoes – plus a large number of patrol vessels, minelayers and minesweepers. There are also contingency plans to convert and arm the country's merchant fleet in the event of war.

In 1982, this system of defence cost Yugoslavia US $2,870 million – the equivalent of $126 per person or 4.6 per cent of the GNP. This is a higher proportion of GNP than Sweden or Switzerland, but still much lower than Britain.

Under the strategy of 'general people's defence', the Yugoslav People's Army would bear the brunt of an initial attack and seek to repel the aggressors by the tactics of frontal defence. However, if it was not possible to push them back owing to their vast numbers and firepower, the regular army would at least attempt to delay their offensive to give the Territorial Defence Forces time to mobilise.

At the early stages of an invasion, the YPA and territorial units would fight both along fronts and in depth. But if they were in danger of defeat by an overwhelmingly superior aggressor, the YPA would execute what the Yugoslavs call a 'descending transformation', i.e. transfer partially or completely from regular and frontal defence to partisan warfare with the central mountainous region of the country forming the core of a liberated base area. This shift to guerrilla tactics would not exclude the possibility of using heavy weapons, large mobile formations and frontal warfare in particular theatres of engagement when appropriate. Conversely, it is also envisaged that if partisan struggles succeeded in weakening the enemy sufficiently, this would give rise to the 'ascending transformation' of small guerrilla units into a larger, more regular army capable of mounting frontal offensives.

In addition to the military, Yugoslavia also has a civil defence organisation totalling 2.3 million people. Everyone aged between 16 and 60 who is not in the armed forces or the police, except women with children under seven years of age, is required to serve in the Civil Defence Forces.

The Yugoslavs are also committed to non-military resistance. Though the precise form is not officially specified, articles in Yugoslav army journals have referred to hindering an aggressor's attempt to impose a political system through non-compliance with an occupying administration, boycotts, sabotage and the promotion of disaffection amongst enemy ranks.

Whatever criticisms can be made, no one can seriously suggest that the Yugoslav model of territorial defence, or for that matter the Swiss or Swedish examples, are in any way militaristic, bellicose or threatening – let alone the instruments of imperialism or the cause of a spiralling arms race. They do, however, clearly illustrate the possibility of a practical, non-provocative alternative to nuclear weapons.

Protracted Guerrilla Warfare

As the Swedish, Swiss and Yugoslav models indicate, guerrilla warfare is essentially a specialist form of territorial defence based on small scattered units involved in clandestine 'hit and run' military operations to wear down an opponent over a prolonged period of time. Preferring fluidity and dispersal rather than immobility and concentration, guerrillas combine ubiquity with intangibility. By avoiding frontal defence and set-piece battles, they offer an enemy no visible or definable targets to attack. Instead, guided by the principles of mobility and concealment, they suddenly appear out of nowhere, hit their opponents and then melt away just as quickly – a policy of swift strikes, tactical withdrawal and regroupment.

In guerrilla warfare, there is considerable emphasis on the element of surprise to catch the enemy off-guard. Typically, guerrillas attack under cover of darkness or camouflage from mountains, forests, hedgerows, side streets, shadowy doorways and lonely roads. These 'shoot and scatter' ambush tactics are aimed at the enemy's weakest and most vulnerable points – supply depots, communication lines, troop convoys and isolated garrisons. The objective is to distract, disturb and demoralise the aggressors through a war of attrition which saps their will to continue the fight.

Guerrilla strategies have a long history of successful application whereby small nations have been able to defeat far larger great powers. The antecedents of guerrilla warfare can be seen in the battle of Crécy in 1346, where the English victory over the French owed a lot to the use of unorthodox tactics. Faced with overwhelming odds, the English army retreated to a hillside overlooking the pursuing French soldiers. Instead of placing their archers in conventional tight formations, the English commanders scattered them across the hillside. In front of each archer, staves were implanted and holes were dug to fell the advancing horsed armour. By these rudimentary irregular tactics, the English were able to defeat a French army three times greater than their own.

One of the earliest examples of modern guerrilla warfare was the struggle waged by Irish peasant organisations against brutal and unscrupulous landlords in the 1760s. During the War of Independence a decade later, the American 'Minutemen' militias also defied the traditional rules of warfare. Their resort to stealthy sniping, night raids and rural ambushes succeeded in defeating much larger and better equipped British forces. Similar guerrilla methods were also used with great effect by John Mosby's Confederate irregulars in northern Virginia during the American Civil War.

Throughout the Spanish Peninsular War, from 1808 to 1814, guerrilla warfare in the rear areas severely weakened French efforts at the front by forcing them to divert troops from the main battle areas. As Basil Liddell Hart observed: 'The French had beaten, and continued to beat any regular Spanish forces, but the thoroughness of these defeats was of the greatest benefit to the defeated. For it ensured that the main effort of the Spanish was thrown into guerrilla warfare. An intangible web of guerrilla bands replaced a vulnerable military target, while enterprising and unconventional guerrilla leaders, instead of hidebound Spanish generals, conducted operations.'[11] The founder of modern military science, General Carl von Clausewitz, drew the following conclusion from the use of guerrilla tactics in the Peninsular War: 'The Spaniards by their stubborn resistance have shown what the general arming of a nation and general insurgent measures on a great scale can effect.'[12]

Sixty years later, the French themselves turned to these methods when the *francs-tireurs* sprang up to resist the German invasion in 1870; and from 1899, the irregular methods of the mounted Boer militias inflicted major defeats on the British army in South Africa.

During this century, one of the earliest and most spectacular guerrilla campaigns was waged by the British under the auspices of T.E. Lawrence. In his book *Guerrilla Warfare* 'Yank' Levy sums up Lawrence's irregular tactics against the Turks in the following terms:

> Guerrilla attack, Lawrence noted, should be directed against whatever the enemy lacks most. The Turks were very short of material, and therefore his attacks were directed mainly against material. To attack the unguarded railway, the stores almost undefended, was also the best policy for him because his Arab troops would scarcely stand casualties . . . But towards the end of the Arab revolt, when the Turkish Army was breaking, Lawrence saw that the Arabs must be launched as a stinging swarm of raiders against the flank and rear of that army. While he was draining the Turkish strength, he liked to leave the Turkish railways just working, and not more than just working. When Allenby's striking force was ready for the decisive blow, Lawrence sent his Arabs to cut and hold the Turk's railway centres. The guerrillas' target is chosen by the needs of battle, not by any absolute rule.
>
> Captain Liddell Hart's book, *Colonel Lawrence,* is the best description of Lawrence as a soldier and guerrilla leader. In this book Captain Liddell Hart describes the final phase of the war in Palestine as one in which nearly half the Turkish

> forces south of Damascus were distracted by the Arabs. Two Turkish army corps, worn and wearied down until their strength, with that of the railway garrisons, was only about 14,000 fighting men, were pinned east of the Jordan. Liddell Hart writes: 'The most remarkable feature is that, with some relatively light assistance from Chaytor's force, these Turkish masses were paralysed by an Arab contingent that counted less than 3,000 men, and of which the actual expeditionary corps was barely 600 strong.' Allenby's striking force only had to deal with the other half of the harassed and hopeless Turkish Army.
>
> And summarising the whole campaign, Liddell Hart writes: 'The wear and tear, the bodily and mental strain, that exhausted the Turkish troops and brought them to breaking point was applied by the Arabs, elusive and ubiquitous, to a greater extent than by the British forces . . . They severed the line of communication at the moment when it became the life-and-death line, when the fate of the enemy hung on this frayed thread.'
>
> Summarising the man Lawrence, Liddell Hart also writes: 'Military history cannot dismiss him as merely a successful leader of irregulars. He is seen to be more than a guerrilla genius – rather does he appear a strategist of genius who had the vision to anticipate the guerrilla trend of civilised warfare that arises from the growing dependence of nations on industrial resources.'[13]

Between 1918 and 1939, guerrilla warfare tended to be confined to a small number of localised, non-European theatres of conflict in places like Palestine, Abyssinia and China. But during the Second World War, it became a generalised form of resistance in many of the Nazi-occupied countries of Europe. Though most of the partisans had no formal military training and were often short of weapons, they nevertheless played a significant role in the Allied war effort. Numbering nearly two million, the Russian partisans inflicted half a million casualties on the Nazi invaders and contributed to the liberation of sizeable areas of Soviet territory. The partisans in Italy totalled 300,000 – 45,000 of them being killed in action. The French *Maquis* performed the vital function of supplying intelligence and military back-up for the Allied D-Day landings.

There were also substantial armed resistance movements in Bulgaria, Greece, Albania, Yugoslavia, Holland, Belgium, Poland, Denmark and Norway. Their degree of success varied. The Albanians and the 250,000-strong Yugoslav partisans largely prevented the Nazis from ever gaining effective control over their countries and eventually liberated most of their territory by guerrilla tactics. In northern Europe, the resistance was limited to smaller-scale sabotage and ambushes. But even this was effective in that it destroyed key German fuel and ammunition dumps, created a psychological terror and demoralisation amongst the Nazi troops and forced the Wehrmacht to switch large numbers of soldiers away from the frontline, thus taking pressure off the Allied armies.

During the war, the British government officially recognised the value of guerrilla warfare when it established the Special Operations Executive in 1940 to channel aid to the underground resistance movements. Hugh Dalton, the wartime minister responsible for the SOE, specified that its task was to create and support 'movements in the enemy occupied territory comparable to the Sinn Fein'.[14] Accordingly, British advisors and supplies were parachuted into resistance-held areas. In Italy, for example, the British dropped over 2,000 tons of weapons and equipment to the partisans, and in Burma a senior British officer, Orde Wingate, organised the Chindit anti-Japanese guerrilla army.

Another implicit recognition of the importance of guerrilla warfare was the establishment of the Special Air Service in North Africa in 1941 to conduct sabotage missions behind German lines and the creation of the Home Guard. Though the Home Guard predominantly had a 'stand and fight' territorial defence function, most units were also given training in guerrilla tactics and sabotage.

Since the Second World War, many Third World countries have won their independence through anti-colonial guerrilla struggles in environments ranging from the desert of Algeria to the bushland of Zimbabwe and the jungle of Guinea-Bissau. Britain has been on the receiving end of many of these wars of national liberation, being forced out of former colonies such as Kenya (1952–55), Cyprus (1954–58) and South Yemen (1963–68) by determined guerrilla armies.

Contemporarily, despite facing far bigger enemy forces armed with vastly superior weapons technology, highly effective guerrilla campaigns have been waged by the Farabundo Marti National Liberation Front in El Salvador, the South-West African People's Organisation in Namibia, the Eritrean People's Liberation Front in Eritrea and Polisario in the Western Sahara. The South Africans remain powerless to stop the armed rebellion by the African National Congress, the Marcos government has been thwarted in all its attempts to defeat the New People's Army, and the generals in Jakarta are unable to crush the guerrilla armies of Fretilin in East Timor and the Free Papua Movement in West Papua.

But more than any of these liberation struggles, it was the Vietnam war which provided the classic example of a victorious guerrilla army (though conventional tactics were sometimes used, especially during the final push on Saigon). In that war, one of the smallest, poorest and least technologically advanced countries in the world was able to defeat the mightiest military machine in history, the USA. Just as tiny Vietnam bought a nuclear superpower to its knees, today the other nuclear giant, the USSR, is bogged down in an unwinnable guerrilla war in Afghanistan. Nearly 100,000 crack Soviet troops are boxed up in a handful of major cities by largely untrained guerrilla hill-tribesmen with few sophisticated weapons, intermittent lines of supply and no centralised command structure. Since 1979, the rebels have managed to push back seven major Soviet offensives into their stronghold in the Panjshir valley. The latest offensive, launched by the Soviets in April 1984, also failed to dislodge the guerrillas despite high level saturation bombing and an assault led by 500 tanks and armoured vehicles backed up by 10,000 Soviet troops.

Closer to home, the campaigns waged by the IRA in Ireland and ETA in Spain illustrate the potential of guerrilla warfare in urbanised industrial societies. In the north of Ireland, in the cities and countryside which the British state claims as its own, 10,000 British troops and 14,000 RUC police and UDR soldiers can barely contain about 150 IRA fighters who have adapted the principles of territorial defence and guerrilla war to *our geography* of woodland, hedgerows and the urban environment. If a handful of IRA members operating amongst a hostile Unionist majority can force a military stalemate in the six counties, what hope would the Russians have, being stretched out all over Britain (and probably most of Western Europe too) and facing proportionately larger territorial forces enjoying much greater popular support?

Non-Violent Civilian Resistance

Complementary to the strategies of territorial defence and guerrilla warfare, non-violent civilian resistance is primarily a strategy against occupation. In common with the former strategies, it does not accept that occupation means defeat and surrender, but sees it rather as a signal for new forms of opposition. Like guerrilla war, civilian resistance is a protracted form of struggle which seeks to erode the morale and authority of the occupiers and deprive them of all legitimacy and effectiveness. Through a combination of passive non-compliance and active resistance, its objective is to paralyse the occupation administration and ultimately force its collapse and withdrawal.

All governments, even regimes imposed by force of arms,

depend on some degree of compliance by the population for their maintenance. No invading army can organise the whole state apparatus and run all the essential services by itself. It relies on the subjugated peoples being willing to continue to operate the railways, telephone exchanges, power stations, hospitals, docks and mines, etc. Civilian resistance therefore aims to cause maximum disruption to the imposed regime by withdrawing all cooperation and refusing to comply, collaborate or fraternise with enemy officials, through methods such as boycotts, absenteeism, go-slows, strikes, civil disobedience and tax and rent refusals. Resistance can also take more active forms of direct protest: sabotage, mutiny, hunger strikes, occupations, harassment of officials, fly-posting, graffiti, pickets, marches and petitions. These non-violent forms of protest are ideally suited to urban industrial societies with concentrated populations. The complex division of labour in modern economies and state bureaucracies results in a higher degree of interdependence and this makes them extremely vulnerable to disruption.

All the different forms of civilian resistance involve people either undertaking actions which are unexpected and forbidden or refusing to do things which are anticipated and required. Gene Sharp describes this as a form of 'political ju-jitsu' because it throws the enemy troops off balance by reacting in an unorthodox (i.e. non-violent) manner which they are unprepared for and untrained to handle. He suggests that for subjugated peoples to respond with violent resistance, as the invaders expect, only serves to rationalise their presence and justify their repression. It plays straight into their hands because whenever the soldiers of an invading army are attacked, this destroys whatever sympathy they have for the resisting population and intensifies their desire for revenge.

However, with non-violent forms of resistance, it is the occupiers who are put on the defensive. Psychologically caught off guard by unfamiliar tactics, they are also morally disarmed by the spectre of a defiant unarmed civilian population. Even if repression still occurs, through their immense courage and suffering the resisters tend to strengthen sympathy and respect for their cause; not only amongst their fellow countrymen and women, but even amongst the enemy troops. Equally, any repression only serves to highlight the brutal and unjust nature of the occupation regime and further alienate support from it.

Over a prolonged period of time, a sustained campaign of civilian resistance aims to achieve the following results. Firstly, to deter invasion, and if that fails, to make the country ungovernable by a foreign power. Secondly, to render the aggression a costly and fruitless exercise and deny the invaders any gains or benefits from their occupation. Thirdly, to resist the imposition of an alien political system and maintain the values and institutions of the occupied nation. Fourthly, to create demoralisation, divisions and disaffection amongst the enemy troops and civil officials. Fifthly, to mobilise international opinion and sanctions against the attacker. And sixthly, when organised in conjunction with territorial defence, to weaken the invaders' military efforts by forcing them to deploy soldiers away from the main battlefield to quell civilian protests and guard key installations.

Over the last one hundred years, there have been numerous instances of non-violent resistance against repressive regimes and armies of occupation – some of them extremely effective: the Hungarian nationalist rebellion against Austrian rule from 1850 to 1867; a succession of Belgian general strikes in 1893, 1902 and 1913 which extended the franchise; industrial action in Egypt during 1919 to protest against British imperialism; and the German mass strikes of 1920 which defeated the Kapp putsch.

Between 1879 and 1886, Irish republicans organised rent and tax refusals in support of their demand for Home Rule. Later, as the struggle for independence neared its climax, they successfully undermined the authority and legitimacy of British colonial rule by setting up a dual administration, including their own republican police and courts of law.

When Germany defaulted on its 1914–18 war reparations, the French occupied the Ruhr in 1923 to exact repayments. The German trade unions responded by calling for a campaign of passive resistance: 'an unarmed people would still have power and opportunity to demonstrate its will and to disarm every aggressor by striking and closing plants and factories'.[15] The unions' call for the population to refuse to obey the French military and civil authorities was met with support from all political parties, including the Communists. Within hours, the German police and civil servants were acting as if the French did not even exist. They refused point blank to cooperate with the occupation administration, as did the shopkeepers and hoteliers who refused to serve French personnel. To prevent coal and other raw materials and manufactured products being seized and shipped back to France, the unions brought production to a standstill through a wave of strikes. Lorry and railway engines were sabotaged, canals blocked with scuttled barges, railway lines blown up, telegraph wires cut and the electricity supply shut down. Though this resistance failed to prevent the capitulation of the German government, the French never succeeded in their economic goal of extracting the wealth of the Ruhr or in their strategic objective of creating a separate client Rhineland state. Instead, the French withdrew and, chastened by the experience of civilian resistance, never attempted another occupation.

In India, non-violent protest in the form of civil disobedience, non-cooperation with the British administration and the boycott of British goods played a major part in the winning of independence. Urging support for his strategy of 'satyagraha', Mahatma Gandhi argued: 'the government of the people is possible only so long as they consent consciously or unconsciously to be governed'. Symbolic defiant gestures such as the 1930 'salt march' to protest against the British tax on salt and the mass civil disobedience of the Quit India campaign in 1942 were instrumental in arousing pro-independence sentiments amongst the Indian people and convincing the British that their presence was ceasing to be tenable.

During the Second World War, civilian resistance became a significant form of opposition to Nazi rule in several of the western and northern European countries. In Belgium, the underground organisation of go-slows, strikes and sabotage caused a massive drop in industrial production – coal output falling to 64 per cent of its pre-war level. This decline in productivity created endless shortages and delayed the delivery of new weapons and equipment to the Wehrmacht forces. During 1940, there were student strikes in the Dutch towns of Leiden and Delft in protest at the dismissal of Jewish lecturers, and the following February further mass strikes took place in Amsterdam and several other towns in solidarity with Jews facing harassment and internment.

Probably the most sustained campaigns of passive resistance occurred in Norway and Denmark. Following the German invasion of 1940, the Norwegian parliament, the Storting, refused to function and the supreme court resigned. The Nazis responded by dissolving all non-fascist political parties and installing the puppet regime of Vidkun Quisling. This immediately began to clamp down on centres of anti-Nazi resistance such as the student unions. When they refused to obey Quisling's directives, the unions were disbanded and replaced by pro-fascist front organisations. However, these were successfully boycotted and they soon collapsed.

Attempts by the fascists to take over the sporting and cultural associations and impose their own leadership were thwarted when these organisations declared a moratorium on all their activities in protest. Similar efforts to use the churches as an instrument of Nazi policy were rebuffed by the clergy. In protest at fascist interference in religious affairs, the voluntary disestablishment of the church was effected in 1942 when 93 per cent of the clergy resigned their official clerical posts and went on strike against the Quisling regime.

There was also staunch resistance by the Norwegian teachers. In defiance of fascist decrees in late 1941, they refused to display

Quisling's portrait in schools and continued to organise English language classes. When the regime tried to enforce the teaching of Nazi history and propaganda in schools, the teachers called a nationwide strike with the backing of pupils' and parents' organisations. Faced with this strike, plus 200,000 letters of protest from mothers and fathers opposed to the introduction of fascist syllabuses and the compulsory induction of children into the pro-Nazi youth movement, the Quisling regime was forced to capitulate.

Following the fascist takeover of the teachers' union, most of the members resigned en masse, and when they were subsequently ordered to join a state-controlled teachers' confederation in 1942, 80 per cent of them refused. Quisling retaliated by arresting 1,300 teachers and closing all the schools. However, within six months the unbroken resistance of the teachers forced him to re-open the schools and abandon his attempts to control the education system. Effective defeat at the hands of the teachers led the regime to drop its plans for a nationwide corporate labour system of state-run unions.

In Denmark, civilian resistance involved more emphasis on the sabotage of roads, harbours, bridges, telephone cables, electricity pylons, weapon factories, fuel depots and ammunition stores. Organised by underground groups such as the BOPA and Holger Danske, its purpose was to obstruct the Nazi war effort and frustrate the occupation regime. Two of the most successful sabotage raids were the destruction of the Globus aircraft component factory and the Riffelsyndikatet arms manufacturing plant. Industrial sabotage was also clandestinely organised. In the case of one Danish shipyard, workers using go-slow tactics and sabotage delayed the completion of a German minesweeper for twenty-six months when it should have only taken nine. Even then, the finished warship was unusable due to deliberately faulty workmanship.

The resistance also saved the lives of the majority of Denmark's 7,000 Jews. On discovering Nazi plans for their internment, the underground smuggled all but 700 of them safely to Sweden in 1943. During the same year, the Freedom Council organised mass strikes and demonstrations in 15 Danish towns and in July 1944 it led a nine-day general strike in Copenhagen Because of sabotage, strikes and protest marches, 200,000 Nazi troops had to be stationed in Denmark to pacify the population. By diverting these soldiers away from the frontline, civilian resistance greatly assisted Allied efforts to liberate Europe. After the war, the Nazi generals candidly admitted that the non-violent protests in Norway, Denmark, Belgium, Holland and France had been highly effective in undermining German morale and frustrating the fascist war machine.

Since 1945, civilian resistance has become, if anything, yet more common as a method of political protest and opposition to dictatorship and invasion – both East and West. In South Africa, the widespread civil disobedience by the Indian community in 1946 was followed by the African 'Defiance Campaign' of 1952–53, the Johannesburg bus boycott in 1957, the mass rebellion against the Pass Laws throughout 1960, the 1976 Soweto riots and the direct challenge to 'separate development' posed by the Cape Town squatters since the late 1970s. The American black civil rights struggle of the 1950s and 1960s won desegregation and an extension of the vote largely through tactics such as consumer boycotts of racially discriminatory corporations, sit-in occupations of 'whites only' restaurants and the 'freedom rides' to enforce multiracial public transport policies.

In several countries, non-violent protests have been an integral part of the struggle against the fascist right: when the French army generals seized power in Algeria in 1961, their plans to invade France and set up a military dictatorship were abandoned when De Gaulle called for popular resistance, including the blockading of roads and runways, and the trade unions responded with a 10 million-strong general strike. A year later, the Spanish mineworkers' strike in the Asturias gave a major impetus to the establishment of underground anti-Franco unions. In 1963, the Vietnamese Buddhist campaign of civil disobedience and self-immolation drew international attention to the corrupt and brutal nature of the Diem regime. Following the Portuguese soldiers' mutiny which overthrew the Caetano dictatorship in 1974, there were mass trespasses and land seizures by the peasantry in the Alentejo region. And in 1978–79, huge strikes and street demonstrations toppled the Shah of Iran.

Nearer to Britain, the civil rights struggle in the north of Ireland during the late 1960s and the IRA H-Block hunger strike in 1982 performed the important function of galvanising Republican opinion and, in the face of savage repression, winning worldwide public sympathy for the nationalist cause.

Likewise in Eastern Europe: in 1953 Soviet political prisoners went on strike at Vorkuta, and in June of that same year there was a general strike in East Berlin. The strike began as a protest against increased work norms in the construction industry which would have effectively reduced wages. It quickly spread to other industries and the East German government was forced to back down by repealing the new norms and calling new trade-union elections which resulted in the replacement of 75 per cent of the former union officials. Three years later, at the time of the Hungarian uprising in 1956, railway workers at Zahony near the USSR border went on strike in protest at the Soviet invasion. By destroying rolling stock, tearing up rails and removing vital parts from locomotive engines, they successfully delayed the influx of Russian troops and armoured columns. The massive popular resistance to the Soviet occupation of Czechoslovakia in 1968, including human barricades and the sabotage of Russian tanks, compelled the Kremlin to release the imprisoned Czech leaders and negotiate a settlement which kept Dubcek in power until April 1969.

In Poland, strikes, riots and demonstrations in 1970 forced the resignation of the Polish leader Wladyslaw Gomulka and the cancellation of food price increases. Similar rebellions broke out in 1976, also over price rises, and led directly to the formation of Solidarnosc in 1980. Within a few months the new union had 10 million members and had forced the Polish government to accept major liberalisations: the right to form independent trade unions, the legalisation of strikes, a relaxation of censorship, media access for the church and unions and greater freedom of overseas travel. When General Jaruzelski seized power in 1981 and declared martial law, Solidarnosc responded with defiant street demonstrations and mass non-cooperation, including absenteeism and a work-to-rule in industry. Though Solidarnosc was finally driven underground and some of its hard-won reforms were reversed, the strength of the Polish people's resistance undoubtedly deterred a Soviet invasion and the use of far bloodier repression by the Jaruzelski regime.

Though not always wholly successful, even the limited achievements of civilian resistance are remarkable given that they were spontaneous and unplanned. With proper long-term preparation and the education of all citizens in this type of resistance, it could be quite a powerful deterrent to invasion and an effective supplement to a territorial defence strategy.

Such a vision was the inspiration of Commander Sir Stephen King-Hall in the 1950s when he proposed a policy of 'defence without arms' as an alternative to NATO and nuclear weapons. Whilst allowing for small conventional forces capable of putting up some resistance to aggression, he advocated that Western defences should primarily be based on a strategy of non-violent resistance and political and moral warfare – with the latter aiming to psychologically subvert enemy nations and isolate them in the eyes of the international community. Interest in similar ideas has been recently expressed by the Swedish, Dutch, Norwegian and Danish governments and by General Bollardière in France. Many of the new Green parties in Europe have made civilian resistance, or what they describe as 'social defence', the cornerstone of their alternative defence policies. The West German Green Party, for example, is committed to 'non-violent self-defence' and 'active social resistance':

> Non-violence does not mean capitulation, but safeguarding peace and life by political means instead of military ones; and by social defence. Social defence means organising and re-orienting our society in such a way (in the direction of civil courage, resistance, alternative and decentralised structures) as to make it immediately clear to an aggressive foreign power that attempted occupation and domination would entail more difficulties and a greater burden that the increase in power and profit might bring.[16]

Democracy in the Ranks

Running parallel to the tradition of territorial defence, citizen armies and civilian resistance is the concept of soldiers as 'citizens in uniform'. The belief that service personnel ought to enjoy the same rights and freedoms as the civilians they are defending is reflected in the comparatively high degree of internal democracy within the armed forces of most West European countries other than Britain. This was not, however, always the case. Arguing from the standpoint that the defence of democracy requires a democratic system of defence, the European labour movements had to battle long and hard to secure the relaxation of petty regulations and harsh discipline and win extended civil, political and trade-union rights for military personnel.

A majority of the continental left support conscription, believing it to be both a social leveller and an instrument of military democratisation and civilianisation. Typically, the French Communist Party (PCF) argues that conscription creates an 'authentic popular defence' which unifies the people with the army and counters the elitism and authoritarianism of the professional forces. In its view, the opposition of the French conscripts was at least partly responsible for deterring the generals' coup in 1961. For these reasons, instead of opposing conscription the PCF has put its emphasis on a 'New Democratic Code for Army Personnel' which has been incorporated into its political programme since 1975. Principally, the PCF advocates a system of Soldiers' Committees with equal numbers of officers and rank-and-file delegates elected by their units. In Italy, the trade unions have proposed Joint Military and Civilian Commissions to examine questions of service pay and conditions. Amongst the West Germans, the radical Working Group of Democratic Soldiers (ADS) has issued proclamations calling for greater freedom in the ranks and, in 1974, the Soldiers For Peace organisation issued a manifesto declaring their refusal to bear arms against the civilian population and outlining a programme of army reforms: improved pay, a reduction in the length of conscription and the election of soldiers' delegates with the right to take up complaints with senior officers and act as counsels on behalf of colleagues facing disciplinary charges.

More recently, many of the unofficial soldiers' movements have come together in the European Conference of Conscripts' Organisations (ECCO) which represents conscripts in all the West European countries. The ECCO Declaration of November 1979 stated:

> We believe that soldiers are citizens in uniform who are entitled to enjoy the same rights as the rest of the population; there being no justification for soldiers to be treated as third-class citizens ... We share the conviction that only those military personnel who live through democracy and believe in it will feel obliged to defend it ... The authoritarian discipline, based on harsh punishment and the all-embracing power of the commanders, must be replaced by a new discipline based on dialogue, persuasion and reasoned orders which respects soldiers' human rights. Only in this way can the armed forces accomplish the role that most European constitutions assign them: the defence of national territory and the people's sovereignty ... As soldiers, we must be committed to the submission of the armed forces to the people's will and promote amongst our comrades a respect for democratic principles to prevent the army being used in the service of authoritarian and minority interests ... We will also strive to prevent the armed forces being used against the people or in colonial wars and ... oppose the increasing professionalisation of the armed forces.

ECCO's programme includes demands for new individual liberties for servicemen and women: the right to personal privacy; choice of residence; freedom of travel; authorisation to form self-help and interest groups; participation in decisions affecting the organisation of barracks and recreational activities; abolition of separate military penal codes and their inclusion as a specialist branch of civil law under the jurisdiction of the civil courts; and the military's adoption of the principles enshrined in the European Convention on Human Rights.

ECCO proposes an extension of political liberty in the services through the recognition of political, religious and conscientious objection; freedom of speech and demonstration; the right to vote, stand for public office and actively participate in political parties and trade unions; the abolition of censorship; and the banning of fascist and racist propaganda in the armed forces.

In seeking to improve conditions of employment, the ECCO programme calls for the military to comply with International Labour Organisation regulations and urges the reduction of conscription to a minimum; the conformity of barracks to national housing standards; the enforcement of fire, health and safety regulations within the armed forces; the upgrading of wages to at least the national minimum level; the regularisation of working hours; and compensation for overtime in the form of additional pay or time off in lieu.

In the Dutch army, the conscripts' union, the Vereniging Van Dienstplichtige Militairen, has already won many of ECCO's demands. Established in 1966, more than 50 per cent of all conscripts are members. The VVDM has chapters in every barracks, a monthly newspaper with a circulation of 20,000, and its executive is officially granted time off military duties to perform their trade-union work. Each year, when the defence budget is being set, the VVDM makes representations to parliament on behalf of the conscripts. Together with the ten other military unions representing the different services and ranks, the VVDM negotiates with the minister of defence under official auspices.

Between 1966 and 1980, the VVDM won a ten-fold increase in wages; the abolition of obligatory military hairstyles and salutes; a standardised seven-hour working day; compensation for overtime and irregular duty; liberalisation of the barracks regime; the right for soldiers on charge to have a legal counsel representing them; and the freedom to actively participate in political parties and protests.

Amongst non-conscripts in the Dutch forces, 60 per cent of officers and 80 per cent of other ranks belong to unions. Far from causing a decline in military effectiveness, the scrapping of 'bull' and excessive discipline has greatly boosted morale so that the Netherlands now has one of the highest efficiency ratings of any NATO army.

In West Germany, as well as a military ombudsman to investigate individual grievances, there are two soldiers' organisations. Firstly, there is the Bundeswehr Verband, or soldiers' association. Though it is not a full trade union, it does take up issues of pay and conditions. Secondly, all ranks can belong to specialist military branches of the main trade unions such as the Professional Soldiers Department of the Public Services and Transport Union.

Under the Danish Constitution: 'Citizens are entitled – without previous permission – to form unions for any legal purpose.' Accordingly, well over 90 per cent of Denmark's servicemen and women belong to the 14 separate associations for officers and the one main union for other ranks. The figures for unionisation are only slightly lower in Belgium, Norway and Luxemburg.

In Sweden, the trade-unionisation of the forces has existed

since 1936. Under the State Officials Act of 1965, military personnel were also granted the right to strike. They briefly exercised this right in 1970, together with tactics of mass sick-listing, demonstrations and the occupation of military premises. The underground soldiers' news-sheets which were produced during this period of militancy have since become permanent and officially accepted. Since then, the Swedes have taken military democratisation a stage further by legalising political activities on base by off-duty personnel and introducing the principle of 'codetermination' between officers and men – a form of industrial democracy in the forces which requires officers to consult with lower ranks in decision-making.

Swedish conscripts are represented through a 'soldiers' parliament' consisting of delegates elected from each regiment. This 'parliament' discusses grievances, considers resolutions and draws up policy recommendations which are forwarded to the ministry of defence. Nearly 96 per cent of Sweden's professional soldiers belong to one of the three main military unions, all of which are affiliated to national trade unions. The Union of Swedish Officers (SOF) is affiliated to the National Federation of Government Employees; the Swedish Union of Warrant Officers (SUOF) and the Union of Non-Commissioned Officers in the Defence Forces (FUF) are affiliated to the Organisation of Salaried Employees – Civil Servants Section. In addition, specialist personnel like army engineers are members of specialist associations such as the union of Civil Engineers (CF) which is affiliated to the Organisation of Swedish Professional Workers.

Trade-unionisation in Sweden's armed forces has resulted in tangible improvements: the defining of regular working hours; introduction of overtime pay; an independent parliamentary ombudsman to handle complaints; the jurisdiction of civilian courts over all crimes committed by soldiers; and the right of appeal against internal military discipline via the civil law.

Unlike Sweden, in France trade unions have always been illegal. As a result, with no effective redress procedure, unrest amongst troops in 1975 boiled over into big demonstrations by discontented soldiers in Draguignan and the French Army of the Rhine at Karlsruhe. The government responded by liberalising the disciplinary code and establishing consultative committees representing groups of soldiers; though unions are still banned despite the pressure of the left-wing CFDT union federation.

Britain is today, therefore, one of the handful of West European countries without any military democracy or trade-unionisation. As well as showing up Britain as an exception to the rule, the contemporary army reforms in nearby countries with social systems comparable to our own illustrate that democracy in the ranks is a practical and winnable goal to aim for.

Chapter Six:

British Precedents for Popular Defence

The Militia Tradition

Whilst many other West European countries quite clearly have a long lineage of territorial defence and citizen armies, the 'nations in arms' tradition seems quite alien to Britain. Nevertheless, it *is* an integral part of our pre-twentieth century history. The permanent standing army was not established until 1689. Prior to that date, Britain had been defended largely by amateur volunteer militias. In Anglo-Saxon times, the defence of the realm was undertaken by a locally organised military force known as the fyrd. It consisted of free landowners between the ages of 16 and 60 who, by custom, served in its ranks for two months each year. Under King Alfred, this system was slightly modified when all landowners were required to do 'thane's service' and provide their own arms. During the reign of Edward I, the first truly national force of amateur soldiers for the purpose of home defence was created. This later became variously known as the trained bands, fencibles, militia or volunteers. Throughout the feudal era, the English armies which fought against the kings and princes of Europe were only raised temporarily for specific campaigns and were then disbanded. This was due to a long history of English antipathy towards the creation of a standing army on the grounds that it would require onerous taxation and could become an instrument of despotism and tyranny. Besides, with Britain being an island state protected by the navy, it was felt that there was no need for a regular army.

It was not until the English Civil War and the foundation of Cromwell's New Model Army in 1645 that Britain first acquired a professional army. Later, in the 1660s, to meet the growing demands of empire, the first permanent standing units were established. To Parliament, their formation symbolised the beginnings of arbitary rule and they were only accepted on the strict condition that they were never stationed in Britain. James II, however, ignored this stipulation and diverted the militia budget to finance the formation of a home-based regular army which grew in size to 34,000 men. This aggrandisement of military power was seen by Parliament as being incompatible with political freedom and a threat to popular liberties. Memories of the virtual military dictatorship under Cromwell and fears that the king was assuming absolutist powers led to James being deposed by William of Orange in the 'Glorious Revolution' of 1688. The principal charges against James included 'the raising and keeping of a standing army within this Kingdom in time of peace without consent of Parliament and the quartering of soldiers contrary to law'. Parliament was determined to ensure that whilst William and his successors might remain the titular head of the army, they should enjoy no independent control of the military. To make the army accountable to the people and prevent it from ever again growing too large or being used for oppressive purposes, the Declaration of Rights in 1689 decreed that the army budget and Mutiny Act had to come before the House of Commons every year for approval and renewal.

Despite this sanctioning of a permanent standing army, the militia system continued in parallel and was strengthened by the 1757 Act requiring militias to be recruited in each county by compulsory ballot and financed out of the rates. Militia members did three years service, training each Sunday between February and October plus a few days drill at Whitweek. Discipline was imposed by the civil authorities, with the militias only coming under the jurisdiction of military law in times of war. During the Napoleonic wars, the militia was again boosted by the Levee En Masses Act of 1803 which called for the mustering of all men aged 17 to 55; though this mandatory levee was never enforced following the spontaneous voluntary enlistment of 463,000 recruits. Simultaneously, however, the combination of the Napoleonic wars, together with the rapid rise of colonialism abroad and working-class discontent at home, led to a massive expansion of the standing army. Thus, after the militia's brief revival in the first decade of the nineteenth century, it was soon relegated to an auxiliary role and gradually ceased to be seen as an alternative to the regular army. This change was greatly lamented by radical commentators of the day, who continued to regard the standing army as an instrument of tyranny to thwart the people's will. Writing in the *Political Register* in December 1816, William Cobbett noted:

> There is no need of a standing army in a country where the very lowest classes are so well off as to have no desire and no interest to disturb the public tranquillity. This was formerly

> the situation of our now miserable country. 'The English Constitution,' says Blackstone, 'knows nothing of standing armies.' Then he goes on in a triumphant strain to say that 'No fortresses, no barracks: nothing to keep soldiers distinct from the people – nothing of this sort belongs to England.' Alas! My Lord Mayor, what would this great commentator on our laws have said if he could have lived to this day?

Throughout the nineteenth century, the militia continued to decline as the basis of defence; though it was briefly revived and re-popularised in the late 1850s and 1860s when there was a widespread fear that Napoleon III was planning to invade Britain. To meet this threat, in May 1859 General Peel, the Secretary of State for War, proposed the creation of a Volunteer Corps for home defence. By the end of 1860, 119,000 volunteers had enlisted. In Liverpool, for example, there was a Borough Guard of municipal employees and a Press Guard of local journalists; plus special corps of millers, artisans, engineers, railway workers, etc. The formation of these different corps was entirely spontaneous. Subject to the formal approval of the Lord Lieutenant of the county, any group of 60 to 100 men could form themselves into a company. Within each company there was a good deal of democracy and autonomy, with the volunteers being empowered to elect their own officers and organise their own training sessions two or three nights a week. Frederick Engels, however, was one of the most outspoken critics of the election of officers. He argued that senior ranks in the Volunteers ought to be held by full-time professional soldiers and based on qualifications and merit. Nevertheless, despite his criticisms of what he saw as excessive democracy and local independence, Engels was generally enthusiastic about the principle of a Volunteer Corps. Indeed, he wrote a series of articles for the *Volunteer Journal of Lancashire and Cheshire* in 1860 in which he advocated government funding to give all volunteers two weeks training a year at Aldershot to improve their skills and efficiency.[1]

Support for some form of militia or citizen's army was also strong amongst other early socialist pioneers. In 1831, for instance, the radical working-class weekly *The Poor Man's Guardian* published an article written by Colonel Francis Macerone entitled: 'Defensive Instructions For The People'. A radical Italian exile who had formerly fought in the royal Neapolitan army, Macerone argued: 'It is essential for a free people to be armed. To hope that liberty and justice can be preserved with all the means of power and coercion existing in the hands of the governing minority is an infantile delusion . . . An armed people cannot be subdued by any faction. They require no paid army to protect them and none can coerce them. Arm, then oh British people and you will be safe.'[2] Accordingly, Macerone urged the creation of a people's militia and outlined some rudimentary territorial and guerrilla tactics for the defence of working-class districts against the army and the police – the fortification of fields and buildings, street and house-to-house fighting and the construction of improvised weaponry. Such ideas were subsequently embraced by the insurrectionary wings of the Chartist and Irish Republican movements.

During a later era, in the early 1900s, a similar view was echoed by radical socialists such as the MP for Colne Valley, Victor Grayson. A vigorous opponent of conscription, he favoured the creation of a citizen's militia and the reorganisation of the armed forces on a more democratic basis. In circumstances of widespread police and army suppression of strikers and the possibility of German aggression, Grayson even went so far as to agitate for workers' armed self-defence: 'The workers themselves must take steps to procure rifles, revolvers, ammunition and other popular accessories.'[3]

Grayson's revolutionary ideas were adopted by the Social-Democratic Federation in 1908 and were widely debated amongst the left, as indicated by the following correspondence which appeared in the columns of *The Worker* on May Day, 1909:

> 'Recently there has been a large amount of talk about the Citizen Army. As a substitute for the present standing army under capitalism, and also as a weapon for the working class in the transition from capitalism to the Cooperative Commonwealth, it has found warm advocates in Messrs Gee, Grayson, Northcote, and other socialist lecturers.
>
> Briefly stated, the Citizen Army scheme amounts to a proposed democratisation of the military forces: the substitution of our present voluntary army by a national militia, democratically controlled . . .
>
> The arguments put forward by the advocates of this scheme are briefly: (i) That it would prevent the use of military force against the will of the majority of the people, since the army and the people being the one and the same thing, the will of the majority of the nation would be the will of the majority of the army. In other words, if the majority declared for the Social Revolution they would have the army at their back and not against them. (ii) That the Citizen Army is the only alternative to conscription.
>
> But, sir, it seems to me that a parliament in which the landlord and capitalist class is dominant would not be at all likely to grant to the working class a weapon which would be used for the overthrow of the first named. It does not seem likely that the master class will forge and sharpen a

weapon for their own throats.

Of course, it may be argued that the statute establishing the Citizen Army will be carried, not by a bourgeois majority, but by a parliament containing a majority of revolutionary working class representatives. But long before the new scheme had time to materialise, the bourgeois would use the existing military forces to overthrow the anti-militarist government and re-establish his power.

The author of this critique of the citizen army system concludes by advocating an alternative policy of civilian resistance based on the trade-union movement:

> The soldier in the field, equipped with rifle and cartridge-pouch, is merely the final phase of a long and complicated social process. He has been placed there, equipped and fed by the labour of the working class. His continued efficiency depends on a regular supply of food, clothing, and the necessities of life from that source. He has been transported to the field of battle by a whole army of railway workers. The intelligence which directs his movements is dependent upon the workers in the telegraphic and other kindred agencies. Well, sir, this being the case, I contend that the working class, organised in some such union as the Industrial Union, would be able to paralyse any army which the capitalist class could put into the field. It could put the army in quarantine: it could cut off the supplies of food, clothing and fuel.

Two years later, *The Worker* also reported the unsuccessful attempts of radicals to commit the 1911 Trade Union Congress to support the replacement of the standing army by volunteer citizen's forces:

> At Wednesday's sitting of the Trade Union Congress at Newcastle Town Hall, Mr J. Stokes, of the London Glass-blowers, moved:– 'That this Congress, realising that militarism and the existence of a regular standing army constitutes a menace to popular liberty, is of the opinion that the time has arrived for the institution of a real citizen army, free entirely from military law during times of peace, officered entirely by the selection of the rank and file, such citizen army to be used for defensive purposes only.'
>
> Mr Stokes said . . .
>
> A volunteer citizen army would defend the rights of the people against the military caste. There had never yet been any great change in any country in the world that had not been brought about by the social reformers bringing over the army to their side. If at the present day there were war and

> England were invaded, then he would be prepared to do his share. Any man who stood on one side and did not attempt to repel invasion because of some idealistic notion about arbitration would not be a coward, but he would be a fool . . .
>
> Mr Will Thorne, MP, seconding the resolution, said the country had to realise that it had to choose at present between a professional army and a citizen army. Even in times of good trade 80 per cent of the young men who enlisted in the army enlisted simply because they could not get civil employment, and in times of bad trade 90 per cent joined for that reason. If the principle of the Right-to-Work Bill was admitted, and if the Right-to-Work Bill were carried, where were they going to get their army from then?
>
> The country would be compelled to choose between conscription and a citizen army. Such a citizen army would be officered by men of their own class. There was nothing impossible in that. If the children of the working class were given the same facilities as were given to the men who officered the army and navy at present, they would have a navy and army which would be better maintained than it was by the cads who officered the army today.

However, despite such radical agitation periodically throughout the 1920s and 30s, it was not until the Second World War that socialists were able to push the armed forces in a more popular and democratic direction.

The Home Guard – An Army of the People

The Home Guard of 1940–45 provides a relatively recent British example of an alternative model of defence. Based on a territorial military strategy and a militia system of organisation, the Home Guard represents a brief moment, not so long ago, when Britain raised a 'people's army' to fight a 'people's war' against fascism.

With the threat of Nazi invasion on the cards in the summer of 1940, it fell to left-wingers such as Tom Wintringham to play a leading role in the development of the Home Guard. A former Royal Flying Corps engine-fitter during the First World War, Wintringham had been involved in a minor mutiny in France during the summer of 1918. Two years later, he became a founder member of the Communist Party, and from 1923 till the late 1930s he variously served as a journalist, deputy editor and editor for party publications such as *Worker's Weekly*, *Labour Monthly*, the *Daily Worker* and *Left Review*. In 1925, Wintringham was arrested along with eleven other leading communists following an article in the *Worker's Weekly* which urged the armed forces to refuse to break strikes or wage an imperialist war. He was convicted of Incitement to Mutiny and sentenced to six months' imprisonment. Following the outbreak of the Spanish Civil War, Wintringham was one of the originators of the idea of an 'international legion' to support the Republican forces. Indeed, he went to Spain and was commander of the British battalion of the International Brigade in the celebrated battle of Jarama.

Wintringham returned from Spain in 1937 with personal experience of the much more popular and democratic system of defence which had been practised by the *brigadistas* and the Republican armies. With the prospect of German aggression looming ever larger on the horizon, Wintringham published early in 1939 a pamphlet called *How to Reform the Army* in which he proposed the democratisation of the British armed forces and their reorganisation around 'volunteer battalions' of a new type: 'An army strong enough to defend Britain . . . is possible if the British people are given a new liberty, that of learning the handling of arms.'[4] Wintringham suggested the creation of a volunteer short-service light infantry of 150,000 men – half made up of 40–45 year old ex-servicemen from the 1914–18 war and the other half of younger men. All volunteers would do a brief four to eight week basic training period, followed by a three week refresher course every three years.

Wintringham put these ideas to War Office officials, together with the lessons he drew from his experience of fighting the German and Italian generals in Spain. But they were not interested. It took the Nazi blitzkrieg across Europe, particularly the occupation of Holland, to awaken their rather reluctant interest in the idea of a home defence force.

By early 1940, the fascist tide seemed unstoppable, with the appeasing western governments unwilling to take the offensive against the Third Reich and the allied armies proving largely ineffectual on the battlefield. After the German occupation of Norway and Denmark, the attacks on Belgium and France and the Nazi parachute landings in Holland, a fascist invasion of Britain appeared imminent. Spontaneously, thousands of unofficial 'watch' committees sprang up all over Britain to scour the coast and skies to give warning of an invasion. By 14 May 1940, Churchill's Coalition government, which had just replaced the appeasing Chamberlain administration, could no longer resist public pressure for action. Echoing the call of William Pitt nearly a century and a half earlier, Anthony Eden, Secretary of State for War, appealed over the radio for 'local defence volunteers' – soon to be known as the Home Guard. Even before he had finished speaking, police stations were besieged with volunteers – 250,000 signing up in the first 24 hours and 1.5 million by the end of June. Though the Home Guard was only open to male recruits, many women also wanted to bear arms. Indeed, some succeeded in joining the Home Guard unofficially in the first few months and others formed a private 'Amazon Defence League'. Dr Edith Summerskill requested in Parliament that women should be allowed to join the Home Guard on equal terms with men, but this was flatly rejected by the government. Eventually, however, a 22,000-strong women's Home Guard Auxiliary was formed, though it was explicitly restricted to non-combatant tasks.

In the initial weeks of its formation, the Home Guard was full of a glorious chaotic enthusiasm, with few weapons and little effective training, but a huge popular will to resist fascism. The local units which sprang up enjoyed a large degree of independence. In many towns, they were effectively autonomous municipal armies under the command of local council leaders. The mayor of Southend, for example, led an army of nearly 2,000 volunteers.

Wintringham realised that in the new atmosphere of national emergency, any initiative which contributed to the cause of national defence was suddenly acceptable; no matter how much it might have been frowned upon, even proscribed, a few weeks earlier. He saw the possibility of taking advantage of this changed climate of opinion to transform the Home Guard into a genuine people's army to resist fascist aggression.

Following discussions with Edward Hulton, millionaire publisher of the left-wing weekly *Picture Post*, the two of them came up with the idea of an unofficial Home Guard Training School under Wintringham's leadership. Hulton agreed to put up the initial funds, while another friend of his, Lord Jersey, placed his estate at Osterley Park in West London at the School's disposal. Wintringham recruited a wide range of experts to work with him at Osterley. His two closest colleagues were former comrades from the Spanish Civil War: Hugh Slater and the Canadian 'Yank' Levy. Slater, a writer and painter, had worked for the International Brigade's general staff. At the Home Guard School, he became an instructor in the street-fighting tactics of barricading, sniping and 'mouseholing' from house to house. Levy taught unarmed combat and knife-fighting. Prior to Osterley, his chequered career had included illicit arms trading in Mexico, service with Sandino's forces in Nicaragua, trade-union organising in the merchant navy and a stint as a machine-gunner in Spain. Through Slater came another painter, Roland Penrose. With no direct fighting skills to impart, this surrealist artist was nevertheless an expert in camouflage. The former Labour MP, Major Wilfred Vernon, combined socialist politics with officer experience in the 1914-18 war and was the School's principal lecturer on the improvisation of mines, grenades and molotov cocktails. Another staff member, Stanley White, was a leader in the Boy Scout movement. His knowledge of the simple skills of scouting – stalking, patrolling and outdoor survival – was an invaluable part of guerrilla instruction. Three Andalusian miners who had fled to Britain as refugees after the Spanish War taught sabotage, including the use of explosives to immobilise tanks and demolish bridges, roads and railway tunnels, etc.

The new School was opened on 10 July 1940. Its format of instruction was a two-day course repeated three times a week. Within the first three months, 5,000 volunteers had already passed through it. There were even instances of Regular army units attending for unauthorised training in defiance of a War Office ban. Indeed, the War Office and official Home Guard leaders were extremely hostile to Osterley and their attempt to shut down the School was only narrowly averted. But by October, Osterley's reputation was so formidable that the government was forced to officially recognise it as the No.1 Home Guard Training School and adopt it as the model for all subsequent training. Not that the opposition was just from the establishment. The Communist, Trotskyist and Independent Labour parties were all united in their condemnation of the Home Guard. George Orwell rebuffed their arguments in a *Tribune* article of 20 December 1940:

> Conversation with an ILP member:
> 'Are you a pacifist?'. 'No, certainly not. I would fight in any war for the establishment of Socialism, or the defence of genuine democracy.' 'You don't think the present war is a war of that kind.' 'No.' 'Don't you think it is capable of being turned into that kind of war?' 'It might, but not till the workers are in control. The workers must have the weapons in their own hands.' 'Well, then, why not join the Home Guard? They'll give you plenty of weapons.' 'The Home Guard! But that's just a Fascist organisation.' . . . The Communists, ILP, and all their kind can parrot 'Arms to the Workers', but they cannot put a rifle into the workers' hands; the Home Guard can and does.

Orwell concluded his case for the Home Guard by warning that it is 'childish to suppose that there might not at some time be an attempt at treachery by an English equivalent of the Pétain government; or possibly post-war chaos in which it would be necessary to use violence to restore democracy and prevent some kind of reactionary coup d'état. In any of those circumstances, the existence of a popular militia, armed and politically conscious and capable of influencing the regular forces, will be of profound importance.'[5]

Despite the combined opposition of both left and right, the demand for Home Guard training continued to soar. Wintringham described his impressions of the early days of the Home Guard School in an article for *Picture Post,* then Britain's most popular weekly magazine. Under the title 'The Home Guard Can Fight' (21 September 1940) Wintringham wrote:

> As I was watching yesterday 250 men of the Home Guard take their places for a lecture at the Osterley Park Training School an air-raid siren sounded, and a dozen men with rifles moved to their prearranged positions as a defence unit against low-flying aircraft. The lecturer began to talk of scouting, stalking and patrolling. And as I watched and listened I realised that I was taking part in something so new and strange as to be almost revolutionary – the growth of an 'army of the people' in Britain – and, at the same time, something that is older than Britain, almost as old as England – a gathering of the 'men of the counties able to bear arms.'
>
> The men at Osterley were being taught confidence and cunning, the use of shadow and of cover, by a man who learned field-craft from Baden-Powell, the most original irregular soldier in modern history (with the possible exception of Lawrence of Arabia). And in an hour or two they would be hearing of the experience, hard bought with lives and wounds, won by an army very like their own, the army that for year after year held up Fascism's flood-tide towards world power in that Spanish fighting which was the prelude and the signal for the present struggle. I could not help thinking how alike these two armies were: the Home Guard of Britain and the Militia of Republican Spain. Superficially alike in mixture of uniforms and half-uniforms, in shortage of weapons and ammunition, in hasty and incomplete organisation and in lack of modern training, they seemed to me more fundamentally alike in their serious eagerness to learn, their resolve to meet and defeat all the difficulties in their way, their certainty that despite shortage of time and gear they could fight and fight effectively.

Later in the same article, Wintringham summed up the skills taught at Osterley:

> Modern tactics in general, and German tactics present and future. The use and improvisation of hand-grenades, land mines and anti-tank grenades. The use of various types of rifles, shot-guns, pistols, etc. Camouflage, field-craft, scouting, stalking and patrolling. Guerrilla warfare in territory occupied by the enemy. Street tactics and defence of cities; the use of smoke-screens. Troop-carrying aircraft, parachut-

> ists, and defensive measures against them. Field works, road-blocks and anti-tank methods. Observation and reporting.

Wintringham and his colleagues subsequently wrote a synopsis of their lectures which was published as an official handbook in 1941 under the same title – *The Home Guard Can Fight.* A sort of do-it-yourself guerrilla guide outlining what was taught at Osterley, this included advice on the use of home-made explosives to knock out German tanks, as well as detailed instructions on the subject of street fighting.[8]

In the same year, 1941, Penguin Books published a handbook on *Guerrilla Warfare.* Written by 'Yank' Levy, in collaboration with Wintringham, it was intended to acquaint the general population with guerrilla tactics. Included in this ABC of irregular warfare was the following advice on industrial sabotage:

> Find out about the drainage system of important factories, whether by means of it you can enter the factory when the enemy is in occupation, to commit acts of sabotage. Don't forget to examine the coal-chutes of the local power station – a hefty charge of explosive can be sent down into the building by this route. A lump of clay with explosive embedded in it and coal dust patted thoroughly into the outside looks exactly like a lump of coal. Such a charge can be dropped down a coal-chute or onto a pile of coal. Firemen will then shovel it into the fire-box with the ordinary coal and up goes your power house.[9]

Also for the benefit of the wider public, Wintringham wrote up many of these ideas in regular articles for *Picture Post.* In a feature on 26 July 1941, for example, he reported on the Home Guard's success in weapons improvisation under the headline 'We Make Our Own Mortar For 38/6':

> From those early days of July, 1940, we have been making many homemade mortars. We have dropped the heavy base plate; all that such a weapon needs is a spiked tail that sticks firmly in the ground. We became experts at kicking a mortar stuck in the ground, or wedging it with a piece of stone, in such a way as to alter the range or angle of fire, to get the second shot on target if the first one went a little wide. And with our fifth or sixth mortar, we got the idea of making the tail end in the form of a spade, so that the man handling it can dig a hole for it quickly and easily. Powder taken from fireworks is not realistic. So we made our own gunpowder . . . This particular weapon, a four-inch mortar capable of throwing a six-pound shell, cost us 38 shillings

and 6 pence. A similar weapon, not much more efficient or more accurate, of regulation pattern and bought through the Ministry of Supply, would cost more pounds, considerably more, than mine cost in shillings.

Other ingenious improvisations were devised by Home Guard units all over the country: cars and trucks were converted into tanks by cladding them with steel plating, and ARP firefighter's stirrup-pumps were filled with petrol or dry-cleaning fluid for use as flame-throwers. A Sussex unit equipped itself with lethal wooden crossbows which fired grenades; and in the Bolsover collieries, the miners' Home Guard manufactured 'backyard' anti-tank guns out of scrap metal – scoring a 90 per cent kill ratio in field practice against fast moving targets.

During this period, Wintringham became the country's foremost advocate of urban guerrilla warfare to resist Nazi occupation. In a *Picture Post* feature on 24 January 1942, he spelled out to millions of readers the A to Z of 'This Question of Street Fighting':

> In the last war villages and towns could be flattened by artillery; that war moved slowly and men fought mainly in the mud of fields. This war moves fast; armies attack on wheels and tractor; therefore, mainly on roads. And the roads cross in villages and towns.
>
> An army that can hold built-up areas can prevent its opponent using vehicles for manœuvre; and manœuvre by vehicles is the essence of modern attack. On the other hand an army that does *not* learn street fighting cannot attack in Belgium, or the Ruhr; it must fight in empty deserts.
>
> Our enemies win battles and campaigns by the use of two principal weapons; the tank with a gun and the dive-bomber. We have all too few tanks with more than a fairly light gun; and we have no dive-bombers. And that is another reason for learning street-fighting; for in the streets these weapons are at a great disadvantage.
>
> Tanks are of little use in streets against a vigorous resistance; no tank carries enough ammunition to smash down the houses on each side of a fairly short street. Therefore, infantry opposing the tanks can always be hidden, on either side, at very short ranges. Streets are, for tanks, long and dangerous 'defiles', like passes through hills where the enemy can lurk, not only close on each side, but also above the vehicles. Tanks have never scored success in street-fighting – when opposed by the obvious methods.

Warsaw showed the reason for their failure: the civilians and half-trained recruits of Warsaw, without fortifications of a later period than Napoleon's (and happily released from control by their War Office, which was engaged in running away) defeated a German armoured division which reached the suburbs of the city at the end of the first week of fighting, and did this entirely with improvised methods. These methods occasionally got mixed, as when some enterprising men in a garage tried to use a petrol pump as a flame-thrower, at the same time as the Warsaw fire brigade from a side street opposite were trying to blind the tanks with water from their hoses. But they were effective enough to throw Reinhardt's Panzer division and its supporting troops out of the suburbs in 24 hours; and they stayed out until the main German army came up many days later.

Before an actual attack is made on a city it can, of course, be heavily bombed. If the authorities have refused to make suitable air raid shelters, the military effect of this bombing will be considerable. But as soon as the enemy begins to try to enter the city, he must cease bombing it. Street fighting soon becomes so confused, there is so much smoke from burning buildings and so on, that it is impossible for bombers to operate as close support for their infantry.

Therefore, in street fighting the weapons in which our enemy have been allowed to build up superiority are not of much value. Street fighting is mainly infantry fighting. But it is not mainly fighting *in the streets*. It is mainly fighting within buildings or from within buildings.

Naturally, if there is no opposition in the streets – as happens if the defending commander has put all his forces in a line round the city – the German attacking forces can march or run through the open streets to the rallying point. That is why the defence of a long perimeter, by a thinly spread line of troops, is of little use.

If on the other hand the defending commander has wisely organised defensive strong points within the city itself, a defence in depth with snipers commanding long streets and machine guns placed for enfilade fire down side streets, the Germans have a much more difficult task. They will have to try the 'mousehole method' . . .

Advance along streets held by modern machine weapons is suicidal. These weapons are now very accurate, little likely to jam at the critical moment, and very numerous: frontal advance against them does not work.

In defence against an attack or counter-attack of the type described, it is necessary to realise that the rifle is a long-range weapon (as ranges go in streets) and the rifleman cannot defend himself at short ranges against a determined rush from the other side of the street. The machine gun, and still more the tommy-gun, can normally defend itself against a rush of men who get out of cover 25 yards away.

The rifleman, therefore, should normally be placed relatively high up in a building, where he cannot be quickly rushed, and should be supported by grenadiers. The machine gun or tommy-gun is usually best placed at ground level, because it then gets grazing fire throughout its effective range. As the Irish have shown, snipers with rifles on roof-tops can be of great value.

Roofs and cellars should be considered possible routes for counter-attack against a force that has penetrated a row of buildings.

Just as field-craft in open warfare includes hundreds of different hints and tips, so 'street-craft' also is made up of a great number of fairly simple rules which are not very difficult to learn. It would be useless to put them all down here; but it may be mentioned that windows are seldom safe to fire from if your weapon protrudes into the street beyond the window; your enemy will be at such short range that he will spot you at once. Barbed wire can be thrown across a street; the best way is to sling half a brick from a house you hold to a house on the other side held by your comrades; to the brick a string is tied; they pull on the string, and haul the wire across. Flares are very useful at night, and much street fighting is done at night. Troops who cannot get forward in any other way will try to smash a building near their objective with mortar shells, and then rush this building, which will be easier to enter than one that has not been knocked about. Pages of such hints and tips could be given.

But, when we were engaged in giving this sort of information to Home Guard officers and men at Osterley over a year ago, a very great gentleman who had been a Cabinet Minister met a friend who said he had just been to Osterley. *'Terrible !' said the great gentleman, 'I hear that Anthony Eden is going to take them over and legitimise them. And they're teaching street fighting – just planning to murder us in our beds.'* There speaks the real voice of the Unteachable Tory.

From Osterley and the pages of *Picture Post,* these revolutionary ideas fanned out across Britain from the summer of 1940. Whilst the often-caricatured buffoonery of 'Dad's Army' may have had a grain of truth to it in the early days and in the more benighted rural districts, for the most part the *real* Home Guard was deadly serious and capable of delivering a crippling blow to any Nazi invaders. In the industrial areas, it had a predominantly working-class membership and was often organised directly on a workplace basis (through the Dockyard Defence Volunteers, Factory Defence Sections, etc.) to defend the railways, mines, shipyards and manufacturing plants in the event of fascist aggression. Within the Home Guard, there were specialist units for journalists, postal staff, civil servants, taxi drivers, Thames lightermen, etc. At the House of Commons, MPs and clerical staff had their own Home Guard, as did BBC employees at Broadcasting House. On the Southern Railway, a Home Guard was formed to defend the tunnels, bridges, viaducts, signal boxes and locomotive depots. In Essex, the Rivers Catchment Board unit patrolled the marshes and stationed lookouts along the coast.

The strongly democratic character of the Home Guard was evidenced by the way in which many units initially enjoyed a high degree of autonomy, elected their own officers and resisted the imposition of War Office nominees and procedures. Even when the Home Guard was regularised and finally made an official part of the British Army on 6 August 1940, saluting was optional, there was relatively little 'bull', officers had no powers of summary punishment and insubordination could only be penalised by dismissal in the most serious cases. The popular character of the Home Guard was also obvious by the relish with which many local units set up road blocks to harass the pleasure vehicles of the upper classes – private motorcars in those days still being seen as symbols of leisure and class privilege.

Contrary to the 'Dad's Army' mythology, most Home Guard units reached a high level of proficiency and would have presented a serious stumbling block to Nazi pacification of the country. In an article for the Army Bureau of Current Affairs,[10] Major Geoffrey Cotterell rated the Home Guard fitness level as 75 per cent of that achieved by regular troops and its operational efficiency as being 'almost' to professional army standards. This judgement was based on his investigation of a cross-section of units around the country. One of his accounts described a Home Guard Anti-Aircraft unit in North-East London. It consisted of 1,500 members organised into eight A.A. batteries on a rota system. Each battery practised for two evenings every eight days – one evening for A.A. training and the other for weapons instruction. Cotterell noted the very low level of absenteeism as proof of enthusiasm and high morale. He also detailed the techniques of 'town defence' practised by Home Guard units in Lancashire. These included the fortification of buildings and the burial of secret arms caches, and involved training in sewer-crawling, wall-scaling and house-to-house street fighting.

In a further series of *Picture Post* articles and his book *New Ways of War,* Wintringham began arguing for the expansion of the Home Guard to a maximum strength of 4 million, the mass improvisation of weapons in 'backyard' workshops, the establishment of a Home Guard Council separate from the War Office to oversee organisation and weapons procurement, and for the right of Home Guarders to carry their rifles with them to their homes and their workplaces. These demands were also taken up by Hugh Slater in his Penguin Special *Home Guard For Victory*. He suggested that a 'fully developed Home Guard' would be 'an absolute guarantee against both the crude fascism of a Mosley and the more insidious Fifth Column activities of any would-be British Pétain'.

At the same time, Wintringham began formulating an 'anti-blitzkrieg' strategy specifically for the Home Guard:

> The Germans have greatly developed the tactics of attack in depth, by the use of armoured divisions, of troops landed from the air and of Fifth Columnists. These tactics can best be resisted by a force which is naturally disposed by the conditions of its formation across the whole depth of the country. We can possess an army that is so thick a line that it fills the whole map. The Home Guard can be such an army . . . The Home Guard will be mainly holding forces, providing part of our outposts, and most of our defence in depth. They will be strategically static in most cases. Even in the event of invasion, most of the Home Guard must stay close to where they are raised. But if they are to take over from the Regulars some part of their duties, strategical mobility for a certain proportion of the Home Guard will become necessary. And even those units which do not move far from their home quarters must be tactically mobile. Tactical immobility is today suicide. It is the Maginot Line. Those who 'sit in a pill-box' seldom get a chance to shoot, either straight or crooked; they find the enemy floods them, and they become isolated.

Wintringham later went on to refine these early ideas and develop the theories of 'web defence' and 'islands of resistance', set out in the following terms in *Picture Post* on 17 May 1941 under the title 'Train the Home Guard For a Modern War':

> The invasion of Britain, carried out by blitzkrieg tactics of attack in depth, would not consist only or mainly of a landing on the beaches, but would consist mainly in its first phases of a number of attacks from the air, aimed at making such a landing or several landings possible. During these opening stages of invasion any important point in Britain would be threatened with attack, not from one direction only, but from any direction. The military answer to this is to have active garrisons everywhere of importance, a web of

defended 'islands' that can be held firmly, from which patrols and stronger groupings can sally out, to mop up weak raiding parties and to harass larger enemy forces. In addition to these active garrisons we need forces capable of counter-attacking and destroying any large Nazi concentration.

I believe that the Home Guard should form almost all the active garrisons; the Regular Army in its formed units should be reserved for counter-attack; Regular troops that have not completed their training should supplement the Home Guard garrisons. And I am certain that it is far more economical, in money and man-power, for these active garrisons of tank-proof 'islands' to consist of men who work productively in industry until they are needed, rather than that they should consist of immense numbers of Regular soldiers immobilised in relative inactivity, and losing their keenness because of this inactivity. Our ability to make these active garrisons out of man-power usefully employed in the production of war goods puts us, on this field of defence, right ahead of the Nazis in the development of the technique of war.They have developed attack in depth; we answer with a new form of defence in depth that only a democracy can achieve.

The Nazis cannot arm workers in factories and offices, in the countries they have conquered or in Italy. If they arm the factory workers in Germany they arm the revolution which will eventually destroy them. Because they are not a democracy, they cannot achieve the new form of defence that checkmates the new form of attack. We can achieve it, if we realise that the British people once again, as so often in their past, have had the initiative to invent and develop something new and powerful – and, as so often in the past, have done so without realising theoretically what they were doing.

A blitz *attack* can be compared to a great flood rolling on a narrow front down a valley. The dam has broken in the mountains; what shall we do? It is coming quickly, sweeping down to the plains where we live. Shall we put a frail barrier of sandbags across the edge of our plain, to wall in this flood? It will be broken 'like lightning'. It will be useless as soon as it is broken. No; we will take to the hill-tops, to each little hill in the plain. We will strengthen these against the flood. These little hills, dotted here and there, will split the flood into smaller channels, into streams that can be tamed. And we shall sally out from our hills, on anything that will float, to open a sluice here or close one there, to master the waters that come after the first rush of the flood.

In other words, we shall fight by forming our tank-proof islands everywhere, by counter-attacking on a small scale from one or several of these islands, by building (after the enemy tanks have passed and are struggling in some other part of the net) zones of resistance linking our islands to hold up the Nazi infantry coming after them.

Then our own counter-blitz will be loosed. For this every tank we have, every well-equipped soldier, will be needed. Our Regular Army as a whole, or almost as a whole, will be needed. It will be fatal to fritter this army away chasing parachutists here, forming a 'stop line' there against a small raid, holding a town at a third place. It must be used like a spear.

And the Home Guard must hold most of the islands of defence. But if the Home Guard is to do the full job it must be able to move a little, as well as hold. Its level of training must be raised considerably. During the winter it has learned its weapons; it is capable of being passive garrisons of strong points. Now it must concentrate on tactics; it must learn how to be tactically mobile at short distances, five or seven miles, away from its main centres of resistance. This tactical mobility makes all the difference between passive garrisons and active garrisons.

If the Home Guard remain mainly passive garrisons of strong points organised for all-round defence, they will be able to play a considerable part in resistance to heavy German attacks that come within their area. But such positions cannot do more than delay smaller raiding parties of troops, possibly including armoured troops, landed from the air. These raiding parties will slip through any defence that is passive and restricted to its islands; they will wriggle through the wide gaps between these strong points. There is need for mobile units of the Home Guard, battle patrols, units capable of local counter-attack and of rounding up raiders.

If the Home Guard cannot do this job, the raiders will be successful in their main task, that of distracting considerable forces of our Regular Army, scattering forces about the countryside and preventing them from taking part in a rapid counter-blitz against any Nazi lodgement in force.

The future of the Home Guard is to be recognised as democracy's answer, and an effective answer, to the Nazi technique of aggression. If we choose only to copy totalitarian methods, we shall never catch up or surpass the Nazis. But if we set free and mobilise the initiative of our own people in a democratic way, in a way similar to that in which this defensive army of volunteers was raised and

> trained, I believe we shall find and develop ways of taking the offensive also, new methods of war, which the Nazis are doomed by their ideas and their organisation never to be able to understand or copy.

Had it not been for the active opposition of much of the left, the Home Guard might have grown much larger, and become far more radical, and perhaps even permanent. But without a concerted political campaign to defend this embryonic citizen's army, the War Office was able to impose restrictions and eventually wind down its activities once the threat of Nazi invasion had subsided.

Tom Wintringham – Left Strategist of 'People's War'

The Home Guard era and the particular contribution of Tom Wintringham are important as positive examples of a radical reconciliation of democratic and socialist ideas with the task of national self-defence. Wintringham can be credited with the development of a theory of 'people's war' which corresponded to the traditions, geography and culture of British society in the mid-twentieth century. His unorthodox combination of military theory and revolutionary socialism started with a series of articles in the early 1930s. In'Modern Weapons and Warfare', published in *Labour Monthly* in August 1932, Wintringham first began evolving a concept of popular defence applicable to the modern industrial states of Europe:

> The more highly mechanised and technically developed a force is, the smaller is the percentage of its men that it can put in the firing line, the more sensitive are its lines of communications, and the greater are its difficulties in occupying territory if the population are hostile, possess some arms, and are determined to fight.[11]

This idea was further developed in a follow-up article in January 1933 under the title 'Modern Weapons and Revolution'. 'Since a modern army is dependent on the whole of heavy industry for its munitions, and in the field on an uninterrupted stream of supplies,'[12] Wintringham concluded that the nature of modern warfare made popular forms of resistance to aggression more possible than ever before. He also became convinced that human will, and the social relations within the armed forces and the resisting nation, were critical factors in war – at least as significant as military organisation and armaments technology.

In *English Captain,* an account of his experiences in the Spanish Civil War written in 1938, Wintringham noted that the

International Brigaders had to do their fighting 'mainly in a mosquito-cloud of tiny, almost independent units spontaneously alert to every change in a film of events moving at winged speed'.[13] This led him to begin outlining a new theme: 'modern war demands a type of army that feels free; an army in which the corporals, sergeants and lieutenants in particular are men skilled in an art and carrying their skill into practice, not drilled 'robots' obeying mechanically the rule-book, the blue-print, and the boss'.[14]

In turn, Wintringham reasoned that military victories were increasingly dependent on troops being 'managed, led, organised in battle by commanders who snatch at opportunity, alter plans rapidly, bluff, use surprise, switch forces and transport from one line to another'.[15] The German and Italian fascist generals recognised this in theory, but they contradicted it in practice by their blind adherence to the authoritarian '*Führer- Prinzip*' which Wintringham saw as an 'idealisation of the rare old British "theirs not to reason why" business':

> Individual initiative . . . based on understanding and consultation, is the central feature of the discipline and tactics that can win modern war. And this sort of initiative can only be produced by a democracy . . .
>
> It follows that the soldier who has suffered least at the hands of drill-sergeants is often the best soldier for the difficult business of modern attack, and for the almost equally difficult business of defence by strong-point, withdrawal and counter-attack.
>
> The young soldier who has escaped drill and played a good deal of fast football has had a better preparation for modern war than most.
>
> And the soldier who has been trained to have one leader and no individual thoughts is utterly unfitted for modern war.[16]

Wintringham elaborated these ideas further in a *Fact* pamphlet of April 1939 titled *How to Reform the Army*, which argued that lower ranks and junior officers 'must have developed to their fullest capacities qualities of independence and understanding, of intelligence, and of initiative. They must be free men, standing on their own two feet, considering, criticising, and making part of themselves the things they are told. They must not be "robots", obedient, automatic men.'[17]

Premising all his ideas on the concept of democracy, which he suggested was an essential complement to military efficiency, Wintringham contended that 'throughout two thousand years of warfare the majority of successful armies have been created by communities relatively freer and more democratic than their opponents',[18] and that 'modern war makes voluntary, understood and thinking discipline, and elastic tactics based on initiative and independence, more valuable than ever before'.[19] Accordingly, he advocated a system of army discipline based not on 'bull', unquestioning obedience, fear, brutal punishments or the denial of soldiers' rights, but rather on the free will of troops who are informed, consulted and respected by their officers. In his opinion, the essence of democratic discipline is the self-discipline of soldiers who feel free and who share common aims and principles.

Wintringham specifically proposed the formation of a special Corps of Adjutants, under the Adjutant-General's branch of the British Army (responsible, among other things, for welfare), so as 'to have alongside the commander of any but the smallest units a type of leader whose principal duty is to explain, to hear complaints, to remedy injustices and take some part in punishment'.[20] This was broadly the function of the 'agitator' in Cromwell's New Model Army, the 'delegate' in the armies of the French Revolution, the 'political commissar' in Soviet Russia and the *'comisario de guerra'* in the armies of the Spanish Republic. Wintringham did not suggest that the Adjutant-General's branch 'should be encouraged immediately to appoint "political commissars" throughout the Army'; but rather that the adjutant of the battalion should be an officer of a special corps, trained to do his particular job, which must above all be one of explanation: 'convincing his men that there is some sense in the orders and regulations under which they live'.[21]

Believing that the army's rigid class divisions were an impediment to military efficiency, Wintringham urged more egalitarian relationships between officers and men. He also favoured a drastic reduction in the amount of time troops wasted on drill. In his view, drill taught the exact opposite to the creative initiative required by soldiers in battle:

> You can get absolute obedience without drill. It can arise from enthusiasm, from a consciousness of common aim, from the desire for efficiency and victory, from the mutual respect that links, in any army, good officers to good men; these things drill stifles and overlays with a grudging reluctance to do a single thing beyond what is directly ordered.[22]

Wintringham saw football as being far superior to any form of drill because it developed the 'tactical sense and the ability to cooperate from different positions in slightly different functions'.[23]

With the outbreak of war later in 1939, Wintringham got to

work on expanding many of these early themes into two new books which were published in 1940 – *Armies of Freemen* and *New Ways of War.* In *Armies of Freemen,* he argued that an authoritarian society and armed forces were a major obstacle to military victory and that the democratic organisation of the army and the popular will of millions of free men and women to resist invasion were decisive influences in the waging of successful wars:

> Freedom is a gain for which to fight; that is understood. Freedom is also, or can be, a weapon with which to fight . . . One can point swiftly around the world, to the places where the freedom of fighting peoples has been rigidly restricted, their confidence destroyed, their liberty of intercourse cut down, their organisations abolished and their spirits crushed – just before a debacle. The attack on a people's freedom from within is a formula for losing wars. Freedom, felt and making a difference, making a people eager, is almost a formula for winning wars.[24]

> Freemen can be made into better soldiers and better armies than men who are relatively not free. This is because the essential qualities needed in battle . . . are qualities of initiative and self-reliance, together with the qualities that give unity of action. Freemen can develop these qualities to a higher level than is possible to men whose lives are full-shaped by a higher authority – men who never have, outside the army or within it, the chance to develop the basic qualities of initiative, never have any practice in combining freely their activities with the free activities of other men.[25]

In support of these arguments, Wintringham cited the example of the defence of Paris in 1793 when Captain Carnot urged democratic discussion and persuasion amongst the defending troops, and trust in the enthusiasm of the Parisian masses and their fury against tyranny to defeat the invading armies. Another example he referred to was the battle for Madrid during the Spanish Civil War. Following the Franco uprising, half a million Spaniards turned out on the streets of Madrid demanding arms to defend the Republican government, and people's militias were formed in every district to resist the fascist army. Against overwhelming odds, thousands of workers stormed the Montana barracks, seized its armoury and distributed guns to the citizens of Madrid. Within hours, thousands of people had streamed out of the city to attack the advancing 10,000-strong fascist column led by General Mola. Despite the lack of officers, heavy weapons and military training, these spontaneous democratic militias managed to halt Mola's forces at Sierra Guadarama. It took Franco two years to conquer Madrid and even then he only succeeded with the help of Hitler and Mussolini.

The notion of democracy as an essential component of military efficiency was taken up again in *New Ways of War* where Wintringham reiterated that most of the victorious armies in the past have been relatively freer than the unsuccessful ones:

> Tiny Greek armies of citizens defeated enormous Persian forces of slaves. Alexander the Great, with his companion cavalry, rode over despotisms much more autocratic than his Greek-influenced principality. The armies of the Republic of Rome were freemen in form, and more nearly free men in fact, than the Carthaginians they destroyed. The Germanic and Gothic tribes that overran the Roman Empire had a primitive democracy of their own. The English archers at Crécy and Agincourt were already, because of the looser feudal structure of England, becoming semi-independent yeomen; they beat the French serfs and knights who were still in every sense 'their Lord's men'. Cromwell's army, which appointed its 'agitators' and sent them to argue politics with the Lord General, was more democratic than that of King Charles. Washington's poorly trained national militia beat the Hessians of King George. The ragged armies of the French Revolution fought most of Europe with success.'[26]

In recommending a strategy of popular resistance against Hitler, *New Ways of War* referred to the methods of 'people's war' as being instrumental in the foundation of the Dutch Republic, the liberation of Italy by Garibaldi and Napoleon's defeat in the Peninsular War at the hands of the Spanish guerrillas. Accordingly, Wintringham outlined the first beginnings of his 'people's war' strategy for Britain. Calling for mass resistance in the event of Nazi invasion, he set out information on how to make 'backyard' hand-grenades and upgrade the lethality of shotgun cartridges by melting the tiny lead shot into a single armour-piercing bullet. He proposed rendering fields useless for enemy aeroplane landings by digging trenches and implanting heavy stakes in the ground. To decapitate German motorcyclists, he suggested stretching sharp wires across roads where German convoys would pass.

These 'do-it-yourself' examples of military and civilian resistance were also elaborated by Wintringham to the mass readership of *Picture Post*. In his article 'Against Invasion – The Lessons of Spain' (15 June 1940), Wintringham outlined techniques for constructing roadblocks, fortifying villages, preparing bridges for demolition and making molotov cocktails:

> Take a 2-lb glass jam jar. Fill with petrol. Take a heavy curtain, half a blanket, or some other heavy material. Wrap this over the mouth of the jar, tie it round the neck with string, leave the ends of the material hanging free. When you want to use it have somebody standing by with a light. Put a corner of the material down in front of you, turn the bottle over so that petrol soaks out round the mouth of the bottle and drips onto this corner of the material. Turn the bottle right way up again, hold it in your right hand, most of the blanket bunched beneath the bottle; with your left hand take the blanket near the corner that is wetted with petrol. Wait for your tank. When near enough, your pal lights the petrol soaked corner of the blanket. Throw the bottle and blanket as soon as this corner is flaring. (You cannot throw it far.) See that it drops in front of the tank. The blanket should catch in the tracks or in a cog-wheel, or wind itself round an axle. The bottle will smash, but the petrol should soak the blanket well enough to make a really healthy fire which will burn the rubber wheels on which the tank track runs, set fire to the carburettor or frizzle the crew.

Wintringham also recommended forms of non-violent civilian resistance. Under the headline 'Your Job in an Invasion' (24 May 1941) he advised hiding all food to starve the invaders, and in 'Arm The Citizens!' (29 June 1940) he urged the littering of roads with broken bottles to puncture and delay advancing German motorised columns.

With the chiefs of staff bereft of any strategy for resisting Nazi invasion, in one of his more theoretical *Picture Post* features, 'Blitzkrieg and the Answer' (10 May 1941) Wintringham put forward his own defensive plan. It proved to be the *only* coherent plan for opposing fascist aggression and occupation that was ever drawn up in Britain during the Second World War and owed a lot to Wintringham's collaboration with the Free Czech officer F.O. Miksche who had also fought with the Spanish Republican Army:

> German tactics we have outlined. Now what can be done about framing a system of defence against them? There are two basic needs that this defence must meet. It must split the spear or cut it out of the hand of the man wielding it. Secondly, it must delay the spear itself and hold it up until the defending army can launch its own spear, its counter-blitz. The first job is to divide the tanks from the motorised infantry, and, if that fails, to divide the mechanised forces from the foot-soldiers following them. Tanks alone cannot win lasting success. Tanks accompanied only by small parties of motorised infantry cannot hold the ground they overrun.

Our system of defence must be like a sieve that lets some part of the attack through (because this part cannot be effectively stopped on a line, and because this part cannot alone finally succeed) but holds the other part of the attack, which cannot penetrate the sieve.

Or it must be like a web in which the mobile forces are caught and netted, until they break themselves to pieces thrashing about within the web. To cut the tanks off, and the motorised infantry off, from fuel and other supplies, is also part of the aim of this defensive system.

Some soldiers may say: 'Oh, this is just defence in depth again. We know all about that; we use it.' It is true that the British Army has learned that defences must be in depth. But so, to some extent, did the French Army; and their idea of defence in depth was that of line after line, one behind another, each line losing its purpose and effectiveness if pierced or turned by armoured units. That is not what we are proposing. We propose a *web* of defence made up of tank-proof islands of resistance, these islands joined by minefields, and protecting each other by their fire. Behind this main web, made out of Regular troops, another web with wider meshes: the whole area behind any defended line being garrisoned by men who work as civilians until danger nears, and by troops in training or on transport and similar jobs. The second part of the web we shall deal with in next week's article when writing of the Home Guard. It is an essential part of the system of defence advocated. Here we deal with the other two essentials: the closely woven web formed of normal infantry divisions, and, separate from this, the strategic reserve of armoured and motorised forces, of planes and specialised artillery.

A division in the line (roughly 12,000 men in three brigades) forming part of this main defensive organisation would choose a covering position for its outposts, whose duty it is to give warning of enemy movement and to delay enemy infantry attack. Behind these outposts the division would have a 'filtration zone', a zone occupied by two infantry battalions out of the three in each brigade. These battalions would hold, not a line or series of lines, but those bits of territory of varying sizes that are best adaptable for proofing against tanks. Little woods that the tanks cannot enter; villages; steep hills; or positions within the loop of a river – these are the tank-proof islands of resistance which must be manned. They will be manned not only by infantry but by guns: anti-tank and anti-aircraft guns, field and some medium artillery. They will be protected by minefields at points where they are weak against tank attack, and these minefields will also join island to island, along lines that can be covered by fire from the islands.

The second thing needed is a scrapping of the water-tight compartments that separate infantry from other arms. Each infantry battalion should know 'its own' anti-tank gunners, 'its own' field gunners, engineers for mines and fortifications, etc. They must know them as well as they know the officers and men or other companies in their battalion. Each battalion must be able to be – even in some cases each platoon must be able to be – a little independent army on its own, holding its own island, cooperating in fire or counter-attack with other little armies. For this, more independence in the lives of small units is needed, and a more highly developed interdependence.

In early 1941, Wintringham brought out yet another lengthy pamphlet, *Freedom Is Our Weapon – A Policy for Army Reform*, in which he insisted that class privilege and private profiteering had to be challenged because they were undermining the war effort, and that the army had to shed its traditional conservatism and introduce greater 'freedom and cooperation' if it was to have any hope of winning against the forces of fascism: 'A Conservative ruling class is incapable of fighting modern war effectively because war is changing very rapidly. And Conservatives do not admit change. They do not understand it. They cannot take advantage of it.'[27]

Wintringham urged that the war be waged as an 'anti-Fascist revolution' in which the British army learnt the 'tactics of irregular warfare' and how to 'aid in the organisation and armament of an improvised popular militia' in the countries under Nazi domination.[28] For this purpose, he advocated a new 'light infantry for landing parties from the sea, a light infantry for landing parties from the air, a light infantry that can fight alongside peasant guerrillas in the mountains or alongside workers' militias in the cities'.[29]

Wintringham also suggested that Britain's fighting capacity would be greatly enhanced if the army was released from its oppressive policing duties in the colonies: 'a revolutionary democracy would set free these parts of the Empire'[30] because 'if this war is to be won it must cease to be one in which the conservative British Empire attempts to defend its possessions from German attack. It must become a war for the liberation of Europe and the world from Nazi and fascist domination and aggression.'[31]

This theme of turning the war into an anti-fascist and anti-imperialist war surfaced again in Wintringham's *People's War*. This book, published in 1942, called for a Second Front based on a 'people's war' strategy of combining British landings on the continent with support for simultaneous partisan uprisings in the occupied nations:

> It is useless for them to pretend that the British Army has sufficient good modern equipment to make headway against German forces by purely 'regular' methods. The best we can hope for is a position similar to that of Wellington's small expeditionary force in the Peninsula, in the years before 1812. That small force was able to do its job because it had the backing of the Spanish guerrillas. In the same way a British force landed today on the Continent could do its job, at the much greater speed of modern war, if supported by a popular revolt which we help to arm. But we cannot expect that men who believe a popular revolt to be worse than Fascism will arm or organise it. That is why all who really desire that we should pull our weight in the war, and help the Russians to save their country and our own, ought to be working for the idea of a People's War, rather than for the idea of a Second Front as a sort of repetition of Lord Gort's expedition to France.[32]

Wintringham slated the conventional conception of a Second Front as a 'slow business of landing cautiously and "fencing off" an entrenched bridgehead'. However, a Second Front as part of a people's war would be 'a forest fire jumping across Europe, spreading through the air when blocked on the ground, and becoming an explosion when it reached the big cities'.[33] In the final chapter of *People's War*, 'What Are We Fighting For?', Wintringham suggested that apart from the defeat of fascism, the object of the war must be Roosevelt's 'four freedoms' and Marx's 'classless society'. He argued that American war production had shown that the problem of want could be decisively solved. All that was needed was common ownership and planning and in this the Russians led the way: 'The absence of large-scale private property has made it possible for them to "scorch the earth" more effectively than it has been done anywhere else.'[34] In Wintringham's view, Britain needed to emulate the Soviet example by taking major industries into common ownership – both to ensure maximum efficiency and military victory and to guarantee a more equal society after the war. What he wanted was a 'merger between economic and political democracy'.[35]

The development of these ideas followed Wintringham's break with the Communist Party. In 1938, he had been expelled from the party for 'maintaining . . . personal relationships which are considered dangerous to the interests of the Party and the working class'.[36] In those days, the Communist Party organised an iron discipline over every aspect of its members' lives. In

Wintringham's case, his 'crime' was to separate from his Communist wife to live with a left-wing American journalist who was not a party member. Despite his expulsion, he remained a Marxist, albeit an increasingly democratic and non-sectarian one.

Wintringham's political break with official Communist policy came at the beginning of the war. Initially, the British and French Communists supported the Allied effort as a natural continuation of their fight against fascism throughout the 1930s. However, within a month Moscow condemned this line as fundamentally 'incorrect' in the light of the Molotov-Ribbentrop pact. Though tactically astute as a means of giving the Soviets a breathing space to prepare for war, the pact unhappily echoed the appeasement policies of the western governments which the Communists had for so long denounced. Stalin nevertheless insisted that the whole international Communist movement had to be subordinated to this tactical manœuvre and that the Communist parties must therefore abandon their anti-fascist popular front strategies. The British Communist Party duly obliged with a 'peace policy' against the 'imperialist' war and in so doing converted itself into little more than a branch of the Soviet Communist Party in Britain. Both the Soviet and British Communist policies towards the war flatly contradicted all their previous declarations as illustrated by the following quote from *Pravda* on 11 January 1939 which was also hailed in the *Daily Worker*:

> Consistently fighting against war, the working class does not stand for peace at any price. Faced by Fascist aggression, the proletariat rouses the masses of the people for a national, anti-Fascist war . . . The struggle of the proletariat of the bourgeois-democratic countries is unbreakably linked up with its struggle against foreign Fascist aggression.
>
> War against the Fascist aggressors is a just war.

Wintringham highlighted the Communist Party's 'somersaults' of policy with the charge that 'dialectics are not acrobatics'. In a letter to the *New Statesman* on 5 July 1941 which set out his political break with the Communists, he alleged:

> The failure of the Communist Parties from October, 1939, to June, 1941, to make this war an anti-Fascist and popular war was a deliberate failure; they did not try. They did not try because they lacked independence and courage in thought and action – and Marxism. Lacking these, they could not apply the basic ideas of Communism to this changing world; so they retreated to the past, taking the application made by Lenin in 1917 – very effective then – as equally good for the different war of 1939. Dutt wrote in

November, 1940: 'This war is a continuation of the war of 1914–18 . . . it is a war of rival capitalist Great Powers, like the last war.' He sneered at the idea of a People's War as the invention of Horatio Bottomley. At a time when no political party in Europe – Fascist, Conservative, Liberal or Socialist – pretended that the world situation was the same as in 1917, or could be dealt with in the same way, the Communist Party here tried to apply mechanically the Bolshevik policy of 1917 to a vastly altered world. They became the only true Conservatives left in Europe.

What, in fact, *is* this war, in Marxist terms? Every Marxist knows that it began in 1936 in Spain. It was then an imperialist war, yet at the same time a war between Fascism and anti-Fascism. It was thus defined by the *History of the CPSU.* With the defeat of anti-Fascism in Spain, and the opening of the Polish campaign, the war became dominantly imperialist. But having once been an anti-Fascist popular war, it could become so again, if popular forces were organised to make it so. To understand how a war can change or be changed in its essential character, read Lenin's reply to Luxemburg's *Junius Pamphlet.*

To work for this change in the war is, of course, the only Marxist way to apply today Lenin's policy of 1917, changing this policy to meet the new developments that have occurred. Lenin's policy was: 'Turn the imperialist war into a civil war.' The principal new developments are, on a world scale, the existence of the Soviet Union and of Fascism. Because of these, the only form of civil war that a Marxist could aim at, in 1940, was sure to become international civil war – i.e., anti-Fascist war. Instead of which the Communist Parties said that anti-Fascism was illusion, said that the distinction between Fascist and Democratic states 'had lost its significance'; if these parties aimed at any form of civil war, real or figurative, in Britain and France, it was war against their own governments rather than war against the Fascist aggressors.

Naturally, any anti-Fascist force that wants to win against Fascism must fight the friends of Fascism here, where we can reach them. We must also fight those reactionaries who cannot win this war. But we must fight against these reactionaries not as war-makers 'spreading the war'; but as half-hearts who are losing it.

I have the right to make this attack on the Communist leadership because, since May, 1940, publicly, and before that privately, I have stood for making this war into an international civil war. Or, rather, I have tried to make clear the fact that Hitler (with his Fifth Columns) has already made this into an international civil war – which up to now he has been winning because the governments trying to fight him have failed to see what sort of war he was waging, militarily and politically.

Last summer I published in a Penguin an outline of the policy of a People's War; the CP rejected it. With the help of men from the Spanish Republican Army and the International Brigade, I taught the Home Guard how to fight Fascism; the CP refused to let its members help. For a year I have been advocating a Home Guard 4,000,000 strong, of which the numerical majority would necessarily be from the industrial working class. The CP did not lift a finger to achieve this, and some of its members ridiculed themselves by calling the HG a 'vigilante force'. Today the Communists call for aid for Russia. The only real aid that can be given is for our Regular army to carry the war back into Europe. How have the CP helped to prepare the Regular army for that job? I have tried to make available to it the military experience of Spain; have they? With many others I have worked to make a strong Home Guard, whose main duty I have always put as the protection of this country while our Regular army attacks Fascism abroad in alliance with European revolt. By their failure to help in any of these directions – and in many others – the CP has made action, in fact, more difficult, action that can help to save Soviet cities from the Nazi bombers.

In the industrial field the CP could have mobilised every force, including trade unionists and technicians, to produce the goods in spite of capitalist inefficiency and profit-seeking. In the USA, Walter Reuther of the Automobile Workers (CIO) produced a plan for making more planes than capitalist industry dare contemplate. The opponents of this plan were Wall Street and the Communists. No similar plan has been proposed for any section of British war industry, because good brains have been confused and immobilised by a caricature of Marxism.

In Greece and Jugoslavia the Communist Parties backed the war, as our Chinese comrades have done. They had to work under governments more definitely repressive than Mr Churchill's. And therefore it is no use Communists here and in America saying that they have acted, in the past 18 months, out of loyalty to the International. The International, which allowed or encouraged three of its parties to take the line of a People's War, could have been persuaded of the need for the British and American parties to take the line of making this war an anti-Fascist one – particularly as such a line would have made the resistance to Fascism stronger

> than that which can be organised by anaemic ruling classes. True loyalty to an International always includes insistence on applying the line of that International to meet the needs of each national working class – not sacrificing those needs for 'diplomacy.'

In the same year, 1941, this critique of the Communist Party's war policy was expanded into a book, *The Politics of Victory*. It defined an alternative policy of supporting the war against fascism whilst at the same time opposing the Churchill coalition government and fighting for a radical socialist administration – a strategy of combining unity and struggle. Whilst conceding that the war had elements of inter-imperialist rivalry, Wintringham saw that its distinguishing feature was not so much 'a war for the division of the loot', but hinged instead around 'aims and purposes [that] relate more to the exploitation of the working class of Europe, and to their revolutionary resistance to exploitation, than they do to the exploitation of colonial peoples'.[37] Summing up the character of the conflict, Wintringham describes it as 'a war waged by Fascism to secure power on a world scale as a counter-revolutionary force in the first place, and as an expanding imperialism in the second. In this war the main reactionary section of British finance capital either helps Fascism or is unable to oppose it effectively, because British imperialism supports the counter-revolutionary nature of Fascism more strongly than it can oppose its quality as an expanding imperialism.[38]

He went on to portray the 'revolutionary situation' which existed in Britain during the summer of 1940 and how in the absence of leadership and organisation it was diffused and the ruling class recovered control:

> In May and June 1940 British finance capital met with severe defeat. Its army was unceremoniously bundled out of Europe. Its great ally France was destroyed as a fighting power. This defeat of the British bourgeoisie led to a great increase of the possibility of turning the war into an anti-Fascist war. It became necessary for the British bourgeoisie to take steps towards the arming of the civilian proletariat. It became necessary for them to appeal to Social-Democracy for its aid, and to take Labour leaders into the Cabinet, at the same time pushing somewhat to one side the most reactionary representatives of British finance capital, Mr Chamberlain and his close associates. It became necessary for them to appeal to the industrial proletariat for unexampled efforts in the production of armaments. And within the ranks of the bourgeoisie there was dismay and division; they could not stand up easily to any heavy pressure towards a change in the character of the war.

This is the period in which J.B. Priestley began his Postscripts on the wireless, and I helped to found the Osterley Park School for the Home Guard, to which thousands of armed civilians came to hear the tactical instruction of International Brigadiers. During this period the London *Evening Standard* became at intervals a revolutionary Socialist paper. British imperialism's main aim was clearly defeated; there was some danger of a total defeat as complete as that of France; and because imperialism's plans were wrecked there was a swing forward by the forces of anti-Fascism. This swing forward happened without any leadership or organization, or any support from the Communist Party.

We cannot tell how far the swing forward of anti-Fascism would have gone if it had been led and organised. It did not achieve any considerable success during the three or four months of its spontaneous upsurge. Then in September or October 1940, having no clear aims or organisation, it fell away, and the British bourgeoisie recovered from their fright. Priestley was dismissed from the BBC; recruiting for the Home Guard could be shut down; the *Evening Standard* became what it had always been.

. . . anyone who was in contact with the feeling of the army, the factories and the air-raid shelters in 1941 will surely agree with me that there is a volume of discontent and a willingness for action which could be led towards a programme of anti-Fascist war, but cannot be led towards a programme that is felt to be likely to include a surrender to Hitler.[39]

The missed opportunity for socialist advance in mid 1940 led Wintringham to restate in *The Politics of Victory* that the left ought to fight to 'turn the imperialist war into an anti-Fascist war' and through a 'new Popular Front' seek to 'unite the struggle against imperialist and Fascist tendencies in Britain with the struggle against the Nazi Party'.[40] To this end, he raised the slogan of 'victory by democracy'. Modelling his ideas on the lessons of the Spanish Civil War and the Chinese Revolution, he conceived this slogan as combining 'victory by means of democracy, and democracy's victory over Fascism and Imperialism'.[41]

A few days after the German invasion of the USSR in June 1941, Wintringham added a Postscript to *The Politics of Victory* which warned the Communist Party against going from one extreme to another – from sabotaging the war effort to wholehearted uncritical support for the Churchill government: 'Acceptance of any form of political truce would be such a mistake; refusal to recognise and lead the anger of the British people against the majority of the present cabinet would be such a mistake.'[42]

Despite Wintringham's warnings, this was precisely the second great error of the Communist Party during the war. It totally subordinated the struggle for social justice in Britain and the interests of the British working class to the task of defending the Soviet Union. With the Communists compounding their first mistake by a second, Wintringham made his decisive break with his former party. Whilst remaining a committed Marxist, he turned his energies to founding the radical Commonwealth movement in July 1942. This scored a number of sensational by-election victories during the war, fighting on what seemed at the time an almost revolutionary programme of greater social equality, common ownership of industry and wealth, abolition of patronage and corruption in government supply, workers' councils in industry, elimination of government red tape and bureaucracy, the defence and extension of civil liberties, a British offensive in Europe as part of an anti-fascist war by mass resistance and revolution, repudiation of revenge against the ordinary people in the fascist states and immediate planning for radical post-war social reforms and reconstruction. Wintringham stood as a Commonwealth candidate in the North Midlothian by-election in 1943 on a programme of people's war and the immediate liberation of Europe and the colonies, and came within 869 votes of unseating the Solicitor-General for Scotland, Sir David King Murray. In 1945, he won 36 per cent of the vote at Aldershot. But following the Labour landslide, he urged the disbanding of Commonwealth and the commitment of its members to work through the Labour Party. Soon after the war he died from a heart attack.

Whilst the specifics and concrete actualities of war may have changed since the 1940s, many of the basic principles have not. For this reason, Wintringham's contribution to democratic military theory and the concept of popular resistance to aggression still has a continuing relevance for industrial, urbanised Britain in the late twentieth century as we consider alternatives to nuclear weapons.

Chapter Seven:
Radicalism in the Armed Forces

Leveller and Chartist Beginnings

As the Home Guard and Wintringham years indicate, at particular moments in history the British armed forces have been open to, and part of, radical social change. Indeed, despite their present authoritarian bias, the military services of Britain have a long history of radicalism, progressive ideas and democratic agitation within the ranks, dating right back to the primitive army democracy of King Arthur of the Round Table who consulted with and was advised by his fighting men.

It was, however, in Cromwell's New Model Army, for a brief period during the English Civil War, that one of the most revolutionary upsurges in the armed forces occurred. Like so many armies before, the New Model Army included both press-ganged men who largely comprised the infantry, and volunteer artisans, yeomen and peasant farmers who made up the cavalry. Amongst many of the volunteers, there was an extraordinary spirit of democracy and a strong affinity for the Leveller movement with its radical demands for social reform and political and religious freedom. The attitude of the volunteers, which later came to be shared by much of the infantry as well, was summed up in one of their 'representations' to Parliament: 'We were not a mere mercenary army, hired to serve any arbitrary power of a state, but called forth and conjured by the several declarations of Parliament to the defence of our own and other people's just rights and liberties. And so we took up arms in judgement and conscience to those ends.'

The democratic character of the New Model Army was evidenced by the election of 'agitators' by the rank-and-file soldiers – two from each regiment – and the formation of a Soldiers' Council which demanded that all officers be elected by the ranks. This later became a parliament of the whole army with the establishment of the Council of the Army where privates, officers and generals gathered together in complete equality to debate questions of theology, the political and military objectives of the war, and to deal with the grievances of the troops.

In 1647, agitators from the New Model Army were involved in drawing up the Levellers' 'Agreement of the People'. It was a republican manifesto with democratic demands. Favouring an alliance between the army and the people, it envisaged the monarchy and the existing Parliament as being superceded by a new form of government from below which would be bound by a charter of human rights guaranteeing personal liberties and freedom of religious expression.

In the following two years, representatives from the army leadership were involved with the Levellers in revising and radicalising this document. The final Agreement of the People, issued in 1649, was a truly remarkable programme which in many respects heralded two or three centuries in advance the subsequent demands of the Chartists and the Labour Party: manhood suffrage (except for servants who were thought to be susceptible to their master's manipulations); abolition of rotten boroughs and property qualifications; annual parliaments and government by representative committees; disestablishment of the church and religious toleration; an end to tithes and indirect taxation and their replacement by a system of progressive tax in proportion to income; repeal of conscription and capital punishment (except for murder); equality for all citizens before the law; a ban on martial law in peacetime and on the extortion of confessions; the right to trial by a jury of twelve men chosen from the defendant's neighbourhood; and the election of judges, army officers and clergy by the local community. Amongst the other proposals later attached to this Agreement of the People were the provision of public hospitals; free primary education for all children; agrarian reform to encourage freeholds and recover for the poor their enclosed common land; freedom of the press; codification of civil and criminal law; decentralisation of government administration; and on the initiative of the Derbyshire miners, the right to work.

In some regiments, soldiers openly wore the green ribbons of the Levellers and in their hats they paraded copies of the Agreement of the People bearing the slogan 'England's Freedom, Soldier's Rights'. Eventually, however, all these principles were betrayed when Cromwell used the New Model Army to crush the Levellers, enforce his virtual military dictatorship and ruthlessly colonise Ireland. But not all units willingly complied. Several regiments mutinied against Cromwell rather than betray the ideals of the English Revolution and be used for the bloody suppression of the Irish. In the words of the *Soldier's Demand* of 1649: 'Fellow soldiers . . . Oh! the ocean of blood we are guilty of! Oh! how these deadly sins of ours do torment our consciences!

What have we to do in Ireland to fight and murder a people and a nation which have done us no harm? We have waded too far in that crimson stream already of innocent and Christian blood.'[1]

Two centuries later, during the Chartist era, there was similar ferment in the army in support of the workers' cause. General Napier, commander of the army in northern England, wrote to his brother in July 1839: 'There are many Chartists amongst the Rifles.' And later the same month: 'At Hull, soldiers and the mob joined to thrash the police. The soldiers started the attack crying "Damn your eyes, we are all Chartists".'[2]

Prior to this period, most of the army had been billeted in people's homes or in common alehouses. But after the outbreak of Chartist sympathies amongst his troops, General Napier urgently requested that the government build barracks to keep his soldiers separate from the civilian population which he saw as a source of rebellious sentiments and incitement to disaffection.

At around the same time, the radical journalist William Rider observed in the *London Democrat* that 'the army as a body will not serve corruption's cause'.[3] He reported that many soldiers regularly read the Chartist press – the *Northern Star* and *London Democrat* – and that in some parts of the country, troops elected delegates to the local Chartist movement and held frequent secret meetings with Chartist organisers.

The First World War Mutinies

The next great period of radicalism in the forces occurred in the early 1900s in parallel with the rising industrial militancy of that era. In October 1906, several British naval barracks were destroyed by rioting ratings. Three years later, in 1909, discontent in the navy over poor pay and conditions reached fever pitch. At a time when naval enlistment totalled 100,000 personnel, there were 116,000 'breaches of discipline' recorded amongst the sailors in a single year.[4]

However, the most sensational rebellions in the ranks occurred in the closing stages of the First World War. They were sufficiently serious for Field-Marshal Sir Henry Wilson to recall that 'an unofficial Cabinet meeting took place in the form of certain "conversations". The case was put strongly by Churchill that discipline was disappearing fast in the army and Haig added that if things continued there would be no army left in France'.[5]

Under the impact of the Russian revolution, for example, there were a number of half-hearted and short-lived attempts to form Councils of Workers and Soldiers within units of the British army. These, however, came to nothing. But at Etaples and

Boulogne, between September and December 1917, demonstrations and strikes by troops in protest at appalling mistreatment resulted in scores of mainly Chinese and Egyptian soldiers in the British Expeditionary Forces being shot and wounded after they refused to work and tried to break out of camp.[6] Even more serious and widespread mutinies erupted in 1918 when a total of 676 troops were officially court-martialled and sentenced to death for acts of sedition and mutiny. Though not all of these death sentences were carried out, unofficially many other rebellious soldiers were summarily shot on the spot.

The first of the big mutinies on the British mainland occurred in early 1918 when machine-gunners in the Guards staged a mass strike at Pirbright in Sussex. For three days, all soldiers refused duty and instead organised their own voluntary training sessions.[7] Towards the end of the year, the spate of rebellions accelerated. On 13 November there was a mutiny at Shoreham when troops marched out of base camp in protest at brutality and degrading treatment by the officers. The army responded by demobbing a thousand soldiers the following morning and another thousand each week thereafter.[8]

Amongst overseas troops, the fervour of dissent was equally pronounced. At Le Havre, Royal Artillery units rioted on 9 December 1918, burning down several army depots in the course of the night.[9] The most sustained mutiny of all took place at army camps surrounding Calais. Unrest within the units stationed there had been building up for several months beforehand over issues such as cruel and humiliating punishments, the censorship of news from home, bad working conditions in the Valdelièvre workshops, the savage ten-year sentences imposed on five teenage soldiers for relatively minor breaches of discipline, and the harsh regime in Les Attaques military prison where the detained soldiers were flogged and manacled for trivial offences such as talking to each other and were only issued with a single blanket, even during the severest of winters. In January 1919 these grievances exploded into agitation for improved conditions and speeded demobilisation. At Valdelièvre camp, troops elected a Soldiers' Council and called for a general strike. To a man, they refused to go on parade at reveille. Instead of their normal guard duty, troops manned picket lines and set up defensive positions throughout the camp. At another base in nearby Vendreaux, 2,000 soldiers walked out in sympathy and marched to Valdelièvre as a gesture of solidarity. After a mass meeting, the 4,000 mutineers descended on the army headquarters at Calais and seized control. Within three days, 20,000 troops had joined the mutiny, including women's units of the Queen Mary Army Auxiliary. In a wave of spontaneous unionisation, a Calais Soldiers' and Sailors' Association was established, which linked up with similar soldiers' committees in other units of the army by affiliating to the newly formed Soldiers', Sailors' and Airmen's Union. For the duration of the strike, each unit elected delegates to a Camp Committee and each camp in turn sent delegates to the Central Area Committee which coordinated the strike and issued orders from the occupied army headquarters. This committee secured the support of the local French civilian population, including the railway workers who put an embargo on the movement of all British military goods. When General Byng arrived with troops to put down the mutiny, his soldiers were unable and reluctant to suppress the strikers and many of them eventually joined the rebellion. Powerless to crush the mutineers, the army brass was forced to concede to the soldiers' demands for improved food, new barracks, greater freedom of leave and the abolition of weekend work.[10]

This successful mutiny at Calais had an immediate ripple effect throughout the British forces. In January 1919 there was a tidal wave of mutinies at Southwick, Folkestone, Dover, Osterley Park, Shortlands, Westerham Hill, Felixstowe, Grove Park, Shoreham, Briston, Aldershot, Kempton Park, Southampton, Maidstone, Blackpool, Park Royal, Chatham, Fairlop and Biggin Hill, as well as at several London railway stations where troops refused to embark for Russia and France.

On 3 January 1919, virtually the entire garrison at Folkestone refused to attend reveille in protest at poor food, excessive officer privileges and orders that they return to France. At a huge demonstration, 10,000-strong, the troops voted to form a Soldiers' Union. The *Daily Herald* on 11 January described the events as follows:

> On their own signal – three taps of a drum – two thousand men, unarmed and in perfect order, demonstrated the fact that they were fed up – absolutely fed up. Their plan of action had been agreed upon the night before: no military boat should be allowed to leave Folkestone for France that day or any day until they were guaranteed their freedom.
>
> It was sheer, flat, brazen, open and successful mutiny. Pickets were posted at the harbour. Only Canadian and Australian soldiers were to be allowed to sail – if they wanted to. As a matter of no very surprising fact they did not want to. One officer tried to interfere. He leapt across the gangway and got a rough-house. 'I am a relative of Sir Douglas Haig,' one of the officers pleaded. 'We are all King's messengers,' said another party. But nothing of that kind availed them.
>
> Meanwhile troop trains were arriving in Folkestone with more men returning from leave and on their way to France.

> They were met with pickets . . . in a mass they joined the demonstrators.
>
> On Saturday an armed guard of Fusiliers was posted at the quays by the Army authorities. They carried fixed bayonets and ball cartridges. The pickets approached. One rifle made a show of going up: the foremost picket seized it, and forthwith the rest of the guard fell back.
>
> The mutineers visited the station in a body, after having posted their own harbour guards, and tore down a large label marked 'For Officers Only' . . .
>
> On Saturday a great procession of soldiers, swelled now to about 10,000, marched through the town. Everywhere the townspeople showed their sympathy. At midday a mass meeting decided to form a soldiers' union. They appointed their officials and chose their spokesmen.

At nearby Dover, 4,000 troops staged a simultaneous demonstration in the town centre in support of the Folkestone mutineers. Following a mass meeting in the harbour station, they marched on the town hall to present their demands to the military authorities.

Three days later, 1,500 men from the Army Service Corps at Osterley Park commandeered military vehicles and drove them into Whitehall where they held a rowdy rally demanding demobilisation. Within four days, they were all demobbed. This gave encouragement to troops at Shoreham. Over 7,000 of them refused duty and marched out of camp to a mass meeting in the centre of Brighton where they were joined by a mutinous detachment of Royal Engineers from Southwick.[11]

In mid-January 1919, 20,000 striking soldiers seized control of the Southampton docks and 500 men at RAF Biggin Hill went on strike over dirty and leaking barracks, food shortages, the existence of only five washbasins between 500 men and the total absence of baths or showers. As a result of their actions, the mutineers won an immediate ten-day leave and dramatic improvements in camp conditions.[12] The following month, the War Office was besieged by 3,000 soldiers who defied orders to board the boat-train for Calais, and units of the Guards were used to disarm the Durham Light Infantry at Colchester when its members refused to sail for Russia.[13] Amongst the troops that were eventually sent against the Russian revolution there was widespread passive resistance. Soldiers in one British battalion stationed at Baku, for example, refused to carry out their duties until they were allowed an Anglo-Russian interpreter to read them copies of *Pravda.* After two weeks of these readings, the War Office hastily called the battalion back to Britain.[14]

Over 9,000 reservists were recalled to Aldershot in May 1919 as part of the government's contingency plans for dealing with the coal strike and a threatened rebellion in Ireland. Unwilling to act as a tool of civil repression, several hundred of them prepared for an uprising, predicting that 'soon the Red Flag will be flying over this town'. However, after sporadic rioting and looting by a hard core of troops, the planned insurrection was thwarted by the arrest of the conspirators.[15]

In the Luton Riots of June 1919, soldiers and war veterans went on the rampage after being excluded from municipal celebrations in honour of the Versailles Peace Treaty. At the end of the official procession, the mayor and his entourage were chased by an angry crowd, including soldiers, into the town hall which was later ransacked and burnt to the ground.[16]

Around the same time, a mass meeting of several thousand troops who had served continuously for over three years without leave at Kantara in Egypt, voted to go on strike and set up a Soldiers' Council to express their dissatisfaction at the slow pace of demobilisation. Two men from each unit were elected as delegates to a Central Committee which organised the refusal of all official duties and the establishment of an alternative camp administration.[17]

During this period, there were also a large number of mutinies in the navy over grievances such as low pay, overcrowded conditions at sea and intervention against the Russian revolution. Between 1852 and 1917 naval wages had only been increased twice – by a penny a day to nineteen pence in 1912 and by a further two pence a day in 1917. Even these minor increases were grudging and largely due to the initiatives of lower-deck benevolent societies. These societies had evolved over the years into a nascent form of trade unionism whereby each individual society issued an annual appeal on behalf of the ratings. Their separate appeals were brought before an inter-port joint committee and coordinated into a so-called 'Magna Carta' or 'Loyal Appeal ' on behalf of all lower-deck sailors throughout the navy. These appeals were widely reported in the press and taken up by sympathetic MPs. Fearful that they would encourage dissent, the government suppressed the societies' activities during the war and made sure they were never resurrected again after it was over.

With the safety valve of the lower deck benevolent societies effectively denied, mutiny became an increasingly common method of protest towards the end of the war. The first significant naval rebellion occurred in the summer of 1918 when sailors spontaneously and defiantly began electing Ship's Committees on fighting vessels and Port Committees in naval towns, often with active support and liaison from the local trade-union movement. These committees demanded the unionisation of the forces, affiliation of the Sailors' Union to the Trades Union

Congress and official negotiating rights with the Admiralty on behalf of all naval personnel. The Portsmouth committee's plan for a general strike to end the war and secure improved naval pay and conditions was only averted by the government's swift action in attending to the sailors' complaints – including a 200 per cent wage increase.[18]

But even this was not enough to prevent subsequent mutinies elsewhere. Soon after the armistice with Germany, the crew of a light cruiser stationed at Libau on the Baltic Sea mutinied, and other crews were so unwilling to fight a war of aggression against Russia that several ships had to be recalled to Britain from Archangel and Murmansk because their ratings were regarded as unreliable.[19]

Throughout 1919, sailors at Invergordon, Portsmouth, Devonport and Fort Edgar repeatedly disobeyed orders to weigh for Russia. At Rosyth, when the ratings on a large battle cruiser were alerted by dock workers that their destination was Russia, they refused to set sail. After a three-week strike, the Admiralty put their ship into Portsmouth and discharged the entire crew. Simultaneously there were mutinies on minesweepers at Rosyth and the red flag was hoisted over the patrol vessel *HMS Kilbride* at Milford Haven. When 150 sailors walked off their ships at Fort Edgar on hearing that they were scheduled to sail to the Baltic, the First Destroyer Flotilla remained port-bound and its return to the war zone was delayed until the crews were replaced.[20]

Later, in November 1919, rebellion spread to the aircraft carrier *HMS Vindictive* moored at Copenhagen. Ratings demanding shore leave were involved in acts of sabotage and a mass strike. A detachment of marines had to be sent on board to quell their protest. During the following month, three-quarters of the crew on the flagship *HMS Delhi* refused to embark for Biorko in the Gulf of Finland and sailors on the gunboat *HMS Cicala* mutinied in the White Sea.[21]

Though 1919 was the zenith of naval revolt, sporadic mutinies continued right up to the Second World War, hitting another high point in 1930–31. In 1930, there were six major rebellions involving *HMS Revenge, Vindictive, Royal Oak, Lucia, Repulse* and *Ramillies;* a year later, the celebrated Invergordon mutiny occurred in protest against cuts in pay. Following a strike by ratings centring on *HMS Rodney* and *Norfolk*, the Admiralty was forced to reduce its wage cuts and accede to their other demands for improved naval conditions.[22]

Largely as a reaction to such immense dissatisfaction in the forces, the Labour Party took an increasing interest in the issue of military democratisation throughout the 1930s, culminating in the publication of Lewis Clive's book *The People's Army* in 1938. With an introduction by the Labour leader Clement Attlee, it called for an 'anti-Fascist army' with a 'democratic spirit' and presented a strong critique of the inter-war British Army: 'Imperialism is its raison d'être'[23] and it has been 'built up on ancient traditions of oppression and of the most far-reaching class distinctions'.[24] Railing against the deprivations and humiliations of army life, Clive quoted Captain Liddell Hart's damning exposure of barrack accommodation in 1936: 'Everything is hard, rough and uncouth in the extreme . . . There is not the slightest atom of privacy or comfort; nor the faintest thing resembling a home.'[25]

Distinguishing between the army's latent and manifest purposes, Clive argued: 'This army pretends to be one thing and is another. It asserts that it is directed against the foreign Fascist and in reality it is more concerned with the British colonial peoples and the British working class. It contains that working class within its ranks and is therefore compelled to maintain the most rigid distinctions between the commissioned and non-commissioned [ranks] . . . [and] repression is carried to appalling lengths'.[26] He concluded: 'If . . . Fascism may compel us to rely some day upon our armed forces, then those forces must be fitted to resist Fascism. They must be acquainted with the virtues of the democracy which they are being asked to defend.'[27] Without an education in democracy and the benefit of greater individual freedom for troops, Clive feared that 'the more the soldier is deprived of liberty the more willing he will be to strike down the liberty of others'.[28] He noted that the 1936 Annual Conference of the Labour Party 'referred to the need for maintaining defence forces to preserve the people's rights and liberties and the continuance of democratic institutions. If these are really to be ensured, the first precaution must be an introduction of a greater measure of those liberties and institutions into the Services themselves, upon which for their defence we may be forced to rely.'[29]

To this end, Clive recommended a series of reforms including promotion solely on the basis of qualifications, merit and open competition; and the reorganisation of the army's promotional structure to ensure that at least half the officers are drawn from the non-commissioned ranks. He also urged the establishment of two sets of 'machinery for the collective expression of grievances'. Firstly, 'authorised committees for each small unit should be elected by the men themselves' to deal with issues such as food, barrack conditions, recreation, etc. Secondly, the setting up of a regular government 'Review of Service Conditions' which military personnel would be able to lobby via elected spokespersons and committees.

These radical ideas embodied in *The People's Army* were the principal catalyst for the Labour Party National Executive

Committee statement entitled *Labour and Defence* which was introduced by Hugh Dalton MP and overwhelmingly adopted by the 1939 Annual Conference as official Labour policy. (And since it has never been rescinded, it still *remains* official party policy.) This statement affirmed that 'a democratic state must have democratic Forces to serve it'.[30] It proposed that 'a democratic force is one which will, as far as possible, reproduce in its own organisation and conditions of life, the democracy of the nation it serves, and which is as little as possible segregated from civil life in all its aspects – political, economic and social'.[31] To narrow the gulf between military and civilian society and ensure that the military was more accountable to the public, the *Labour and Defence* statement called for representatives from trade unions, local authorities and other community organisations to be involved in the administration and management of the armed forces. It went on to suggest the need for soldiers to be positively educated in democratic ideals: 'The forces of democracy exist to defend the freedom of the human spirit and those democratic institutions of law and order which safeguard it; and they perform their task better for knowing the supreme value of that which they guard, and for realising their unity with the people they serve.'[32]

Criticising the way in which the army functioned on the basis of a 'small staff corps elite' and a 'large body of regimental drones,' *Labour and Defence* stated that 'there must be no class distinctions and the cleavage between the commissioned and non-commissioned ranks should be made as small as possible'.[33] It specifically recommended the abolition of separate messes for officers, NCOs and lower ranks. Urging a relaxation of unnecessary petty regulations and severe discipline, the Labour Party document said 'there should be as little military discipline as possible in leisure hours'[34] and there ought to be full freedom of democratic debate and discussion within the forces. It quoted with approval the words of one of Cromwell's lieutenants, Thomas Fuller: 'To make good infantry, it requireth men bred, not in servile or indignant fashion, but in some free and plentiful manner.'

Calling for an extension of soldiers' rights, especially pertaining to discipline, it argued for Judge Advocates independent of the military to preside over court-martials and for all troops on charges to have access to free legal aid and a Court of Appeal. But most scathing of all was the statement's condemnation of the lack of adequate redress for grievances. It concluded that 'there should be full freedom for members of the armed forces to join trade unions and professional associations' so that each soldier can have 'some say in the determination of his pay and conditions of service'.[35] It proposed a negotiating machinery along the lines of the old Admiralty Welfare Committees, with rankers having the right to elect and instruct their representatives. For the officers a Whitley Council system was commended.

1939–45: Soldiers' Parliaments and Strikes

The *Labour and Defence* policy and Clive's book *The People's Army* both heralded and symbolised the popular mood which was to sweep through the armed forces during the Second World War. Whilst in the late 1930s the British army was still weighed down by reactionary 'blimpish' officers, as the war progressed a far more democratic and rebellious spirit began to prevail. According to the former tank commander E.P. Thompson: 'I recall a resolute and ingenious civilian army, increasingly hostile to conventional military virtues, which became – far more than any of my younger friends will begin to credit – an anti-fascist and consciously anti-imperialist army.'[36] Indeed, such was the transformation of attitudes during the war that it was the decisive vote of the forces which gave Labour its massive majority in the 1945 general election. An estimated 80 per cent of service personnel voted Labour and most of them did so out of a genuine commitment to wide-ranging social reforms. Far from being ready to move against the election of a radical socialist government, a small section of the army contemplated a military coup against the Tories if Churchill was re-elected. They even went so far as to discuss the possibility of asking Field-Marshal Montgomery to head a military-backed anti-Tory government.

Right from the outset of the war, it became obvious that military conservatism was an impediment to the Allied effort and that radical changes in the forces were essential for victory. One of the first innovations of the war was in the field of army education. In 1941, the Army Council agreed that all soldiers, even those in operational fighting units, were entitled to three hours' education per week, including one hour on 'citizenship'. This was intended to maintain morale, especially in idle units awaiting postings and battle orders, and also to create an army of soldiers familiar with democratic ideals, with an awareness of what the war was all about and why fascism had to be defeated.

Accordingly, the Directorate of Army Education produced a series of monthly booklets under the title *The British Way and Purpose* which formed the basis of lectures and discussions amongst the troops. Compiled in three sections – 'Soldier-Citizen', 'Report to the Nation' and 'Today and Tomorrow' – these booklets were a mixture of popular history, facts and figures on contemporary social issues such as poverty and ill-health, and alternative ideas about the future shape of post-war Britain. They included the presentation of radical proposals to reform the education system, establish a health service and social security scheme, demolish inner-city slums and re-settle the inhabitants in new garden cities.

The British Way and Purpose series generated so much interest and enthusiasm amongst the troops that it led to the formation of the Army Bureau of Current Affairs. In its handbook of 1942, the aim of ABCA was defined as creating a 'modern democratic army' in which there was good morale, open debate and a sense of 'comradeship' between the troops. Under the sub-section entitled 'Training Democrats', the ABCA manual stated that 'the British Army dares to be democratic because we know that it is through being citizens of a democratic country that we shall win'.[37] To this end, it advised officers that soldiers should feel free to air their grievances and express their opinions through setting up unit wall-newspapers and magazines to which all ranks should be encouraged to contribute. To stimulate discussion, ABCA published throughout the war a regular bulletin called *Current Affairs* which formed the basis of weekly political education classes organised for the troops by Army Education Officers posted to each unit. Amongst the topics covered were: 'Work For All', 'Our Ally Russia', 'The Beveridge Report', 'Scottish Nationalism – Independence or Devolution?', 'Partisan Resistance in Yugoslavia', 'How Can We Abolish War?', 'The United Nations', 'Cripps on Indian Independence', etc. A regular feature of these bulletins was ebullient praise for Stalin and the Red Army, glowing accounts of Soviet economic planning and heroic stories written by Russian soldiers and translated straight from Soviet army journals.

Current Affairs continued to appear for a short time after the war before it was wound down by the army's brass hats who feared that it was encouraging subversive sentiments within the ranks. Some of its last editions in 1946 included features on poverty in the Third World; the need for international cooperation to resolve problems of war, famine and unemployment; outline plans for the creation of a National Health Service; a critique of racism and sexism in British society; and a damning exposure of continuing post-war class inequalities.

It was largely following ABCA's initiatives that committees of soldiers from the ranks were elected in most units of the British army to produce duplicated unit magazines with names such as *Rapid Fire* (15th Royal Fusiliers) and *Smoke* (Smoke School of the Pioneer Corps). Together with the wall-newspapers, these magazines published a mixture of news from home and the battlefield, poems and short stories, cartoons, political viewpoints and complaints concerning petty restrictions, unnecessary 'bull' and the abuse of officers' powers.

Groups of soldiers also banded together to set up Welfare Committees. These were elected by the men at platoon, company and battalion level to represent the troops' interests and initiate action to improve the conditions of barracks, standard of food, availability of leave and entertainment, as well as providing financial aid to any member of the unit whose family was in hardship as a result of being bombed out of their home during the blitz. Unofficially, Welfare Committees established a de facto consultative machinery between officers and their men and gave the lower ranks some input into the organisation and administration of the unit's affairs.

Typical of the new radical awareness which engulfed the forces between 1939 and 1945 was the experience of the 15th battalion of the Royal Fusiliers. On one occasion, news of Soviet victories over the Nazis in early 1942 prompted members of a mortar platoon to parade through the streets of nearby Barnstaple with clenched fist salutes and red flags in their mortars. In the same battalion, copies of the Communist *Daily Worker* were sold openly and soldiers joined up with civilians in Barnstaple to form a *Medical Aid for Russia* committee which held regular collections amongst the troops and organised benefit concerts in the town. In 1942, members of the 15th Fusiliers arranged a public debate in Barnstaple in which they not only called for a Second Front to oppose fascism and support socialism in the USSR, but they also demanded that the army set up special training sessions to prepare them for continental landings and the liberation of occupied Europe. Proposed by fusilier Bill Brooks, a resolution to this effect was carried by about 200 votes to 12. However, such public left-wing agitation within the ranks resulted in the intervention of the War Office which ordered the battalion to be disbanded. In their last unit wall-newspaper, the 15th Fusiliers announced defiantly: 'Disbanded, dispersed: in tanks, gliders, lorries, in other units: we will still fight fascism – For Victory!'

On many of the battlefronts, the issues raised in the ABCA lectures led to soldiers establishing informal political discussion groups. In some cases, these became formalised with the setting up of Soldiers' Parliaments in Cairo, Burma, Selevang and Deolali. In Cairo, from 1943 onwards, a number of troops began meeting for regular political discussions. They eventually decided to put their exchange of views in a more formal debating manner by establishing a Forces' Parliament open to all troops. Right from the outset, it clashed with the army establishment. The secretary of the parliament, Sam Bardell, recalled how a colonel padre buttonholed him at one of the parliament's opening sessions: ' "I have been sent along by the Brigadier to read prayers". I replied: "I am sorry sir, we don't have prayers in this parliament".'

After the Cairo Parliament proceeded to vote in favour of a sweeping programme of nationalisation, there were protests from the senior officers against its alleged left-wing bias and subversive character. To satisfy its critics, the Forces' Parliament agreed to hold a mock general election amongst the troops in March 1944. Labour won with 119 votes, followed by Commonwealth with 55, Liberal 38 and Tory 17. A pre-war Labour councillor, Harry Solomons, was elected 'prime minister' of the Cairo army. The first bill passed by the new parliament was proposed by the future Labour MP Leo Abse, and decreed for the banks to be taken into public ownership. According to Sam Bardell: 'We proceeded to nationalise the Bank of England more or less on the same terms as Mr Dalton, except that we were not so generous with the compensation.' Top army officers and the War Office became alarmed after Hitler's propaganda chief, Dr Goebbels, claimed in a German radio broadcast that British troops in Cairo had mutinied and were setting up soldiers' soviets. Sir Edward Grigg, the minister of war, swiftly denounced the parliament as 'an attempt to subvert discipline' and ordered the chiefs of staff to reassert military authority. They responded by insisting that debates had to be conducted on Oxford Union lines and that all speeches had to be submitted for vetting in advance. The Forces' Parliament rejected this ultimatum by approximately 600 votes to 1, and soon thereafter, those soldiers most closely involved with its activities were arrested and re-assigned to faraway postings.[38]

Though usually not formalised on parliamentary lines, similar fiery debates and radical resolutions were frequently organised by British army units elsewhere. On the troop ship *Andes* which was bound for India in early 1945, a mass meeting of over 500 soldiers voted overwhelmingly in favour of immediate independence for India. Resolutions calling for the decolonisation of empire and the nationalisation of industry were also carried by troops stationed at Comilla in East Bengal, and the Selevang Soldiers' Parliament in Singapore issued a declaration of support for bombed-out London families who organised the seizure of properties for illegal squats in defiance of the authorities. In the run-up to the 1945 general election, many units staged their own mock polls where rival candidates issued manifestoes and canvassed for support amongst the troops; these usually resulted in Labour, and sometimes Communist, candidates being elected. One of the more radical developments occurred in Singapore during the closing stages of the war when British soldiers helped form the East-West Society. Its purpose was to foster friendship and solidarity with the Malayan people and oppose the British suppression of our former allies in the anti-Japanese guerrilla army. In some cases, this opposition even went as far as soldiers giving the Malayan Communists advance warning of attacks being planned against them by the British forces.

As in the First World War, there were a substantial number of open mutinies.[39] The most significant of these were in the latter stages of the conflict. In March 1945, for example, RAF aircrews at Kallang in Singapore went on strike in protest at delays in demobilisation and repatriation. For his part in leading the strike, Aircraftman Norris Cymbalist was sentenced to ten years' penal servitude. Five months later, at Kluang, 263 members of the 13th Parachute Regiment were charged with mutiny and court-martialled, though their sentences were subsequently quashed on 'technical' grounds. Nine corporals were tried at Lichfield in January 1946 on charges of mutiny after they had walked off the troopship *Empress of Scotland* in Liverpool in protest at lice-infected blankets and a ten-hour wait between meals. The next month, two ships of the Royal Indian Navy in Bombay mutinied against the poor conditions of service and in support of the Indian Congress demand for independence. The murder of striking sailors provoked the Bombay trade unions to declare a general strike, and at Deolali, the British Forces' Parliament adjourned in solidarity with the mutineers and in protest at their massacre. In November 1946, dozens of troops at Tel-El-Kehir were arrested and imprisoned in a ex-German POW camp after they had organised a mass strike to demand immediate demobilisation.

The postponement of repatriation was also the cause of a rebellion at Drigh Road RAF camp in Karachi; though this grievance was compounded by dissatisfaction over the lack of news from home, bad food, excessive overtime and harsh discipline. The strikers elected a committee of 20, chaired by Leading Aircraftman Attwood, which presented a list of complaints to the Air Commodore. Whilst he responded by acknowledging most of the men's grievances and conceding most of their demands, Attwood and two others were nevertheless arrested on charges of mutiny. Within forty hours, the aircrews raised £223 for their defence. At his court-martial, Attwood was found guilty. But following a huge protest campaign by soldiers throughout the forces, the RAF overturned his conviction and Attwood was released.

After the war, in response to these outbreaks of dissension amongst aircrews, the Air Council recommended the setting up of RAF Station Committees of officers and ordinary ranks to 'share in the general running of their station'. This proposition was, however, abandoned after resistance from the chiefs of staff. The same fate befell plans by the Attlee government to require all commissioned officers to serve a spell in the ranks.

The Soldiers' Charters of 1946 and 1971

The continuing demand for major democratic reforms in the armed forces inspired serving soldiers, ex-servicemen and women, and the National Council for Civil Liberties to draw up a Forces Freedom Charter in 1946. Written by ex-Staff Sergeant R.J. Spector, it was published as a pamphlet under the title *Freedom for the Forces*. Critical of the 'unnecessary narrowness and restrictions of military life', it drew on the many examples of soldiers being deprived of their civil liberties during and after the war: the ban on International Brigaders from Spain serving in the forces; the MI5 blacklist of 'subversives'; the purge of left-wing officers in the Army Education Corps and the Army Bureau of Current Affairs; the witch-hunt against interpreters at the Control Commission in Germany on the grounds that they were members of the Fabian Society or married to socialist women; the 112-day prison sentence passed by the RAF on Corporal Bastin in Bangalore, India, for the 'crime' of selling four copies of an Indian Communist newspaper; and the court-martial of Corporal Sherman of the Army Service Corps on a charge of distributing copies of a pamphlet by the agricultural workers' union which advocated a national minimum wage.

With the intention of preventing a repetition of these injustices, the Forces Charter called for 'the elementary freedoms of speech and thought for the citizens in uniform'. It recommended that the government 'rewrite the whole body of King's Regulations and the Army Act which was devised for the nineteenth century'.[40] Based on a 'citizen-soldier' philosophy, the Charter demanded four freedoms for all service personnel: freedom of speech, freedom of representation, freedom of trial and freedom of development. Specifically, it called for: '1) Fullest political and civil rights; 2) The right of free organisation, association and discussion; 3) Revision of the code of military law, in particular, court-martials and summary punishments; 4) Improved educational and welfare services, including vocational training for civil life.'[41]

Since the Forces Freedom Charter, military democratisation has virtually ceased to be a political issue. It was briefly revived in 1971 when a small group of soldiers, together with the Young Chartists and the Leeds University Labour Club, issued *The Soldiers' Charter*. Reported in the *Daily Mail* under the headline 'Troops Bid for Own Union',[42] the Charter detailed examples of the denial of liberties to members of the forces and outlined a 12-point programme for reform:

1. We demand the absolute right for all servicemen to form soldiers' committees and to join a trade union.

2. It is at company level (or equivalent) that the soldiers' committees should be set up . . . with the chairmen of the different committees forming a higher committee at regimental level. Elections should take place, say, every six months. There should be one man, one vote, with all officials subject to immediate right of recall, and with at least the chairmen of each committee being 'full-time', i.e. freed from other duties.
3. One of the most bitter complaints of soldiers is that the 'fatigue' system can be abused (and often is) by officers wishing to discriminate against individuals. It is 'official' army policy that dirty jobs (cleaning latrines, etc.) should be spread out evenly. To ensure that this is done, each Commanding Officer must, in our view, be required to keep a book that records every fatigue that each man is doing; the soldiers' committee to have daily access to this book to ensure fair play. People who think they are being victimised should be able to take their grievance to the committee . . .
4. The Soldiers' Committee should have access at any time to the Company Commander who must give a decision on an issue within 24 hours. If that decision should prove unacceptable to the Committee, then the case may be taken up by the Regimental Soldiers' Committee, which would have immediate right of access to the Commanding Officer. If he does nothing, or his decision is not accepted, then the Soldiers' Union nationally may take up the matter and sanction a work-to-rule until satisfaction is obtained.
5. 'Military crimes' are 'crimes' that would not be considered such in civilian life, e.g. insubordination, failure to salute an officer, disobedience, threatening a superior or 'conduct prejudicial to good order and military discipline'. The greatest number of these are dealt with by the Company Commander or Commanding Officer (i.e. courts-martial are rare); the object is not to establish justice, but to maintain and enforce discipline. Perhaps this explains why we have never known such a case, once brought by a soldier's superior to the CC or CO, dismissed. The first aim of the CC or CO is to 'back up' the person bringing the charge. There is no way to ensure justice, in our view, other than by allowing a Soldiers' Committee representative to be present at Company Commanders' or Commanding Officers' Orders. This representative

could advise the accused after the charge had been read and before the 'award' (in civilian language, 'sentence') had been given . . .

Where an offender is court-martialled (until such time as a Labour government can abolish this procedure altogether) the president of the court-martial should confine his duties to those of 'judge' as understood in a civilian court. There should be a jury made up of a cross-section of servicemen. This would bring courts-martial more closely into line with civilian courts, abolishing the present situation in which the president of the court-martial (usually a major in a district court-martial and a brigadier in a general court-martial) performs the functions of both 'judge' and 'foreman of jury'. The accused should have the right to declare a jury 'biased' if he thought a disproportionate number of officers comprised it. Any complaints of this or any other sort could be taken up by the Soldiers' Committee, which would have a representative and advisor present throughout.

The Soldiers' Committees and the Union should negotiate a full review of the Manual of Military Law to abolish vaguely-worded 'crimes' such as 'conduct prejudicial to good order and military discipline', etc.

6. Complaints by officers about subordinates' hair length are in some cases a form of victimisation and an unnecessary source of friction. There should be negotiated an agreed haircut and hair length standard . . . The regulation that 'the hair on the head shall be kept neat and tidy' should mean just that, and not mean 'short' unless this is the will of the soldiers themselves.
7. The mess system must be abolished. There should be one dining room for both officers and other ranks, and no segregation of sleeping quarters. There should be a communal social centre with public and saloon bars open to both officers and other ranks alike. The Soldiers' Committees should have a say in the management of this social centre. Advantages would be (a) the abolition, or at least reduction, of class discrimination and (b) vast savings in expenditure on quite unnecessary 'luxury' officers' facilities.
8. A soldier is entitled to some privacy in his living quarters. Every soldier should have the right which at present only married soldiers have, i.e. the right to a 'home', a room which is his own personal concern, in which he may receive visitors, including those of the

opposite sex, and where his furniture, shelves, drawers, etc. are exempt from 'bull' inspections by officers. Nobody inspects the officers' quarters, and this 'privilege' should be the right of all soldiers.

9. There must be no interference with leisure hours (e.g. starting exercises on Sunday mornings), or, if a day is lost unavoidably, a free day in lieu must be given later in the week. There must be an end to compulsory attendance at sporting and social functions (officers' parties, etc.) . . .
10. Officers' batman facilities should be abolished. If an officer wants a batman, let him hire a civilian at his own expense instead of being provided a man at the tax-payer's expense. A soldier wants to be a soldier, not an officer's personal servant, whether full-time or part-time . . .
11. The overall job of the Soldiers' Committees should be to guard against any victimisation or over-zealous enforcement of ambiguous rules. The Committees should act as watch-dogs over the warrant officers. They should, with assistance from the union nationally, negotiate set and reasonable *standards* of cleanliness, neatness, etc. for all military equipment, including vehicles, garages, outside areas, barrack rooms, accommodation, stores and personal uniforms. Once reasonable standards had been agreed, the role of the Soldiers' Committees would, of course, be to ensure that they were not overstepped or 'bulled' by overzealous NCO's . . .
12. The first right to establish must be the right to organise. We demand the right of all soldiers to join or form a trade union eligible for affiliation to the Trades Union Congress. This in itself would be a small gain unless the union were democratically run and had real power: the Soldiers' Committees should be the basis of the union on 'the shop floor'. The Committees and the Union should have access to all files except those governed by the Official Secrets Acts (which should themselves be abolished by a Labour government as soon as possible). In addition, servicemen should be free to join political parties, with the right of free assembly, freedom of speech (the right to send letters to the press, etc.) and freedom to publish and circulate journals, leaflets, etc. within the army. There should be a vote by post for all ranks whether in the UK or abroad, effectively carried out.[43]

This long tradition of military radicalism illustrates that the call for democracy in the ranks is not some new and extreme proposal, but an integral part of the history of the British armed forces – a hidden part of their history which the labour movement has largely neglected and ought now to revive.

Chapter Eight:

A Democratic Defence Strategy for Britain

Re-Orienting the Military to Strict Self-Defence

All the evidence points to the need for a radical restructuring of Britain's defences around a non-nuclear and non-provocative defence strategy which is unmistakably defensive, self-reliant and democratic – an alternative model of defence more appropriate for a medium-sized parliamentary democratic state with limited resources available for defence expenditure and a genuine commitment to de-escalating the arms race.

Britain's current defence strategy continues to be steeped in the history of our imperialist past. Relatively unprepared for self-defence, our armed forces are instead predominantly biased towards offensive weapons, overseas engagements and a repressive internal policing role against the British people. We are overwhelmingly dependent on an increasingly uncertain American military umbrella and a suicidal and illegal nuclear weapons policy which gambles with the future of human civilisation and is contrary to international law. Within our deeply authoritarian and class-ridden armed forces there is widespread brutality, sexual and racial prejudice and the denial of civil, political and trade-union rights to service personnel.

This aggressive-inclined and anti-democratic system of defence does not, however, *have* to be. It is not fixed and immutable. There are plentiful practical precedents in our own history and the experiences of other European nations which point to the feasibility of radical alternatives: partisan and civilian resistance in 1939–45, the British militia tradition and the Home Guard, radical soldiers' movements and democratic army reforms during the two world wars, and the contemporary territorial defence strategies and citizen armies of Switzerland, Yugoslavia and Sweden.

The starting point for the development of an alternative non-nuclear defence strategy is a redefinition of Britain's basic military objectives in terms of an unequivocal commitment to strict self-defence, i.e. acceptance of the principle that the protection of our country against attack, invasion and occupation is the sole legitimate objective of military policy. The fulfilment of this objective is presently obstructed by Britain's lingering pretensions to junior superpower status, our reluctance to let go of the remnants of empire and the preparation of the armed forces for the defence of British economic interests abroad and for an internal security function at home. These diversions undermine effective national defence because the greater the army's international and internal policing role, the less is its capacity for the real protection of our island from foreign aggression and invasion. It stands to reason that the more troops we send abroad to places like Belize and Hong Kong, the fewer troops we have at home to defend the UK. If imperialism and self-defence are thus contradictory, then opposition to the vestiges of British colonialism and support for a truly self-defensive posture are complementary. Successful anti-imperialist demands for the recall of the armed forces from their peripheral global commitments have the spin-off effect of strengthening our central home defences. Conversely, the reorganisation of the military around a genuinely self-defensive capacity is implicitly anti-imperialist in that it limits the possibility of the army being used as an instrument of external expansion and conquest. Resolving the conflicts in Ireland and the Falklands/Malvinas, and withdrawing from NATO support in Germany and the last outposts of the Pax Britannica in Cyprus, Gibraltar, etc. are thus essential elements in regrouping and concentrating our military efforts around the UK mainland; thereby consolidating our self-defensive capabilities and clearly signalling our non-aggressive intentions to other countries.

The shift to pure self-defence does not, however, mean that we have to do away with the principle of deterrence. Deterrence is not, in itself, necessarily a bad thing. It *is* preferable to have adequate defences to deter an attack in the first place, rather than having to fight a war to prove the point. But there are three fundamental flaws in our current nuclear-based deterrent. Firstly, its offensive character makes it threatening and provocative to other states and this in turn incites an accelerating arms race. Secondly, it is a catastrophically devastating deterrent which potentially endangers the very existence of life on earth. And thirdly, the nuclear deterrent has become a substitute for effective defence. As an aggressive deterrent based on a retaliatory 'deep strike' ability, it has little or no defensive value. What we need instead is an unambiguously *defensive deterrent* which is non-provocative and works in tandem with, or better still, as part of, a concrete anti-invasion and anti-occupation capacity. In other words, a combined strategy of deterrence *and* defence – the deterrence of aggression through an effective defensive capability.

Probably the most appropriate model of non-nuclear defensive deterrence is a two-pronged strategy of frontier and territorial defence; similar to the Swedes and designed to make Britain a 'tough nut to crack'. There are, of course, some people who would argue in favour of a wholly territorial strategy. However, not even the Yugoslavs have gone that far and it would be foolish for us to make no attempt to avoid the pain of invasion and occupation. We ought therefore to capitalise on the advantage of our island position whereby the ocean acts as a natural obstacle to invasion and provides favourable circumstances for effective border-based defence against sea and air attack. Equally, our defences need to be able to cope with the disadvantages we face as an island nation; particularly our vulnerability to blockade and the cutting off of vital food supplies, etc. For both these reasons it makes good sense to have an element of frontier defence capable of protecting our merchant shipping and repelling intruders at the perimeter of our territory – or at least causing them the maximum possible damage and delaying their advance to give our reserves and territorial forces time to mobilise.

Adopting a combination of frontier and territorial defence, based on defensive 'anti-weapon' systems and reinforced by mass civilian resistance, would render Britain an unattractive target for aggression because it would give us the ability to impose immense hardships and huge costs on an invading army. By ensuring that our country was *difficult to dominate* and that an attacker would suffer unacceptably great losses, this dual strategy would provide both a disincentive to invasion and an effective defensive ability.

The rationale of frontier defence is to put a sharpened defensive shield around the UK; making penetration difficult and exacting a 'high entry price' from aggressors by the use of high technology and high firepower 'anti-invasive' armaments including mine-layers, frigates, interceptor fighter planes and anti-tank, anti-aircraft and anti-ship missiles. This frontier defence would be undertaken by mobile regular forces alerted by early-warning systems and able to move swiftly to the point of attack where they would employ conventional 'stand and fight' defensive tactics with the support of the reserves following their mobilisation.

If an enemy assault can be likened to a fast moving clenched fist, the goals of frontier defence are firstly to halt its thrust, secondly to sever the vital arteries and tendons, thirdly to force the fist open and spread its separate vulnerable fingers to weaken its strength, and fourthly to detach the fist from the arm which gives it support and driving power.

To this end, the initial objective of the regular and reserve frontier defenders would be to halt and destroy the incoming enemy assault forces in the sea and airspace immediately beyond our borders before they can reach us and inflict any damage. However, this may not be possible where there is a surprise attack by overwhelmingly superior forces. In these circumstances, frontier defence would aim to confine the invasion to the perimeter of our territory and, through the concentration of heavy firepower, fissure the attacking force into smaller, separate fragments. This would diffuse and weaken its offensive capacity and slow its advance, transforming the aggressor into a softer and more vulnerable target and facilitating the mounting of a successful counter-thrust to expel the invading army.

If, however, our border defences were in danger of being overrun, the regulars and reserves would tactically withdraw inland to both rural and urban areas and switch to a mobile 'deep defensive' territorial strategy combining both conventional and guerrilla methods. In the extreme and unlikely case of vastly superior invasion forces, in order to survive to fight another day, the regulars and reserves might need to withdraw completely from southern England. North of a fluid defensive line stretching from Cardiff to Hull, where the terrain is more conducive to territorial defence, they would establish a permanent base area, sustain a British government relocated from Whitehall and resist enemy penetration.

Most of the time, the regulars and reserves would function to reinforce local in-depth resistance by static territorial units unable, by their own efforts, to defeat major enemy offensives or mount counter-thrusts to drive out large invasion units from their district. Dispersed in a *defensive grid* across the entire country and organised in a vastly expanded community-based Territorial Army, these semi-autonomous units would consist of 'hide and seek' guerrilla infantry armed with automatic weapons, grenades, mortars, land-mines and anti-tank and anti-aircraft missiles. This all-over 'hedgehog' defence would make Britain hard to handle – the hundreds of localised territorial forces acting like so many razor-sharp and stinging spines, puncturing the enemy army with thousands of tiny wounds which would eventually bleed it to death.

In being geared to a sustained war of attrition, the guerrillas would levy a 'high occupation price' using 'fight and flight' ambush tactics to bog down and beleaguer the invaders. The nationwide territorial nature of their resistance would offer no concentrated targets. An enemy would therefore be unable to launch large-scale attacks with sophisticated weapons and intense firepower in the hope of winning a few decisive victories. Instead, it would be compelled to spread its forces thinly over a wide area using its more vulnerable infantry in search-and-destroy operations against our guerrillas. This dispersal would dilute the aggressors' initial strength and superiority, turning their troops into soft targets for the small territorial units operating in their own familiar terrain with local popular support. This combination of factors would put the guerrillas in a favourable position to cut the enemy's elongated communication and supply lines and then pick off their isolated units one by one.

Much of this guerrilla warfare would be waged in urban environments in conjunction with a campaign of civilian resistance. The IRA and ETA have demonstrated the potential of covert urban guerrilla war in contemporary West European societies. With proper training in street fighting, sniping, booby-traps, barricading, etc. our territorial units could certainly improve on their tactics and success-ratio; though the adoption of such methods would need to be strictly confined to military targets and specifically *reject* indiscriminate terrorism endangering the civilian population. In some wooded and hilly parts of the country, conditions would be favourable for rural guerrilla warfare and the establishment of liberated base areas – Scotland, Wales, Cumbria, the Peak District and parts of Devon and Cornwall.

All in all, this combination of rural and urban territorial resistance by local guerrilla units, backed up by regular and reserve forces, would render a foreign-imposed administration unworkable and make life unbearable for the invaders by progressively exhausting them militarily, destroying their morale, depriving the occupying regime of its legitimacy and power, and making the cost of the invasion outweigh its advantages.

A categorically defensive territorial strategy is now financially and militarily more feasible than ever before. Firstly, the new precision-guided 'anti-weapon' systems are highly accurate and lethal. Each glider or rocket in the West German Container Weapon System (CWS) can saturate a designated area with up to 4,000 mini-bomblets or lay down a 600-piece anti-tank minefield. In less than a minute, a single launcher in the Multiple-Launch Rocket System (MLRS) can fire 12 missiles releasing 7,700 grenade-like sub-munitions over an area the size of six football pitches. Both the CWS and MLRS are deadly against infantry, field artillery and lightly armoured support and supply columns. So too are the new generation of Skeet anti-tank weapons. They can locate and destroy a tank through smoke, fog or even several layers of sandbags by homing in on the engine's infra-red emissions. Skeets have none of the indiscriminate destructive power or toxic radiation side-effects of a nuclear bomb, but according to the *Economist*, these defensive 'smart' anti-tank weapons 'are reasonable substitutes for nuclear weapons; 228 Skeets (one rocket load) would have the same effect on a normally dispersed tank formation as a one kiloton nuclear warhead (also one rocket load)'.[1]

Secondly, defence is much cheaper than offence. Most of the new 'anti-weapons' cost less than 1 per cent of the price of major offensive armaments. An anti-tank weapon costs 0.5 per cent of the price of a tank, an anti-aircraft missile costs 0.25 per cent of the price of the latest strike plane, and an anti-ship rocket costs 0.27 per cent of the price of a destroyer. Put another way: the cost of one Challenger battle tank – £1.5 million – would purchase about 200 anti-tank missiles capable of destroying an equivalent number of tanks. The £20 million price tag attached to each Tornado strike aircraft could buy enough surface-to-air missiles to shoot down 400 fighter planes. In place of a £180 million Type 42 destroyer we could acquire 360 anti-ship missiles – each with the potential to send a large surface vessel to the bottom of the ocean.

Thirdly, many of the latest 'anti-weapon' systems are technologically in advance of the invasive armaments they are intended to destroy; so far in advance that major offensive weapons such as battle tanks, combat aircraft and surface warships are on the verge of becoming obsolete as instruments of war. The 1967 and 1973 Middle East wars revealed the vulnerability of armoured vehicles and fighter squadrons to anti-tank and surface-to-air missiles, and likewise, the potency of sea-skimming anti-ship rockets like the Exocet became apparent during the 1982 Falklands/Malvinas war.

And fourthly, the 'contra-intrusion' weapons are ideal for guerrilla-style campaigns since they tend to be relatively simple to use, easy to transport and conceal and can be operated by small, independent military units without the need for elaborate back-up and support.

The adoption of a joint frontier and territorial strategy of non-nuclear defensive deterrence would require a radical restructuring of Britain's armed forces; involving a shift in emphasis to home-based defence by an enlarged infantry equipped with improved 'anti-weapon' systems. Owing to the very substantial changes it would necessitate, this reorganisation would have to be phased in over a 10-year period to allow for the decommissioning of offensive weapons, purchase of new equipment and a large-scale reduction in regular forces personnel.

Taking 1983 as the base year for all figures:[2] at the end of 10 years, in such alternative armed forces total British mobilisable military strength would be reduced from 601,100 to 457,000. This would be the equivalent of just under two military personnel per square kilometre of UK territory – the same troop density as the

Swedes, and twice as great as the Soviets could hope to achieve in an invasion and occupation of Western Europe. Assuming that the Russians would need to continue garrisoning the Eastern bloc, this would spread their forces across East and West Europe in an average density of less than 1 soldier per square kilometre.

In addition to the reduction in total mobilisable military strength, under an alternative defence plan our regular forces would decline from 320,900 to 167,000, regular reserves would drop from 193,400 to 100,000, and the Territorial Army and navy and air force volunteer reserves would expand from 79,700 to 190,000 – 183,000 of whom would belong to a new citizen-style Territorial Army which would thus become the largest single component in the armed forces, accounting for 40 per cent of all mobilisable military personnel. The combination of the Territorial Army and the regular and volunteer reserves would constitute the overwhelming majority of all enlistees at 290,000 or 63 per cent of the total. Overall, the composition of the military would shift away from full-time professional forces to part-time, civilian-based reserves and volunteers.

Whilst the net loss of personnel might seem to substantially weaken our defence capabilities, in fact these would be significantly strengthened by the restructuring of personnel and weapons around a sharpened defensive cutting edge. Following a phased withdrawal from external military commitments in Cyprus, the Falklands/Malvinas, etc., our home-based army would be larger than ever, more densely concentrated in and immediately around the UK and better armed with enhanced 'anti-invasive' weapon systems.

In 1983, the cream of British military personnel – 93,973 servicemen and women – were stationed abroad in 18 different locations around the world. These included 72,176 soldiers, 5,142 sailors and 16,655 airmen. Most of them were posted to West Germany and the 58,800-strong British Army of the Rhine, which easily outstrips our UK-based ground forces of 41,100 troops. This is justified in the name of 'forward defence' – the doctrine whereby the defence of Birmingham begins in Berlin. Whilst it is certainly true that we might wish to assist the West Germans in the event of unprovoked aggression, just as we might want to aid the Yugoslavs or the Angolans, this does not require us to provoke the Russians and undermine our home defences by the *permanent* stationing of military personnel in the Federal Republic of Germany. It is far better that we maintain contingency plans to reinforce the West Germans when attack is imminent – and not before then. A commitment to back up the Germans in the event of attack is probably just as effective a deterrent as us having troops constantly stationed on the Rhine.

Given that 72,176 regular army personnel were garrisoned

Alternative Armed Forces

For a Dual Strategy of Frontier and Territorial Defence[a]

All Services

	1983	*after 10 years*
Regular Forces	320,900	167,000
Regular Reserves	193,400	100,000
Territorial Army, Volunteer Reserves, & UDR	86,800	190,000
Total Mobilisable Strength	601,100	457,000
Total Defence Expenditure	*£15,973 million*	*<£10,500 million*[b]

Army

	1983	*after 10 years*
Regular Forces	160,300	90,000
Regular Reserves	137,700	75,000
Territorial Army	72,600	183,000
Total Mobilisable Strength	387,600	348,000

Combat Arms (Regular Forces)

	1983	after 10 years
Infantry Battalions	56	38
Armoured Regiments	19	7
Engineer Regiments	12	5
Field and Heavy Artillery Regiments	16	8
Air Defence Regiments (SAMs)	3	5
Guided Weapon Regiments	1	1
Missile Regiments	1	1
Independent Anti-Tank Batteries	4	0
Special Air Service Regiments	1	1
Army Air Corps	5	3
Total combat regiments, battalions and corps	118	69
(Total UK-based regiments, battalions and corps	49	69)

Air Force

	1983	*after 10 years*
Regular Forces	89,300	48,000
Regular Reserves	29,100	15,000
Volunteer Reserves	600	1,000
Total Mobilisable Strength	119,000	64,000

Combat and Support Aircraft

	1983	*after 10 years*
Bomber/Strike/Attack	164	10
Ground and Maritime Support	68	72
Maritime Patrol and Anti-Submarine	28	28
Air Defence and Interceptors	111	89
Reconnaissance	44	18
Airborne Early Warning	6	10
Tankers	16	2
Search and Rescue	32	16
Transporters (aircraft)	56	2
Transporters (helicopters)	70	48
Total combat and support aircraft	595	295
(Anti-Aircraft Missile Squadrons	8	12)

Navy *(including marines)*

	1983	*after 10 years*
Regular Forces	71,300	29,000
Regular Reserves	26,700	10,000
Volunteer Reserves	6,500	6,000
Total Mobilisable Strength	104,500	45,000

Combat and Support Vessels

Submarines	31	16
Aircraft Carriers and Assault Ships	5	0
Destroyers	13	0
Frigates	47	12
Patrol/Attack Craft	28	28
Minesweepers/hunters/layers	35	35
Tankers	14	0
Troop Landing Ships	6	0
Replenishment and Support Boats	7	0
Total combat and support vessels	186	91

Fleet Air Arm

Aircraft (Strike and Anti-Submarine)	15	30
Helicopters (Anti-Submarine and Transport)	102	30
Total combat and support aircraft	117	60

Redeployment to Home-Based Defence

	1983	*after 10 years*
Army/Navy/Air Force Mobilisable Strength	601,100	457,000
Less Mobilisable Forces Overseas	93,973	0
Total UK-Based Mobilisable Strength	507,127	457,000
Army Regulars/Reserves/TA/UDR	377,600	348,000
Less Army Forces Overseas	72,176	0
Total UK-Based Army Forces	305,424	348,000
Regular Army, Navy and Air Force	320,900	167,000
Less All Regular Forces Overseas	93,973	0
Total UK-Based Regular Forces	226,927	167,000
Regular Army	160,300	90,000
Less Regular Army Overseas	72,176	0
Total UK-Based Regular Army	88,124	90,000
Regular Navy	71,300	29,000
Less Regular Navy Overseas	5,142	0
Total UK-Based Regular Navy	66,158	29,000
Regular Air Force	89,300	48,000
Less Regular Air Force Overseas	16,655	0
Total UK-Based Regular Air Force	72,645	48,000

[a] The source for current personnel and equipment levels is the *Statement on the Defence Estimates 1983*, HMSO, Cmnd. 8951-I and 8951-II; except for the Air Force weapons inventory which is based on the *Statement on the Defence Estimates 1982*, HMSO, Cmnd. 8529-I and *The Military Balance 1982–83*, International Institute for Strategic Studies, London, 1982.

[b] At 1983 constant prices.

abroad in 1983, their recall from overseas under an alternative defence plan would offset the cut in regular forces, contributing to a net *increase* in the total UK-based army regulars, reserves and territorials from 305,424 to 348,000 and a net *rise* in the total UK-based regular army forces from 88,124 to 90,000.

Of the three services, the navy would bear the greatest cuts. Being a slower, less manoeuvrable, more vulnerable and relatively costly method of defence, its regular enlistment would be more than halved from 71,300 (66,158 of these being UK-based) to 29,000 – all of whom would be stationed in and around the British Isles. The aggressive-tending marine units would be pruned back from 7,700 men to a 1,000-strong amphibious landing force solely for use in the liberation of those parts of our territory, such as the Channel Islands, which might be subject to enemy occupation.

In contrast to ships, aircraft are a faster, more versatile and cheaper type of weapon platform, and for this reason the reductions in the RAF would be proportionately less severe. The 89,300 air force personnel – 16,655 of them posted abroad in 1983 – would be reduced from 72,645 UK-based airmen and women to 48,000 stationed exclusively on the British mainland.

The air force is the frontline of frontier defence. In these alternative armed forces the total combat and support aircraft of the RAF would nevertheless be reduced from 595 to 295 by dispensing with our offensive air capabilities. The remaining 295 flights would be restructured around an enhanced air defence role with anti-ship, anti-submarine, anti-tank and anti-aircraft missiles to prevent the penetration of enemy bombers and naval assault fleets, and to reinforce the army's defensive land operations. This restructuring would require an increase in airborne early-warning aircraft from 6 to 10 to give the maximum possible notice of an impending attack; and an expansion of ground and maritime support fighters from 68 to 72 to provide air cover and strikes to back up our army and naval forces. There would, however, be a reduction in defensive interceptor fighter planes from 111 to 89 on the grounds that these are very expensive and that part of their air defence role can be handled by cheaper and less vulnerable mobile surface-to-air missile (SAM) units. Accordingly, there would be an expansion of the RAF anti-aircraft missile squadrons from 8 to 12 and the equipment of all regular and territorial army battalions with SAMs. The net effect of these changes would be to strengthen very substantially our air defensive capacity.

The major retrenchments would be in the RAF's offensive 'deep strike' and long-range support squadrons. The provocative bomber/strike/attack force would be slashed from 164 aircraft to 10; a token non-nuclear force being retained for exceptional operations where we might need to destroy an aggressor's long-distance supply lines and offensive launch bases, or heavily bomb enemy positions as a prelude to recapturing remote parts of our territory such as the Shetlands which had fallen into their hands.

The withdrawal from remote overseas military engagements and garrisons would obviate the need for our current-sized squadrons of 16 tanker/refuellers and 56 fixed-wing air transporters. Both of these could be reduced to a skeletal complement of two aircraft each. Even with the RAF's helicopter flights being cut from 70 to 48, we would still have an ability to move substantial numbers of mobile regulars and reserves into forward battle areas and mount airborne counter-attacks against enemy strongholds. To deal with crisis situations where we might want to send troops and weapons to aid West Germany or Nicaragua, it would be more cost-effective to make provision for the requisitioning of civilian aircraft than to maintain big and largely unused support squadrons.

There would also be major reductions in our reconnaissance aircraft – from 44 to 18 – and our search and rescue helicopters could be pared down from 32 to 16. The present 28 maritime patrol and anti-submarine warfare planes are probably about right for surveillance and strike in waters adjacent to the UK and the longer distance protection of our merchant fleet.

The navy is the second arm of frontier defence. Though its 1983 complement of 186 combat and support vessels would be cut down to 91, the remaining vessels would be armed with an improved anti-ship, anti-submarine and anti-aircraft missile capacity for the execution of a subordinate merchant shipping defence function, and a dominant coastal defence role involving the destruction of invading warships, submarines, minefields and aircraft and the bombardment of enemy beachheads in support of our ground forces.

Following the redeployment of the fleet in UK coastal waters, an alternative navy could do away with most of the offensive and long-range surface ships which also happen to be very expensive and ever more vulnerable to attack, as demonstrated by the Falklands/Malvinas war and by the latest developments in sea and air-launched anti-ship missiles. This would involve a reduction in our aircraft carriers and assault ships from 5 to zero and in our destroyers from 13 to zero. Many of their tasks such as anti-submarine warfare can be performed far more efficiently and cheaply by faster and more manoeuvrable anti-submarine aircraft and helicopters which also have a better chance of survival. A small fleet of 12 frigates out of 47 would be retained – mainly for counter-attack against naval assault and blockade and to safeguard our shipping routes. The remaining frigates would all carry either anti-submarine helicopters or vertical take-off and landing air defence and strike aircraft.

With submarines being less open to attack than surface ships and more lethal against invading armadas, there is a good case for maintaining an underwater fleet. For purely defensive purposes, however, it is doubtful that we need 31 submarines. Probably about 16 non-nuclear versions would be sufficient; including a mixture of long-distance 'hunter-killers' to defend merchant convoys, and small 'hide and surprise' submarines which can navigate shallow seas and rivers and are thus ideal for in-shore coastal defence. Also cut back would be the navy's long-range support fleet. The 14 tankers, 7 replenishment and support vessels and 6 troop landing ships would be reduced to zero on the grounds that they are oriented to aggressive objectives not required by a home-based naval defence. They could always be made up for by commandeering merchant vessels in an emergency when we might need to launch a naval task force to recapture parts of our territory such as the Western Isles or resupply frigates and submarines guarding the North Atlantic shipping routes.

The Fleet Air Arm would also face a decrease – from 117 flights to 60 – with anti-submarine and air transport helicopters comprising half of these and strike and anti-submarine aircraft making up the other half. Whilst some flights would be sea-based on frigates and the larger patrol/attack craft, the majority would be land-based air support for in-shore naval defence.

In contrast to the cuts in offensive naval units, all 35 of our current minesweepers and minelayers would continue in service to ensure our ability to break any attempt to blockade our ports with mines and enable us to put down our own defensive minefields to protect our coast from seaborne invasion. Whilst the existing numbers of patrol craft are about right, the 28 vessels need to be modified to give them greater speed and an enhanced attack capacity by variously equipping them with anti-submarine depth charges, precision-guided torpedoes and anti-ship and anti-aircraft missiles. In addition, a few of the larger patrol/attack craft could carry anti-submarine helicopters. The potential of these smaller craft as an effective substitute for larger vessels was illustrated during the 1967 Middle East war when an anti-ship missile fired from an Egyptian patrol ship successfully sank the Israeli destroyer *Elat*.

The army is the third line of frontier defence and the mainstay of a territorial strategy. Compared with the 118 main regular combat regiments, battalions and corps in 1983, an alternative army would be slimmed down to 69. But since all of these 69 regular units would be UK-based, this reduction in army forces would still leave the British mainland *better* defended owing to the fact that at present 69 of our 118 regiments, battalions and corps are stationed in West Germany and elsewhere overseas – including 13 of the army's 19 armoured regiments, 19 of its 25 artillery regiments, 8 of its 12 engineering regiments, 25 of its 56 infantry battalions and 4 of its 5 air corps. Thus, whereas only 49 regular regiments, battalions and corps are currently garrisoned in the UK, under an alternative defence plan this would rise to 69.

Proportionately, the heaviest cutbacks in regular army strength would take place in the offensive-inclined and frontier defence units as part of the change-over to a defensive infantry-based 'in depth' strategy. Armoured regiments would fall from 19 to 7, engineering from 12 to 5 and field and heavy artillery from 16 to 8 – the remaining armoured and artillery regiments being primarily geared to intensive frontier defence and counter-offensive operations designed to 'mince and mash' an aggressor army.

Following the across-the-board equipment of all infantry battalions with anti-tank units, there would no longer be any need for the existing 4 independent anti-tank batteries. The army air corps would also lose 2 of its 5 helicopter gunship regiments and squadrons, though the other 3 would need to be retained to ensure a continuing troop transport and airborne anti-tank and ground support capacity. Remaining fully intact with 1 regiment each would be the guided weapon, missile and Special Air Service regiments – the two former being essential for concentrated heavy firepower to splinter invading forces, and the commando skills of the latter being especially valuable for guerrilla-style operations behind enemy lines. To help compensate for the RAF's switch away from high-cost interceptor fighter planes, the army's mobile air defence SAM forces would be increased from 3 regiments to 5.

Whilst there would be an overall reduction in the regular infantry from 56 to 38 battalions, its relative strength would rise from 47 per cent of regular army units to 55 per cent. The net reduction of the regular infantry would be more than offset by the massive expansion of the Territorial Army from 72,600 to 183,000 all-infantry troops. When this is taken into account, both the net strength of the infantry and the infantry as a proportion of total mobilisable army personnel would increase dramatically. The firepower and versatility of the infantry would also be extended and adapted for a guerrilla role; with all regular, reserve and territorial battalions including specialist anti-tank, SAM, mortar, heavy machine-gun and land-mine/sabotage/bomb disposal units; thus transforming each battalion into a semi-independent, self-supporting mini-army.

The cost of these alternative armed forces would be between £9,500 million and £10,500 million at 1983 prices – at least £5,000 million less than the 1983-84 defence budget of £15,973 million. It would only consume between 3.2 and 3.5 per cent of our GDP instead of the 1983 figure of 5.4 per cent. This would bring us closer into line with the percentage of GDP expended on defence in 1983 by West Germany (3.4 per cent), Netherlands (3.3 per cent) and Norway (3.1 per cent). There would be a corresponding decline in per capita defence expenditure from £285 in 1983–84 to between £169 and £187 (at constant prices) per head of population after 10 years.

In addition to military forms of defence, we should not underestimate the effectiveness of non-violent civilian resistance as a deterrent to aggression and a complement to armed opposition in the event of occupation. This combination of military and civilian 'total resistance' would mobilise the *whole population* in the task of national self-defence.

The civilian aspect of this resistance would attempt to isolate and demoralise an occupation administration and, through a campaign of passive non-compliance and active defiance, render it unable to function or achieve its goals. A recent successful example of this was the 1974 Ulster Workers' Council strike. However abhorrent its motives, this strike demonstrated the capacity of popular protest to frustrate the official will and force a reversal of government policy. In a similar vein, though for different reasons, a campaign of civilian resistance against an invading army would seek to obstruct the imposition of enemy institutions and values; defend our civil, political and trade-union rights; deny a puppet government any financial gain or access to strategic materials and information; and covertly aid underground guerrilla fighters with food, clothing, medical supplies, safe houses, etc. Being surrounded by a hostile and non-cooperative population would add to the pressure on an occupation regime, forcing it to divert large numbers of troops away from the battlefield to pacify civilian protests and thereby taking the pressure off our guerrillas and shifting the balance of military forces more in our favour.

In many respects, Britain is ideally suited for non-violent civilian resistance. Firstly, we are a densely peopled country with a large urban concentration of population and a complex division of labour which makes our highly interdependent institutions extremely vulnerable to disruption.

Secondly, the high ownership of photocopiers, duplicators, printing presses, CB and short-wave radios, video cameras and cassette recorders would facilitate the coordination of a large-scale clandestine resistance and make it impossible for an invading army to suppress news and information or spread effective propaganda.

Thirdly, Britain has a huge ready-made organisational base for a campaign of public protest and non-compliance – the 10 million-strong trade-union movement and the hundreds of thousands of local community and voluntary groups with millions of members across the country.

Fourthly, we have a long tradition of political and trade-union protest which, in this century, has included the 1920 dock-workers' strike to block government plans for military intervention against Russia; the General Strike of 1926 when trade-union Councils of Action briefly displaced the state and wielded effective local control in many working-class industrial districts; the mass trespass in 1932 to reclaim public access to Kinder Scout; the 'Hunger Marches' of the unemployed in the 1930s; the 1958–63 Committee of 100's civil disobedience campaign against nuclear weapons; the defiance and defeat of the Industrial Relations Act by the trade-union movement during the early 1970s; the Upper Clyde 'work-in' of 1972 to save the shipyards and the miners' mass picket which closed the Saltley coke depot in the same year; the 1981 Brixton and Toxteth riots in protest at unemployment and police harassment; and the contemporary peace camps to oppose the installation of Cruise missiles.

Though historically civilian resistance has always sprung up *after* occupation and has never been organised in detail in advance as an official part of any country's defence policy, there is no reason why Britain should not take the initiative by drawing up contingency plans and establishing a civilian resistance council to coordinate non-violent opposition by local authorities, trade unions, student and ethnic organisations, churches, tenants' and residents' associations, voluntary self-help groups and sporting and cultural bodies. In the event of occupation, the council would time major acts of civilian resistance to coincide with military uprisings in order to cause the maximum possible chaos, disruption and strain on the enemy's resources. This resistance would include selective strikes and the sabotage of strategic industrial plants to deny an occupation army vital supplies of petrol, military spares, etc. and prevent its exploitation of our advanced technology and natural resources such as gas, oil and coal. Spearheaded through the trade-union movement, this economic resistance would be supplemented by political opposition – strikes and go-slows by civil servants and council officers to obstruct the directives of a puppet regime, and a campaign of tax, rent and rate refusal to deprive a Quisling-style administration of funds so that it would be unable to operate or make any financial gains from its occupation. There could also be public gestures of defiance, including mass demonstrations and civil disobedience against restrictions on liberties, occupations of enemy headquarters and boycotts of the invader's official functions and ceremonies.

A Volunteer Citizen's Army

The switch to a more territorial-inclined defence strategy and a complementary alternative military structure would involve greater reliance on a citizen-style Territorial Army and less dependence on elite professional forces. However, this shift away from a concept of the *armed state* towards the notion of the *armed people* need not and ought not to require conscription. Firstly, it is inherently totalitarian and contradictory for a democratic state to *force* its citizens to defend their liberties. Surely, if the defence of freedom is to carry real conviction, it must be an act of free will by free men and women? And if a society is truly democratic, then surely its citizens will readily defend it without the need for compulsion? Secondly, the existence of national service would encourage the government to take conscripts and poor conditions of army life for granted because it would know that they had no choice. And thirdly, we do not need conscription. The size of armed forces required by Britain to implement a territorial strategy could be achieved without recourse to national service. Comparing Britain with Sweden, which is often cited as a good model of territorial defence, we are about the half the land mass with more than seven times the population and even under an alternative defence plan our regular forces would be two and half times greater. A 183,000 strong Territorial Army – plus regulars, reserves and other volunteers totalling 274,000 – would be sufficient to match the Swedish density of just under two military personnel per square kilometre.

If we thus accept that the state does not have the right to compel people to take up arms, but that the people *do* have the right to bear arms in the defence of their liberties, then the alternative to conscription is a part-time volunteer citizen's army based on a radically reformed Territorial Army.

At present, the Territorial Army is not genuinely territorial at all. It mainly functions as an auxiliary to the British Army of the Rhine and NATO, rather than for the home defence of particular local districts. Under an alternative defence strategy, however, the Territorial Army would fulfil a static territorial role and be reorganised on a decentralised local community basis with units corresponding to parliamentary constituencies – totalling 650 local battalions forming a deep defensive web across the UK and each having a considerable degree of autonomy.

With members recruited from within their own local constituency and having the responsibility for defending it, these territorial units would enjoy the military advantages of being able to mobilise rapidly to defend an area they know intimately and the morale advantages of a passionate commitment which goes with defending one's own 'hearth and home'.

To raise the Territorial Army's strength to 183,000, each constituency unit would be open to men and women on a completely equal basis and comprise an average of 281 part-time civilian volunteers aged 18–45. Representing a major civilianisation of the armed forces, this target ought not be difficult to attain given that the average constituency includes 60,000 electors. But to make certain that the Territorial Army was attractive to a wide range of recruits and ensure that it was representative of all social backgrounds and opinions in society, and not just macho militarists, there would have to be a long overdue liberalisation and democratisation of the armed forces. Volunteers would also need to be granted a statutory right to time off work on a private's rate of pay (£103 p.wk. in 1983) for their initial basic training and periodic refresher courses.

Basic training for the Territorial Army need only last six weeks if all the unnecessary 'bull', square-bashing and drill is eliminated. For the first four weeks all volunteers would learn general territorial and guerrilla skills – the use of automatic guns, grenades, camouflage, building fortification, weapon improvisation and either street fighting or rural guerrilla warfare depending on whether the unit was city or country-based. The last two weeks of basic training would involve specialisation in a particular skill such as anti-tank weapons, suface-to-air missiles, heavy machine-guns, mortars, land mines/sabotage/bomb disposal, radio operation, first-aid or headquarters staff, etc.

After completing the initial course, volunteers would train locally one evening a month under regular army instructors and participate in a weekend local exercise every year and a week-long refresher course every two years – all paid at a private's salary to provide a financial incentive to enlistment.

At constituency level, each territorial battalion would be under the command of its own local officers and organised into 10 platoons – 5 of them infantry and the other 5 specialist (anti-tank, SAM, heavy machine-gun, mortar, and land mine/sabotage/bomb disposal). In addition, there would be a small headquarters staff of about 10 members to direct battle plans and supplies and coordinate with the regular army and civilian resistance. Each local battalion would thus function as its own self-contained army, able to operate independently and exercise a high degree of initiative; rather than being dependent on centralised direction and support.

This part-time army would work out far more cost-effective than large regular forces. Though it would not be up to full regular army efficiency, in the one to three-month crisis period which would precede a war volunteers could undergo intensive training to bring them up to standard. Furthermore, what they lacked in regular proficiency would be largely compensated for in terms of the better morale and motivation which would follow from the knowledge that they were part of a democratic army and defending their own families and communities in a war of genuine self-defence and self-determination. Vietnam's General Giap has described morale as the most underrated weapon in warfare. Indeed, he views the high morale and unshakeable determination of the Vietnamese people as the critical factor which enabled relatively untrained and under-armed peasant guerrillas to defeat the far more powerful and sophisticated French and American armies. Giap describes the battle of Dien Bien Phu as the 'triumph of motivation over machinery . . . They [the French] had modern equipment and air strikes. But the most important thing is people. Troops fighting for independence have inexhaustible reserves of initiative.'[3]

Democratising the Armed Forces

To ensure that the territorial units attracted sufficient recruits and that the armed forces as whole were representative of a broad cross-section of society, a radical democratisation of the military would be a priority. In common with other West European countries, the premise of this democratisation ought to be that soldiers are 'citizens in uniform' and have a right to enjoy all the liberties of the citizens they are defending – including full civil, political and trade-union rights as already won by the Norwegian, Swedish and Dutch armies.

As Clement Attlee wrote in 1938: 'If the citizens of a democratic community are to be asked to serve in the Army, they must be satisfied that the Army will be used for the defence of democracy both at home and abroad.'[4] If Attlee's ideal is to be achieved, then the forces themselves must embody more of the democratic rights and liberties which they purportedly exist to defend. Otherwise, the more soldiers are deprived of freedom themselves, the more readily they will be prepared to deny that freedom to others; thereby threatening the very fabric of our democracy.

This was recognised by the Transport and General Workers' Union when it initiated discussions with the Labour government in 1969 on the issue of trade-union organisation within the armed forces. The union's national officer, John Cousins, declared: 'The unionisation of the services would make the possibility of a military coup d'état more remote.'[5] Following the army's seizure of power in Chile in 1973, a group of 60 Labour MPs came to a similar conclusion. Led by Ron Thomas and Eddie Loyden, they launched a campaign for military unionisation and democratisation in the mid 1970s, arguing that the denial of collective grievance procedures contributed to poor performance and low morale and was contrary to International Labour Organisation regulations and the United Nations Covenant on Civil and Political Rights which codify the right of all employees to belong to a trade union. Simultaneously, their objectives were supported from a less likely quarter. In 1975, NATO's parliamentary assembly and the West European Union called on all member states to look at ways of allowing 'elected representatives of the armed forces to participate in negotiations with the authorities on conditions of service and rates of pay'.[6]

Subsequently, the campaign by Labour MPs led to more than 20 unions expressing an interest in recruiting servicemen and women. When questioned in the House of Commons in December 1977 about whether union organisation in the armed forces was compatible with the maintenance of military discipline, the Minister of State for Defence, Dr John Gilbert, replied that 'it has been found to be so in other countries'.[7] Indeed, following the service of members of the Fire Brigades Union alongside our armed forces on the battlefields of Europe during the last war, the FBU concluded: 'The extension of democratic rights to disciplined men in uniform, if properly and reasonably applied, results in nothing but an improvement in morale and an increase in efficiency.'[8]

The FBU precedent of higher morale and efficiency, and the positive experience of most other West European countries where military unions are permitted, makes a strong case for the trade-unionisation of our armed forces with comparable collective bargaining rights, including the right to strike during peacetime. As with civilian employees, and the experience of other West European countries, there is every reason to believe that service personnel would exercise this right with the utmost responsibility and caution – resorting to such action only as a matter of last resort. Based on specialist military sections of existing trade unions in order to forge links with the civilian population and establish a strong community of interests between military and civilian employees, union membership for lower ranks would be according to each soldier's trade. Transport drivers, for example, could belong to a specialist military branch of the TGWU, mechanical engineers to the Amalgamated Union of Engineering Workers and signals operators to the Union of Communication Workers, etc. Service personnel with less specific jobs such as infantry, with no equivalent civilian occupation, would be members of general unions such as the TGWU or the National Union of Public Employees. Officers could belong to a specialist division of the Association of Scientific, Technical and

Managerial Staffs or one of the higher-grade civil service unions.

Parallel to this national negotiating machinery, there also need to be joint inter-union soldiers' committees elected at company, battalion and regiment level (or equivalent) in all units. Their purpose would be to represent the interests of servicemen and women to the commanding officer and establish a military version of industrial democracy whereby lower ranks are consulted and involved in the administration of the unit – particularly pertaining to the issues of barrack conditions, food, duty rotas, recreational activities, etc. To provide an additional means of redressing individual grievances and safeguarding against abuses such as bullying and victimisation, an independent military ombudsman ought to be appointed to investigate complaints.

Whilst the trade-unionisation of the forces would go a long way towards extending soldiers' rights and bridging the gulf between military and civilian life, several other reforms are also required. Firstly, under the present system of barracks and military housing estates, most service personnel are physically separated from the civilian community. They live, work and socialise almost exclusively in a forces milieu which shuts them off from non-military people, ideas and experiences. This in turn tends to breed an insular and elitist military outlook. To break down the barriers between the armed forces and 'civvy street' and enhance the individual rights of service personnel, barrack accommodation and all-military housing estates ought to be abolished – except for training units. The only restriction on soldiers' choice of accommodation should be that they live within a specified travelling time or a certain number of miles radius from their base. This reform would do more than anything else to integrate military personnel into the wider society. In the case of training units, the introduction of a common mess and sleeping quarters for all ranks would narrow class differentials and foster a stronger sense of collective identity and common interests – these being essential in a fighting unit whose effectiveness depends on cooperation and teamwork.

Secondly, to remove the anomalous legal status of service personnel under military law, whereby they are currently denied many of the basic rights accorded to defendants in civil courts, there should be a repeal of the separate military penal code, the summary discipline powers of officers and the court-martial system. Instead, the essential elements of military law (though not the vague catch-all 'crimes' such as 'conduct prejudicial to good order and military discipline') ought to be incorporated as a specialist branch of civilian law with all personnel on charges having the right to legal representation, a jury trial and a right of appeal – any custodial sentences being served in an ordinary civilian prison.

Thirdly, it is time that the system of 'indentured labour' through fixed long-term employment contracts was replaced by civilian-comparable contracts in which most servicemen and women were granted the right to resign at three months' notice. During peacetime, a 40-hour week and time off in lieu for overtime ought to be standard.

Fourthly, there is no reason why the forces cannot do away with the unnecessary 'bull', square-bashing, routine drill, petty restrictions on hairstyle and the excessively strict dress code. These take up an inordinate amount of time and restrict individual freedom for no practical military purpose. Our soldiers do not defend Britain better because their hair is cut 'short back and sides' and their buckles and boots shine like mirrors. Nor do precision formation marching and impeccable dress uniforms help deter aggression. It is sometimes argued that these frivolities are necessary to encourage an esprit de corps. But this can be far more fruitfully fostered by motivating the army with democratic ideals so that, as Cromwell's maxim put it, soldiers know what they fight for and love what they know. If the forces insist on having shiny buttons, it would save a lot of time if they simply issued permashine ones that don't require polishing.

Fifthly, to ensure a level of civil and human rights compatible with the principles of a democratic society, all military occupations should be open to women on the basis of complete equality with men, and maternity leave introduced so that women can return to their posts after childbirth. Homosexuality ought to be legalised for off-duty personnel – this having the beneficial side-effect of removing the possibility of blackmail. Racism must be rooted out from the forces and a programme of positive action initiated to ensure that black personnel are better represented amongst senior ranks. And lastly, servicemen and women should be accorded the right to actively participate in political parties, elections, public meetings and demonstrations, etc.

Critics will no doubt claim that such radical changes would undermine discipline and render the armed forces incapable of functioning effectively. That is, however, neither the intention nor the likely effect of these reforms. Existing military discipline is organised through inflexible regulations, rigid hierachies of authority, unquestioning obedience, harsh punishment and the isolation of service personnel from what are perceived as the contaminating liberal influences of civilian society. It is a coercive system of authoritarian discipline based on threats and fears in which the rigorous regulation of every minute detail of a soldier's life indicates the officers' profound paternalism, contempt and distrust towards the lower ranks.

In contrast, an alternative system of democratic discipline would be based on consultation, reasoning and consent by servicemen and women who, because they feel free and trusted and enjoy all the democratic liberties they are defending, have the enthusiasm, initiative and self-discipline that only a truly democratic army can release. If the armed forces know and love liberty in their own daily lives, they will surely all the more passionately defend it.

Finally, to encourage this new democratic spirit amongst the forces, current affairs and political education along the lines of the Army Bureau of Current Affairs during the last war should be a regular feature of army life. This would not be of a party political nature, but designed to foster a broader social awareness and replace the traditional military values of aggression, authoritarianism and jingoism with a positive commitment to the democratic ideals of human rights, civil liberties, trade-union freedom, the right of all nations to self-determination, and above all, peace and international cooperation.

A European Self-Defence Organisation

The transition to a democratic non-nuclear defence strategy would require a unilateralist government to set a timetable, of about two years, for the dismantling of Britain's nuclear arsenal and the removal of all US nuclear weapons and bases from our soil and territorial waters. This would provoke a major crisis for NATO, given Britain's present role as America's forward base in Europe and the location of so many key installations in the NATO network. As a consequence of this disruption, it is extremely doubtful that we would be welcome or feel able to remain a part of the Atlantic Alliance.

Regardless of NATO's reaction, however, Britain's commitment to a non-nuclear and non-provocative defence policy would render our continued membership of the Alliance contradictory and untenable. Support for a de-nuclearised and strictly defensive strategy of frontier, territorial and civilian resistance would be incompatible with NATO's offensive nuclear war-fighting doctrine. A non-nuclear Britain would therefore have no choice but to withdraw from NATO in order to sustain the credibility of its non-provocative defence posture.

Though the greater self-reliance afforded by an alternative defence policy would make pulling out of the Alliance plausible, simple withdrawal may not be the best option. It would play straight into the hands of the worst 'Little England' chauvinists and in any case is unlikely to command majority public support. Currently, over 70 per cent of the electorate are opposed to pulling out of NATO. To reassure those who fear that Britain outside of the Atlantic Alliance would be vulnerable to attack, we need to offer a non-nuclear alternative to NATO. An alternative self-defensive alliance of European nations would certainly be more consistent with internationalist principles and would avoid the danger of a retreat into an isolationist and nationalistic 'Fortress Britain' which is implicit in the option of straightforward withdrawal. After all, it would be right for Britain to support Nicaragua in the event of a US invasion and we would certainly expect other nations to rally to our aid if Britain was attacked. Likewise, we ought to be ready to extend those same principles of solidarity and comradeship to other European countries such as Norway, Yugoslavia, etc. if they faced aggression.

Interest in the idea of a strictly defensive and exclusively European alliance was prominent in the wartime Commonwealth movement, and in 1944 the underground European resistance movements issued a joint manifesto calling for a European federal union with unitary armed forces. Subsequently, during the late 1950s, Commander Sir Stephen King-Hall proposed that Britain unilaterally renounce nuclear weapons, leave NATO and form a European Treaty Organisation based primarily on non-violent forms of defence. Whilst such a degree of reliance on civilian resistance is of doubtful practicality, King-Hall's proposal for a solely European collective security agreement, independent of both superpowers, seems feasible enough.

In tandem with withdrawal from NATO, Britain should therefore take the initiative in creating an alternative European self-defence organisation as a non-provocative rival to NATO, open to all European nations, and based upon the following principles: (1) the renunciation of nuclear weapons and the use of force in international relations with the priority aim of establishing a European nuclear-free zone; (2) the commitment to non-provocative methods of defence; (3) the abrogation of all other military treaties and alliances; (4) the removal of all foreign troops and bases; (5) the recognition of the right of all nations to self-determination; and (6) the pledge of mutual support and solidarity in the event of any member state being subject to unprovoked attack or invasion. Unlike NATO, this self-defensive organisation would be a loose decentralised association with no unified command structure; each member state being first and foremost reliant on its own efforts and only as a last resort dependent on external military back-up. Whilst it would preclude the permanent stationing of British troops in West Germany (or any other country), an alternative collective security agreement would not prevent the reinforcement of the German army with defensive anti-tank and SAM units in the period immediately prior to an invasion (usually about three months if the Soviet incursions into Czechoslovakia and Afghanistan are anything to go by). It would also permit military cooperation through the standardisation of weapons and munitions to improve the effectiveness of mutual military aid and combined defensive operations against aggression. Of particular advantage to the smaller and poorer nations of Europe, joint military research and development would help cut costs and the sharing of technology would enhance the capabilities of new defensive 'anti-weapon' systems.

The establishment of this European self-defence organisation could potentially make a dramatic contribution to the fracturing of the two big military blocs which divide Europe, thereby beginning the process of reunifying the continent. It could give countries the confidence to reject nuclear weapons and superpower alliances and encourage them to adopt a more independent and non-aligned foreign policy unconstrained by dependence on the American-dominated Atlantic Alliance. In particular, this alternative defence pact would have an appeal to the small and medium-sized countries of Europe where there are strong anti-nuclear movements, but where many people nevertheless feel hesitant about leaving NATO and standing alone – the Netherlands, Belgium, Denmark, Norway, Greece and Spain. In the longer term, as the divergence of interests between Europe and the United States becomes clearer and a stronger European identity emerges, it could have an attraction for West Germany, France and Italy and even for the more independent-minded East European states of Albania, Romania and Yugoslavia – the latter two countries already being committed to the idea of a Balkan nuclear-free zone. A European defensive alliance might also have favourable repercussions within the rest of the Eastern bloc. Since the Russians use the threat from the imperialist West as an excuse to justify their iron grip over the Warsaw Pact countries, the non-threatening character of an alternative alliance could pressure the Soviets to relax their hold and encourage the East Europeans to assert greater independence from Moscow. By lessening the spectre of Western intervention, a European self-defence organisation is thus likely to encourage democratic movements and liberalising reforms in the Soviet bloc and greater East-West contact; thereby creating the basis for longer-term European unity.

What About Nuclear Blackmail?

This leaves the one remaining problematic issue of nuclear blackmail – the possibility that a nuclear opponent might suddenly attack a non-nuclear Britain or threaten to 'nuke' us in order to compel our submission to its demands. As absurd as the view that it is only our possession of nuclear weapons which preserves our sovereignty is the idea that a non-nuclear Britain would be subject to random, unprovoked and irrational nuclear attack or blackmail. This has never happened to any country during the past forty years of the atomic age, despite all the wars and crises, and there is no reason to suppose it is any more likely in the future.

It is hard to imagine even the staunchest hawks in the Kremlin going to war, let alone nuclear war, on impulse and without logical objectives or provocation. Aggressor nations usually fight wars for quite rational strategic and economic reasons – to gain access to a region and extend their sphere of influence or to acquire new raw materials, technology and skilled labour. Given such objectives, the use of nuclear weapons in conquest is completely irrational and counter-productive because it would lay waste for generations the territory and resources which the expansionist power sought to gain. In the case of the Soviets, they have their own plentiful stocks of natural resources and access to new technology through trade and technical agreements with the West. There is therefore no reason for the Russians to conquer Western Europe to gain by force what they can already acquire through peaceful coexistence. There is even less reason for them to destroy Western Europe in a nuclear conflagration because that would cut off the very supplies of food and hi-tech products on which they depend.

The rationale for a Soviet nuclear attack would be further minimised, and our ability to withstand nuclear blackmail greatly enhanced, by the adoption of a dispersed in-depth territorial defence strategy. Because it offers no concentrated targets, this strategy would render the Russian recourse to nuclear weapons an unattractive and futile proposition.

It is not as if a non-nuclear Britain would be unique amongst the nations of the world. The vast majority of countries do not possess nuclear weapons; yet they have maintained their independence and have neither been invaded, attacked with nuclear weapons nor threatened with nuclear blackmail by the Soviets or any other state. Indeed, if nuclear blackmail is such an easy and likely option, why are the Russians doing things the hard way in Afghanistan?

Throughout the nuclear era there have been numerous wars, invasions and confrontations involving the superpowers – the Berlin blockade and Cuban missile crisis, the occupations of Hungary and Czechoslovakia and the wars in Korea, Vietnam and the Middle East. Apart from the US threats at the time of the Korean and Cuban crises, which were not repeated in subsequent confrontations, neither the Americans nor the Soviets have dared to even threaten nuclear blackmail, let alone actually launch their nuclear missiles. Certainly, neither of the superpowers have ever perpetrated nuclear aggression or blackmail against a non-belligerent state. It is true that the USA repeatedly contemplated the atomic bombing of Korea, Vietnam, China and Iraq in the 1950s and 60s. But even then, at the height of American global military supremacy, successive presidents shrank from activating the nuclear option – including Richard Nixon. Probably the most megalomaniac American leader this century, even he was persuaded that such a course of action against Vietnam was morally untenable and militarily counter-productive because it would have destroyed the very country that the US claimed it was saving from communism. Equally importantly, a nuclear attack against Vietnam would have been publicly unacceptable; provoking widespread unrest at home and abroad and resulting in the USA being isolated and reviled as a political leper by the international community.

This power of public opinion as a constraint against world leaders using nuclear weapons or threatening nuclear blackmail should not be underestimated. The fear of alienating domestic and international support *does* condition the actions of governments and generals. General Sir Charles Keightley admitted as much at Suez: 'In modern days world public opinion is a most important weapon of war.' Indeed, when popular opinion turns against a war, as the American people turned against their government's genocidal policy in Vietnam, then leaders are ultimately driven either to defeat or withdrawal. Even the most power-crazed dictators are conscious of the adverse publicity and international opprobrium which would pour down upon them if they dared to use nuclear weapons or threats as an instrument of war. Being intensely vain men, more so than most politicians, dictators tend to be obsessively concerned about their place in history. Even they would not relish being remembered as the monster who exterminated a defenceless country or reduced European civilisation to ashes and dust.

A further factor which functions as a check and balance on the actions of governments is international law – statutes such as the Genocide Convention of 1948 and the Geneva Conventions of 1949 and 1977 make the use of nuclear weapons illegal. Despite the difficulties of enforcement, these laws *do* act as a restraining influence. Prime ministers and presidents are acutely aware of how the crimes of the Nazis were eventually brought to justice at the Nuremberg trials, and there can be little doubt that an attack involving just a handful of nuclear missiles would result in a scale of genocide far in excess of the worst exterminations by the Nazis.

All these factors add up to make it highly improbable, though not impossible, that a non-nuclear Britain would run the risk of being attacked with nuclear weapons or forced to submit to nuclear blackmail. Whilst we can almost certainly rule out the possibility of irrational and unprovoked nuclear aggression against a non-belligerent Britain, the absolute impossibility of nuclear blackmail is less certain. In the unlikely 'worst case' scenario of blackmail by the Soviets or some other aggressor state, submission would be our only realistic alternative. However unpleasant, it would be temporary and infinitely preferable to the Conservative policy of responding with a nuclear strike against the Russians which would run the risk of a full-scale nuclear holocaust in which both our societies would be permanently annihilated. Once a Soviet occupation had been accomplished, the Russians would no longer be able to use or threaten nuclear weapons for fear of destroying their own occupying forces. In the long term, guerrilla and civilian resistance would sufficiently disrupt the Soviet colonial administration, prevent it from achieving its goals, and cause the Russians so much demoralisation that they would eventually withdraw out of a recognition that it was no longer worth their while to remain in Britain – in much the same way as the Vietnamese forced the French and the Americans to withdraw from their country.

Conclusion

It is encouraging to see the Labour Party taking the first, albeit timid and tentative, steps in the direction of an alternative defence policy with the publication of its *Defence and Security for Britain* statement which was presented to Annual Conference in October 1984. This document commits Labour to a denuclearised and non-bellicose strategy of 'defensive deterrence': 'British defence policy should indicate to any potential aggressor that invasion and conquest of Britain and its allies would be difficult and unproductive. Britain's forces should be deployed for the sake of proper deterrence: to dissuade any state which might be tempted into aggression . . . by mounting forces which are designed as unambiguously as possible, for defensive purposes only.[9]' 'Such a *defence* policy should make sure that any attempt at invasion or conquest is so costly to the aggressor that the latter will not think aggression worth while . . . We require a true *defensive deterrence* which is capable of successful resistance; which exacts a high and unacceptable cost from any aggressor's forces; which as far as possible does not escalate the conflict and which is consistent with a wider policy of promoting security and disarmament.'[10]

Accordingly, *Defence and Security for Britain* proposes scrapping Trident and Cruise missiles, de-commissioning Polaris and removing all US nuclear weapons and bases from British soil. Whilst remaining committed to NATO, Labour seeks to change it from within by pushing for a 'no first use' nuclear weapons policy and the withdrawal of all battlefield nuclear weapons and all dual-capable systems, leading to the creation of a European nuclear-free zone and the eventual dissolution of NATO and the Warsaw Pact.

Though it is unquestionably the most imaginative and radical defence policy adopted by any party since the war, *Defence and Security for Britain* still remains at least partly locked within the parameters of the traditional defence debate by its unswerving commitment to NATO, rejection of an alternative non-nuclear European defensive alliance, opposition to cuts in conventional force levels, abandonment of party policy to reduce defence expenditure to the NATO average of 3.9 per cent of GDP and the lack of any perspective on liberalising the armed forces and extending democratic rights to service personnel.

Despite such shortcomings, the Labour Party *is* moving, however slowly and hesitantly, in the right direction. Whatever its weaknesses, it is the only political party which offers any hope of winning power and implementing a radical non-nuclear alternative. It is up to people who share the vision of a democratic and non-nuclear defence policy to push Labour further and faster in that direction and ensure that it is elected as the next government of this country.

Notes to Chapter 1

1. *Observer,* 1 January 1978.
2. Jim Garrison and Pyare Shivpuri, *The Russian Threat – Its Myths and Realities,* Gateway Books, London, 1983, p.5 and pp.18–20.
3. Owen Greene, Barry Rubin, Neil Turok, Philip Webber and Graeme Wilkinson, *London After The Bomb,* Oxford University Press, Oxford, 1982, p.9.
4. Ibid., pp.8–9.
5. Cited by Philip Bolsover, *Civil Defence,* Campaign for Nuclear Disarmament, London, undated pamphlet, pp.5–6.
6. British Medical Association, *The Medical Effects of Nuclear War,* John Wiley and Sons, Chichester, 1983, p.41.
7. A. Qasrawi, F. Wellhoefer and F. Steward, *Ground Zero,* Scientists Against Nuclear Arms, 1982.
8. Owen Greene et al., op. cit., pp.38–40.
9. S. Openshaw and P. Steadman, 'On the Geography of a Worst Case Nuclear Attack on the Population of Britain', *Political Geography Quarterly,* July 1982, pp.263–278; and 'On the Geography of the Bomb', paper presented to the conference of the Institute of British Geographers, Edinburgh, 5–8 January 1983.
10. Ibid.
11. Ibid.
12. Ibid.
13. S. Butler, 'Scientific Advice in Home Defence', in C.F. Barnaby and G.P. Thomas (eds), *The Nuclear Arms Race: Control or Catastrophe,* Frances Pinter, London, 1982, pp.135–163.
14. Ibid.
15. Carl Sagan et al., 'Long Term Biological Consequences of Nuclear War', *Science,* Volume 222, no. 4630, 23 December 1983, p.1293.
16. A.P. Haynes, 'Possible Consequences of a Nuclear Attack on London', in E. Chivian, S. Chivian, R. Lifton and J. Mack (eds) *Last Aid,* W.H. Freeman and Company, San Francisco, 1983.
17. Carl Sagan et al., op. cit., pp.1293–1300; and 'Nuclear Winter: Global Consequences of Multiple Nuclear Explosions', *Science,* Volume 222, no. 4630, 23 December 1983, pp.1283–1292.
18. Ibid., p.1287.
19. Ibid., p.1286.
20. Ibid., p.1294.
21. Ibid., p.1289.
22. Ibid., pp.1296–1297.
23. Ibid., pp.1283 and 1290.
24. Ibid., pp.1293–1294.
25. Ibid., p.1299.
26. *Guardian,* 22 October 1983.
27. Ibid.
28. Ibid.

Notes to Chapter 2

1. *Guardian*, 19 January 1984; and *Unemployment, Health and Social Policy*, Nuffield Centre for Health Service Studies, Leeds, 1984.
2. *Guardian*, 4 October 1983.
3. *Labour Research*, Volume 72, no. 6, June 1983, p.167.
4. Ibid., p.163.
5. *Dark Days for the Homeless*, Shelter, undated pamphlet.
6. *Guardian*, 15 January 1982.
7. *South London Press*, 23 September 1983, 2 December 1983, 3 February 1984 and 19 May 1984; and *Guardian*, 17 September 1984.
8. *Tribune*, 6 January 1984, p.1.
9. *Labour Research*, January 1984, p.22.
10. Ibid.
11. Michael Meacher, 'As the Rich Get Richer, the Numbers Living in Poverty Soar', *Guardian*, 29 March 1984.
12. *Guardian*, 18 October 1983.
13. *Times*, 6 October 1976.
14. Enoch Powell, 'The Ominous Misunderstanding of Soviet Intentions', *Guardian*, 10 October 1983.
15. Jim Garrison and Pyare Shivpuri, op. cit., p.207.
16. Enoch Powell, op. cit.
17. *World Military and Social Expenditures*, 1981.
18. Jim Garrison and Pyare Shivpuri, op. cit., p. 157.
19. Ibid., p.125.
20. Ibid., pp.132–134.
21. *Challenge*, May–June 1980.
22. *The Military Balance 1981–82*, International Institute for Strategic Studies, London, 1981.
23. Jim Garrison and Pyare Shivpuri, op. cit., pp.162–165.
24. Cited by Jim Garrison and Pyare Shivpuri, op. cit., p.325.
25. *Challenge*, May–June 1980.

Notes to Chapter 3

1. *Statement on the Defence Estimates 1983*, HMSO, Cmnd. 8951–II, p.28.
2. Cited by Sir Stephen King-Hall, *Defence in the Nuclear Age*, Gollancz, London, 1958, p.87.
3. *Statement on the Defence Estimates 1983*, p.11.
4. Ibid.
5. Ibid.
6. Cited in *British Soldiers Speak Out on Ireland*, Information on Ireland, Pamphlet no. 1, 1978, p.6.

7. Frank Kitson, *Low-Intensity Operations,* Faber and Faber, London, 1972, p.2.
8. Ibid., p.3.
9. *Land Operations Manual, Volume 3 – Counter-Revolutionary Operations,* Part 1, p.4.
10. Ibid., p.13.
11. Ibid.
12. *Land Operations Manual, Volume 3 – Counter-Revolutionary Operations,* Part 2, p.3.
13. *British Soldiers Speak Out on Ireland,* p.24.
14. *New Statesman,* 31 October 1980.
15. For a fuller account of all the question marks surrounding the shooting down of the Korean airliner see R.W. Johnson, '007: Licence to Kill?', *Guardian,* 17 December 1983.
16. Marplan Poll, *Guardian,* 26 May 1984.
17. Gallup Poll, 23–28 May 1984.
18. Marplan Poll, *Guardian,* 22 October 1983.
19. Marplan Poll, *Guardian,* 22 November 1983.
20. *Guardian,* 12 March 1984.
21. *Guardian,* 9 April 1984.
22. *Guardian,* 10 February 1984.
23. Ibid.
24. Alexander Haig, testimony to the US Senate Foreign Relations Committee, 4 November 1981.
25. Cited in *The Medical Effects of Nuclear War,* loc. cit., p.26.
26. Ibid., p.26.
27. *International Herald Tribune,* 9 November 1981.
28. Cited in *The Medical Effects of Nuclear War,* loc. cit., p.27.
29. Ibid.
30. Georges Bidault, *Resistance: The Political Autobiography of Georges Bidault,* Weidenfeld and Nicholson, London, 1967.
31. *A Week in Politics,* Channel 4, 30 March 1984.
32. *Guardian,* 13 January 1984.
33. *Guardian,* 29 September 1982.
34. *Panorama,* BBC 1, 2 April 1984.
35. Ibid.
36. For an extended exposition of international law as it relates to nuclear weapons and war, see Lawyers Versus The Bomb, *The Illegality of Nuclear Warfare,* Pamphlet 1, undated; and 'Nuclear Weapons and the Law', *State Research,* Bulletin 31, August–September 1982, pp.170–181.

Notes to Chapter 4

1. F.P. Crozier, *A Brass Hat in No Man's Land,* London, 1950, p.42.
2. *Statement on the Defence Estimates 1983,* loc. cit., p.52.
3. *Sunday Times,* 27 February 1977.
4. Ibid.

5. *Hansard*, 16 June 1981, col. 346.
6. *British Soldiers Speak Out on Ireland*, loc. cit., p.28.
7. Ibid., p.29.
8. Ibid., p.2.
9. Ibid., p.16.
10. *Guardian*, 26 June 1980.
11. *Guardian*, 11 April 1984.
12. Cited by Chris Knight (ed.), *The Soldier's Charter*, Leeds University Union Labour Society, 1971, p.2.
13. *Time Out*, 7–13 April 1972.
14. *The H-Blocks: The New Internment*, Information on Ireland, 1979.
15. Ibid.
16. Ibid.
17. Cited in *New Labour and Ireland*, Volume 2, no. 1, p.9.
18. Ibid.
19. *Sunday Mail*, 17 May 1981.
20. *Socialist Worker*, 17 December 1977.
21. *British Soldiers Speak Out on Ireland*, p.13.
22. Ibid.
23. *The H-Blocks: The New Internment.*
24. *British Soldiers Speak Out on Ireland*, p.18.
25. Ibid., p.18.
26. Ibid., p.24.
27. Ibid., p.25.
28. Ibid., p.20.
29. Ibid., p.25.
30. For more details on these various incidents see *They Shoot Children*, Information on Ireland, 1982.

Notes to Chapter 5

1. Décret No. 62–207 du 24 Février 1962, *Journal Officiel de la République Française*, 25 February 1962, p.1900.
2. Zulfikar Ali Bhutto, *The Myth of Independence*, Oxford University Press, Karachi, 1969, pp.153–4.
3. *The Total Defence of Sweden*, Press Department of the Swedish Defence Staff, Stockholm, 1963, p.2.
4. *Säkerhets Och Försvarspolitiken: Betänkande Avgivet Aa 1970 Ars Försvarsutredning*, SOU, 1972: 4, Stockholm, 1972.
5. Ibid.
6. General Frank Seethaler, 'Reflections on the Defence Concept of Switzerland', *Armada International*, July–August 1980, pp.20–26.
7. *The Dethronement of Stalin*, Manchester Guardian pamphlet, 1956, p.25.
8. Ibid., p.25.
9. Sedmi Kongres Saveza Komunista Jugoslavije, *Kultura*, Belgrade, 1958, pp.357–8.
10. *Introductory Principles of the 1969 National Defence Law.*

11. Basil Liddell Hart, *Strategy: The Indirect Approach,* Faber and Faber, London, 1954, p.339.
12. Carl von Clausewitz, *On War,* Routledge and Kegan Paul, London, 1962, Volume I, p.230.
13. 'Yank' Levy, *Guerrilla Warfare,* Penguin Books, Harmondsworth, 1941, pp.24–25.
14. Cited by K. Macksey, *The Partisans of Europe in World War II,* Hart-Davis/MacGibbon, London, 1975, p.47.
15. Cited in *The Strategy of Civilian Defence – Non-Violent Resistance To Aggression,* edited by Adam Roberts, Faber and Faber, London, 1967, p.111.
16. *Programme of the German Green Party,* Heretic Books, London, 1983, p.26.

Notes to Chapter 6

1. For a more extensive account of the Volunteer Corps see W.H. Chaloner and W.O. Henderson (eds.), *Engels as a Military Critic,* Manchester University Press, 1959.
2. *The Poor Man's Guardian,* no. 44, 11 April 1831.
3. Cited by Reg Groves, *The Strange Case of Victor Grayson,* Pluto Press, London, 1975, p.127.
4. Tom Wintringham, 'How to Reform the Army', *Fact* no. 25, April 1939, p.73.
5. *Tribune,* 20 December 1940.
6. *The Home Guard Can Fight,* HMSO, 1941, p.9.
7. Ibid., pp. 15–19.
8. Ibid., pp.38–40.
9. Ibid., pp.34–35.
10. Major Geoffrey Cotterell, 'The Other Army', *Army Bureau of Current Affairs,* no. 70, 13 May 1944.
11. Tom Wintringham, 'Modern Weapons and Warfare', *Labour Monthly,* August 1932.
12. Tom Wintringham, 'Modern Weapons and Revolution', *Labour Monthly,* January 1933, p.51.
13. Tom Wintringham, *English Captain,* Faber and Faber, London, 1939, p.277.
14. Ibid.
15. Ibid., p.322.
16. Ibid., pp.322–326.
17. 'How to Reform the Army', p.26.
18. Ibid., pp.48–49.
19. Ibid., p.47.
20. Ibid., p.52.
21. Ibid., p.53.
22. Ibid., p.60.
23. Ibid., p.61.
24. Tom Wintringham, *Armies of Freemen,* George Routledge and

Sons, London, 1940, pp.vii–ix.
25. Ibid., p.15.
26. Tom Wintringham, *New Ways of War*, Penguin, Harmondsworth, 1940, p.44.
27. Tom Wintringham, *Freedom Is Our Weapon – A Policy for Army Reform*, Kegan Paul, Trench, Trubner and Company, London, 1941, p.11.
28. Ibid., pp.22–23.
29. Ibid., p.28.
30. Ibid., p.26.
31. Ibid., p.7.
32. Tom Wintringham, *People's War*, Penguin, Harmondsworth, 1942, p.63.
33. Ibid.
34. Ibid., p.91.
35. Ibid., p.92.
36. *Daily Worker*, 7 July 1938.
37. Tom Wintringham, *The Politics of Victory*, George Routledge and Sons, London, 1941, p.28.
38. Ibid.
39. Ibid., pp.51–53.
40. Ibid., p.77.
41. Ibid.
42. Ibid., p.138.

Notes to Chapter 7

1. Cited in *British Soldiers Speak Out on Ireland*, loc. cit., p.4.
2. Cited by Tom Wintringham, *The Coming World War*, Wishart Books, London, 1935, pp. 142–3.
3. Ibid., pp.143–4.
4. Ibid., p.145.
5. *Diaries of Field-Marshal Sir Henry Wilson*, Cassell, London, 1927, Volume I.
6. D. Gill and G. Dallas, 'Mutiny At Etaples', *Past and Present*, no. 69, November 1975, pp.92–103.
7. John Wood, 'The Guardsmen's Revolt', *Guardian*, 30 March 1968.
8. Tom Wintringham, *Mutiny: Being a Survey of Mutinies from Spartacus to Invergordon*, Stanley Nott, London, 1936, pp.312–313.
9. D. Gill and G. Dallas, op. cit., p.112.
10. For further details of the Calais mutiny see David Lamb, *Mutinies: 1917–1920*, Solidarity, Oxford and London, undated pamphlet, pp.14–15.
11. Ibid., p.10.
12. Ibid., pp.12–13.
13. Ibid., pp.12 and 15.
14. Tom Wintringham, *The Coming World War*, loc. cit., p.150.

15. Donald Featherstone, *Conflict in Hampshire,* Paul Care, Southampton, 1976, p.65.
16. David Lamb, op. cit., pp.29–30 (based on an account by Ron Hall, *The Luton Riots: A Reconstruction of the Events).*
17. *Daily Herald,* 4 June 1919 and *Hansard,* 5 June 1919.
18. Tom Wintringham, *The Coming World War,* pp.145–6.
19. David Lamb, op. cit., p.17.
20. Ibid.
21. Ibid., pp.17–18.
22. Tom Wintringham, *Mutiny,* pp.329–37.
23. Lewis Clive, *The People's Army,* Gollancz, 1938, p.57.
24. Ibid., p.163.
25. *Times,* 4 December 1936.
26. Lewis Clive, op. cit., pp.92–93.
27. Ibid., p.231.
28. Ibid., p.205.
29. Ibid., p.114.
30. *Labour and Defence,* 1939, p.1.
31. Ibid.
32. Ibid.
33. Ibid.
34. Ibid.
35. Ibid., p.1 and p.9.
36. E.P. Thompson, *Writing by Candlelight,* Merlin, London, 1980, p.131.
37. *The Army Bureau of Current Affairs Handbook (Mid-East Branch),* 1942, pp.8–9.
38. For more information on the Cairo Parliament see James Clark, 'Secret War Within a War', *Morning Star,* 23 February 1978; and R.J. Spector, *Freedom for the Forces,* National Council for Civil Liberties, 1946.
39. The following examples of mutinies are taken from R.J. Spector, op. cit.
40. Ibid., p.5.
41. Ibid., pp.31–32.
42. *Daily Mail,* 10 May 1971, p.14.
43. Chris Knight (ed.) *The Soldier's Charter,* Leeds University Union Labour Society, 1971.

Notes to Chapter 8

1. *Economist,* 21 May 1983.
2. The source for current personnel and equipment figures is the *Statement on the Defence Estimates 1983,* HMSO, Cmnd. 8951–I and 8951–II.
3. *Guardian,* 7 May 1984.
4. Clement Attlee, Introduction to Lewis Clive, *The People's Army,* p.10.

5. *Times*, 25 February 1970.
6. *Conditions of Service in the Armed Forces*, West European Union, November 1974.
7. *Hansard*, 6 December 1977, Col. 1103.
8. Cited by James Clark, op. cit., p.2.
9. *Defence and Security for Britain*, Labour Party, 1984, p.5.
10. Ibid., p.22.

Index

from the Heretic list:

Peter Tatchell
THE BATTLE FOR BERMONDSEY *UK £2.95/US $5.50*

Preface by Tony Benn

The target of a violent hate campaign stirred up by the gutter press, Peter Tatchell tells the story of the dirtiest by-election in modern British politics. 'Truthful and necessary' (*New Statesman*). 'A frightening document which should be compulsory reading for anybody who still believes that our freedoms are secure' (*Guardian*).

Louis Mackay and David Fernbach (eds)
NUCLEAR-FREE DEFENCE *UK £3.95/US $7.50*

A symposium with 23 contributors, including Frank Allaun, Pat Arrowsmith, Joan Maynard, Peter Tatchell, Stuart Christie and Ronald Higgins. 'The editors have performed a vital task in revealing the true condition of the peace movement and the strands that have to be pulled together if it is to advance further and with credibility' (*Time Out*).

Erik Dammann
REVOLUTION IN THE AFFLUENT SOCIETY *UK £4.95/US $8.95*

Preface by Thor Heyerdahl

'He states clearly the priorities of an authentically radical politics for today's rich nations' (*New Statesman*).

Rudolf Bahro
SOCIALISM AND SURVIVAL *UK £3.50/US $6.50*

Preface by Edward Thompson

'Rudolf Bahro is forcing a consideration of peace, ecology, global human needs onto mainstream Marxism in ways that radicals cannot dismiss' (*City Limits*).

Rudolf Bahro
BUILDING THE GREEN MOVEMENT *UK £4.95/US $8.95*

This new collection of articles and essays focuses on Bahro's struggle within Die Grünen against parliamentary reformism and for a genuinely green radical politics. (Published September 1985.)

Die Grünen
PROGRAMME OF THE GERMAN GREEN PARTY *UK £1.50*

Preface by Jonathon Porritt

A translation of the Federal Programme on which Die Grünen fought the general election of 1983.

For further information, write to Heretic Books, GMP Publishers Ltd, P O Box 247, London N15 6RW. For mail order, please add 10% for postage. In North America, order from Alyson Publications Inc., 40 Plympton St, Boston, MA 02118.